**Nicolas-Louis De La Caille
Astronomer and Geodesist**

Abbé Nicolas-Louis de La Caille (1713–62)
(Anne-Louise le Jeuneux, 1762;
©Bibliothèque de l'Observatoire de Paris).

Nicolas-Louis De La Caille
Astronomer and Geodesist

I.S. Glass
South African Astronomical Observatory

WITHDRAWN

OXFORD
UNIVERSITY PRESS

OXFORD
UNIVERSITY PRESS

Great Clarendon Street, Oxford, OX2 6DP,
United Kingdom

Oxford University Press is a department of the University of Oxford.
It furthers the University's objective of excellence in research, scholarship,
and education by publishing worldwide. Oxford is a registered trade mark of
Oxford University Press in the UK and in certain other countries

First Edition published in 2013

Impression: 1

British Library Cataloguing in Publication Data

Data available

Library of Congress Cataloging in Publication Data

Data available

ISBN 978–0–19–966840–3

Printed and bound by
CPI Group (UK) Ltd, Croydon, CR0 4YY

Contents

———⟨∞⟩———

Introduction

At 10 a.m. on 20 April 1751 one of the greatest astronomers of the eighteenth century, the Abbé Nicolas-Louis de la Caille, Professor of Mathematics at the Collège Mazarin in Paris and member of the Royal Academy of Sciences, set foot on the foreshore of Cape Town, accompanied by his technician, Mr Poitevin, and his dog Grisgris. His principal aim was to measure the positions of objects in the southern sky. That he should travel to such a remote and only partly civilised place was seen by his friends as a risk and a sacrifice. Nevertheless, he had good reasons for his visit, which turned out to be a great success and made his name famous even with the general public.

More than any other astronomer of his time, he saw the value to science of making accurate measurements of the stars and planets. A savant at the time of the 'enlightenment', which was then sweeping the intellectual world, he was one of the first French apostles of Newton, whose theory of gravitation had been looked upon with hostility and scepticism for almost fifty years. Descartes' erroneous theory of fluid vortices in a space filled with an ill-defined medium still held sway. But increasingly precise observations of the positions of the planets, moons and comets were making it clear that their movements could only be interpreted in Newtonian terms. Indeed, it can be said that La Caille and the mathematicians who were his contemporaries in Paris were the true successors of Newton when it came to the development of celestial mechanics and physics as a whole.

Observations at the end of the sixteenth century by the Danish astronomer Tycho Brahe had improved enormously on all previous astronomical knowledge. Two laborious decades of ad hoc theoretical analysis had then allowed Johannes Kepler to show that the planets travel in elliptical orbits and follow his three famous laws.[1] His conclusions had in turn stimulated Newton to formulate his law of gravity, that bodies attract one another in proportion to the product of their masses divided by the square of their distance apart.

It soon became evident that Kepler's simple ellipses were only an approximation to reality. La Caille and a small number of others were

---

[1] See Appendix 1.

able to give more accurate descriptions of the true paths of the planets than Tycho and his seventeenth-century successors, thanks to the development of increasingly better instruments. Without this progress on the observational front, mathematical theories would have remained mere speculations unconstrained by physical reality. La Caille, unlike most other observers, was distinguished by the fact that he had a good understanding of theories and could direct his efforts so that their validity could be checked against the actual behaviour of the planets.

For most of his research career, the Abbé was active as a professor at the Collège Mazarin, the leading institution for mathematical education in France. He wrote several textbooks to go with his courses. These were uncompromisingly pro-Newtonian and, thanks to their many editions and wide circulation in several languages, must have influenced at least two generations of scientists. His firmly logical approach was acknowledged by his most famous student, the chemist Lavoisier.

According to Delambre (1827 p. 529), the historian of eighteenth century astronomy and a leading astronomer himself, 'La Caille was the most courageous calculator and the most zealous observer, the most active and the most assiduous who ever existed'. He was indeed an indefatigable calculator of ephemerides (the predicted positions of planets etc.), mathematical tables, the dates of eclipses and the positions of stars at standard epochs. This was no simple matter in the days before electronic computers. In addition, he re-examined all the historical observations he could lay his hands on to find out how the orbits of the earth, Moon and planets had changed over the long term.

In many ways the high point of the Abbé's career was his visit of two years to the Cape of Good Hope. We are indeed fortunate that we know quite a lot about this period of his life thanks to his *Journal Historique*, a kind of diary of his travels (see Appendix 3). He saw southern hemisphere observations as a necessity if the orbits of the solar system objects were to be measured with exactitude. Investigations of this kind required a knowledge of the positions of the 'fixed' stars because it was relative to them that the paths of the planets were plotted.

When planning his visit, he aimed to examine every part of the southern sky, noting the positions of the stars and anything else he saw, such as clusters of stars and nebulae, or diffuse objects. During his first year he made what must be considered the first ever systematic survey of any part of the heavens. On completing his task, he realised that the existing southern charts were completely inadequate. Accordingly, he felt it necessary to define fourteen new constellations, still in use today, including the only one named after a terrestrial feature, Mons Mensa (Table Mountain).

Because accurate distances for the planets could only be obtained by trigonometry using the longest possible baselines, stretching from observatories in the northern hemisphere to his own temporary one in the southern, he needed to know the precise shape of the earth. Thus he devoted the second part of his stay at the Cape to determining its local radius, the first such measurement to be made from southern latitudes. Here he encountered a paradox: he had to conclude that it was not a flattened ellipsoid, as observations in the northern hemisphere had recently suggested, but instead was somewhat pear-shaped! Though we now know that this result was in error, it was not because of carelessness on his part but rather due to the unappreciated gravitational pull of the mountains near the places where he worked.

La Caille's life was dedicated to work and he wasted no time on idle chat. At the same time he was wonderfully polite, knowing how to interact with people of all classes and how to please officialdom. In particular, while at the Cape, he was admired by the governor, Ryk Tulbagh, a person with a similar outlook who shared his values of honesty, lack of pretension and hatred of corruption. On several occasions, he mentions having been invited, once as the only foreigner, to state functions, probably including the hundredth anniversary of the foundation of the colony, which occurred on 8 April 1752. There is no doubt that his ability to conduct elaborate scientific programmes was greatly enhanced by the Governor's high opinion of him and what he was trying to accomplish.

During his visit, La Caille travelled through the Swartland plains north of Cape Town on foot, on horseback and by ox-wagon, at a time when there were no real roads. With local helpers, including slaves, he climbed mountains and made measurements from remote places, keeping a diary of his experiences and making notes about the customs of the people. This was at a time when the population of the colony was small, few people were literate and even fewer thought of writing social commentaries. In one way or another, he furnished the first fairly objective, non-sensational, account of life in the Colony. As he travelled around, he interested himself in how agriculture was carried on, what fruit and vegetables were grown, what the people ate, the weather and the climate, the mode of transportation, economic conditions, the remaining wild animals, the administration of the law, the condition of the slaves and the reluctance of owners to have them baptised. He looked at the fate of the French protestant families who had emigrated to the Cape following the revocation of the Edict of Nantes in 1685 by Louis XIV.

Unlike some scientists, La Caille was prompt in working up his observations, astronomical, geodetic and otherwise. He published them timeously in the Memoirs of the Royal Academy of Sciences in Paris. These articles contain, besides his science, a great deal of historical information. The main result of his visit to the Cape was a pioneering catalogue of 1942 southern stars whose positions he had measured with extraordinary accuracy for the time. They appeared in a posthumous book called *Coelum Australe Stelliferum* (The Southern Starry Sky) of 1763, edited by his executor, Jean Dominique Maraldi, and assisted by Gabriel Brotier, a classicist literary friend.

La Caille was a unique individual in an age of brilliant individuals. In spite of his formal title of Abbé, he does not seem to have been a particularly religious man. His scientific career spanned only about twenty-five years. Unlike many astronomers, even in those unhealthy times, he did not live to a great age but died in 1762 of an illness, possibly contracted at the Cape. At the time of his death at the early age of 49, he was admired not only by the public but also held in extremely high regard by his colleagues. So much so that he was accorded the unusual privilege of burial in the church of the Mazarin College where he had lived and worked.

The Abbé's signature

1
Early life

Nicolas-Louis de la Caille was born in Rumigny, Ardennes, a small town or village near the border of what is now Belgium, on 15 March 1713.[1] He discouraged people from looking into his origins, saying that real nobility showed itself through proper instincts and feelings and that inheriting a name does not mean the inheritance of anything else. To show a good character, he believed, a person should behave honourably and set an example of probity and virtue.

We know that his family was a well-respected one and had included goldsmiths, advocates, cavalrymen and administrative officials. His grandfather had been Clerk of the Court at Rumigny. His father, Charles-Louis, was a gentleman of the Royal Guard, a position open only to members of the nobility, and had taken part in several campaigns as an artillery officer, in the Corps of Gendarmes. There he had acquired some knowledge of mathematics. At that time he had became known to Louis Henri, Duc de Bourbon, a Prince of the Royal Blood and Prime Minister in the years 1723–6. This was at the time when Louis XV was King of France, long before the Revolution. Society was extremely stratified and nobility of birth made a great difference to one's status. Later in life, when Charles-Louis lost all his money in a failed business venture, the Duke had him appointed to the position of Captain of the Hunts to the Duchess of Maine at her estate of Anet. This was a personal favour typical of pre-revolutionary times.

By his wife, Barbe Rebuy, Charles-Louis had six daughters and four sons. Evidently the family was deeply devout, since three of the daughters became nuns. All the other children except Nicolas-Louis died young.

---

[1] His baptism was however on 29th December 1713 (Boquet, 1913). Since babies were usually baptised within a day of their birth, this throws some doubt on the accepted date.

Education

Charles-Louis was himself interested in science and inventions and encouraged his son in this direction. After some home-schooling, the young Nicolas-Louis was sent to the college of Mantes-sur-Seine,[2] where the headmaster was a friend of the family. Following this, he went as a pensioner in 1729 to the College of Lisieux, one of a number forming the University of Paris, where he studied rhetoric and philosophy for two years. There he was regarded as mature in outlook and was described as having the judgement of someone much older. He was a serious and scholarly person who read widely, especially in the classics. The Latin style that he developed was considered to be very pure and to reflect his admiration for the orator and statesman, Marcus Tullius Cicero.

During these years he had continuous problems with bad health and difficulties in digestion, to the extent that he had trouble eating enough food to stay alive.

When his father died in 1731, the eighteen-year-old Nicolas-Louis was left destitute. He found himself 'very close to that excess of indigence which smothers talents' (Bailly 1770). However, his pleasant character, his general keenness and his good behaviour endeared him so much to his superiors that they applied on his behalf to his father's former patron, the Duc de Bourbon. This noble was graciously pleased to encourage him and take care of his needs.

In 1732 he entered another Parisian College, that of Navarre, where he studied theology for three years, with the idea of becoming a priest. It was during this period that he came across the geometry of Euclid. Like so many other potential scientists he was immensely stimulated by the logical way in which the Greek mathematician had built up a complex set of results in geometry. As a result he found himself studying theology during the day but devoting his nights to mathematics and later astronomy. He had no money to buy books and spent a lot of time deriving results that were already known; this was not time lost but rather a period of self-education.

To complete his theological studies he had to take the degrees of Master of Arts and Bachelor in Theology, if he was to follow the wishes of his father whose memory he greatly respected, though he was by then inwardly directed towards science. His first examination is said to have gone very well and at the end of his second one the examiners praised him highly. The final step was for the Under-Chancellor of Notre Dame, in the absence of the Chancellor, to approve his candidacy, since it was he that would confer the degrees. Unfortunately, this official was attached to the old-style scholastic philosophy of the late Middle Ages. A question that he put to La Caille, who must by now have been

---

[2] Now called Mantes-la-Jolie, this town is 48 km west of central Paris.

infected by the spreading enlightenment that characterised eighteenth-century France, elicited a frank and blunt response that made the elderly official furious. He tried to withhold the degree but his colleagues, fully aware of La Caille's merit, intervened on his behalf and forced him to change his mind, which he did, but under protest. This experience left La Caille humiliated and soured him towards theology and scholastic philosophy, a feeling that remained with him all his life. He never did become a fully-fledged priest but took deacon's orders and became an abbé, a title given in France to certain low-ranking clergy.

Appointed to the Observatoire de Paris

Soon after graduating he sought out Jean-Paul Grandjean de Fouchy, Assistant Astronomer at the Royal Academy of Sciences, who lived nearby. Fouchy was astonished at what La Caille had achieved on his own, without help. Being about to go away for some months he could only offer some general advice and suggest making contact with Cassini II,[3] then the most eminent astronomer in Paris.

La Caille succeeded in bringing his original efforts at theoretical astronomy to Cassini's attention.[4] Jacques Cassini (Cassini II) was the second eminent member of this famous family of astronomers who were effectively the hereditary directors of the Paris Observatory for four generations, though in principle the building was intended to be a place to which all members of the Royal Academy of Sciences had equal access. The founding father, Jean-Dominique Cassini I, had come from Italy to be official astronomer and astrologer to Louis XIV and was largely responsible for setting up the Paris Observatory in the first place.

Cassini granted La Caille an interview and was impressed by his mathematical style and methodology, not to mention his character. 'Live with me; we will calculate as much as you like; I offer you my house and my friendship', he is reputed to have said. Indeed, La Caille's references to the Cassinis and their relations in his letters suggest that he became very much one of the family. This unexpected piece of good fortune, which the Abbé remembered with gratitude for the rest of his life, not only gave him a roof over his head from August 1736 to January

---

[3] To avoid confusion between generations, the Cassinis have traditionally been referred to by Roman numerals.

[4] On the other hand, Carlier (La Caille 1776, p. 11), in his account of La Caille's life, says that it was a mutual friend of La Caille's father and Cassini, a 'respectable ecclesiastic', Mr Léger, Curate of St André des Arts, who recommended him to Cassini. Dr (of Theology) Claude Léger taught at the Collège de Lisieux until he was appointed to St André des Arts in 1738 and must have known La Caille when he was a pupil there (Michaud, J. & Michaud L.G. 1843–65).

Fig. 1.1 César-François Cassini de Thury (Cassini III), with whom La Caille worked at the Paris Observatory. From a miniature portrait of around 1750 by Jean-Marc Nattier, courtesy of Walters Art Museum, Baltimore.

1740, but provided him with a salary of 600 French pounds per annum according to Wolf (1902), who also mentions that at least one reason for bringing him into the household was to set an example to Cassini's second son and heir apparent, César-François Cassini de Thury (Cassini III; see Fig. 1.1). The latter owed his aristocratic name 'de Thury' to the chateâu purchased by his father in 1717 at Thury-sous-Clermont (Oise). César-François was then 27, three years older than La Caille, and was already a member of the Royal Academy of Sciences. Later in life, they unfortunately become rivals (Bailly, 1770). Also then studying at the Observatory was another family member, Jean-Dominique (Giovanni Domenico) Maraldi, known as Maraldi II, who was four years older than La Caille. His uncle, Jacques-Philippe (Giacomo Filippo) Maraldi (Maraldi I) had been a nephew of Cassini I and was also an astronomer. Jean-Dominique had been sent to Paris to join him in 1727 at the age of 18. The Cassinis and the Maraldis had always been, of course, very close, having originated in the same Italian town, Perinaldo, near Nice and the French border.

The Observatory was a crowded place, containing the homes of several families besides the Cassinis. Its large high-ceilinged rooms, designed more to impress the late King than for practical use, had in some cases been subdivided, even vertically (Wolf, 1902), with internal stairs. Jean-Dominique Maraldi for example had nowhere to sleep except the wide embrasure of a window!

For La Caille, the years he spent in the Observatory were the introduction to an occupation that he found infinitely more congenial than the Church. In its stimulating environment he soon showed his ability and by May 1737 he had started making observations. He was already a passionate observer at the age of 24, as can be seen from a memoir in which he complained that astronomical training seemed to be confined to impracticable geometrical methods described as theory. What was needed, he felt, was devotion to fundamental observational work 'which alone was capable of bringing about progress.'[5]

By 1738 La Caille was considered to be a good enough scientist to be put to work on re-measuring the speed of sound, one of the long-term interests of the Royal Academy of Sciences. They felt it necessary to resolve considerable discrepancies between the values that had been found by previous observers in France and England. Perhaps there was some element of international national rivalry involved! On this project he collaborated with Cassini III (Fig. 1.1). Also working with them was Maraldi. Their experiments were carried out in the vicinity of Paris using the most powerful cannons they could get hold of. Observations were made under different conditions of wind, weather, temperature and barometric pressure. Their result was 173 toises[6] per second (337 m/sec) in still conditions, which is the value accepted today for a 'standard atmosphere' and a temperature of 10 °C (Cassini de Thury, La Caille & Maraldi 1738).

It is not quite clear why the Academy laid such emphasis on measuring the speed of sound. It may have been hoped that this knowledge could be used distance measuring purposes. Some doubts as to the utility of their work must have existed in the minds of the young astronomers because their paper ended with the following words:

> What we have said about [the speed of sound] suffices to prove that it is not one of those useless pieces of knowledge but that one can extract several advantages from it, principally for the progress of geography and the safety of navigation (Cassini de Thury 1738).

The advent of Newtonianism

In French scientific circles the 1730s were dominated by arguments over the acceptance of Newtonian ideas, particularly the theory of

---

[5] Memoir dated February 1737 *Dissertation sur l'observation des astres par le seul télescope*, Bibliothèque de l'Observatoire de Paris, ms C 3 27, quoted by Bigourdan (1895).

[6] Toises were French units of length similar to fathoms. One toise = 1.949 m.

universal gravitation. Many scientists, especially outside England, had been slow to accept his concepts, as expressed in the three editions of his *Principia* of 1687, 1713 and 1726. Newton himself had not helped matters by his obscure geometrical approach to mathematics, saying to a friend, 'And for this reason, namely to avoid being bated by little Smatterers in Mathematicks, [I] deliberately made [the] Principia abstruse . . .' (quoted by Westfall, 1980).

La Caille's exposure to Newtonianism probably began during his three and a half years at the Observatory. Before this period of his life he probably could not have afforded to buy many books or socialise in the coffee shops and aristocratic salons where the latest scientific news circulated. At most, he might have been able to attend the few public lectures that were offered. Grandjean de Fouchy, who took a special interest in La Caille's career, may have introduced him to the group of young mathematically minded astronomers then actively promoting Newton's ideas.

This little group within the Royal Academy of Sciences was in effect under the leadership of Pierre-Louis Moreau de Maupertuis,[7] (Fig. 1.2) remembered as an important figure in the history of mathematics and a scientist of great general ability. He was an aristocrat from a merchant corsair (licensed pirate) family in St Malo, Brittany, with a penchant for publicity and was outspoken in his contempt for old-fashioned views. Indeed, the heat associated with the disagreements manifested in the 1730s may have been in part a consequence of Maupertuis' harsh polemics rather than his Newtonianism (Greenberg, 1995).

Those opposed to Newtonian views included La Caille's revered teacher, Cassini II, and several other academicians of the older generation who could not bring themselves to accept the idea of universal gravitational attraction without any obvious physical mechanism. They felt that Descartes' theory of vortices within a 'plenum' or undefined medium in space could account for the movements of the planets, though the theory was weak and unable to predict very much. The aged Bernard Le Bovier de Fontenelle,[8] Perpetual Secretary of the Academy of Sciences until 1741, for example, though once a radical, was another of the Cartesians.[9] He felt that for a Frenchman to propagandise in favour of an English theory was tantamount to disloyalty.

The pro-Newton group included the mathematician Alex-Claude Clairaut and the explorer Charles-Marie de la Condamine. They had begun to meet a few years before as members of a short-lived 'Society of Arts' (Société des Arts), founded to promote the interaction of science and technology. It reached its zenith in the late 1720s and declined

---

[7] See Terrall (2002) and Shank (2008) for accounts of this period.

[8] Fontenelle died in 1757 at the age of 100 years, attributing his longevity to his fondness for strawberries.

[9] Followers of Descartes.

Fig. 1.2 Pierre-Louis Moreau de Maupertuis, the mathematician who propagated the views of Newton in France (engraving based on a painting by Robert Tournières). He is shown here wearing the warm clothes that he used during the geodetic expedition to Lapland (taken from Maupertuis 1768).

thereafter thanks to its emasculation by the Royal Academy of Sciences, who perhaps were jealous of its success or feared the growth of a rival organisation. The Academy's strategy had been to draw away the whole mathematical group by admitting them to their own company and by simultaneously insisting that they leave the Society of Arts. However, within their new forum they enjoyed a higher profile and were able to promote their ideas even more effectively, to the dismay of the old guard.

At the time, the battle over Newtonian science was taking the form of a bitter argument concerning the shape of the earth. This question was considered a very serious one by the Royal Academy of Sciences because of their rôle in the making of accurate maps. Geodetic measurements of France by Cassinis I and II as well as others earlier in the century had apparently proved that the planet was not quite spherical: that it was extended towards the poles, somewhat resembling a rugby ball or an egg.

One of the first and most dramatic actions by the pro-Newton faction was the publication in 1732 by Maupertuis of a little book (Maupertuis 1732) in which, using the clearest language, he showed the weakness of Descartes' vortex theory when compared with Newton's law of gravitation. He applied gravitational theory to find the shapes of rotating stars and planets and demonstrated that the oblate earth advocated by Cassinis I and II was unphysical. Their view was completely contrary to Newton's prediction that there should be a bulge towards the equator due to centrifugal force. In other words, they believed that the earth had to be a prolate ellipsoid.

In 1733 the Academy awarded its medal to an Italian physicist, Giovanni Poleni, who demonstrated that the existing observational data were too inaccurate to decide the question properly. To settle the matter, the Academy resolved to send expeditions staffed by its talented young astronomers and mathematicians to measure the curvature of the earth at two places having widely differing latitudes.

Two techniques were involved in this type of measurement: the precise determination of the latitude and longitude of places by astronomical means and the precise measurement of the distance between them by ground-based surveying. The details of the method will be given in Chapter 3, where La Caille's work at the Cape is described.

Measuring equipment had improved since Cassini I's time, so that there was hope of obtaining much more precise results. An expedition to Lapland (1736–7) was headed by Maupertuis, accompanied by Pierre le Monnier, Clairaut and Anders Celsius, the Swedish astronomer of temperature fame. Another group set off for Peru. It included Louis Godin and Pierre Bouguer with Charles-Marie de La Condamine as leader. The latter expedition took a very long time, from 1735 to 1745, almost long enough to be forgotten. Even though its leaders managed to fall out with one another, both it and the Lapland expedition yielded successful results, at least in the sense that the earth appeared to be flattened at the pole.[10] Maupertuis and his colleagues reported on their return that the earth was indeed flattened at the poles (Maupertuis *et al.* 1738). Needless to say, Cassini II studied the report in detail, trying to find ways to deny the truth of its conclusion.

At the November 1737 public lecture of the Academy of Sciences,[11] Maupertuis seized the moment. To an unprecedentedly large audience he delivered a masterful account of the expedition, designed to answer all criticism. The populist philosopher Voltaire, a strong supporter of the Newtonian viewpoint, declared gleefully that he had flattened the earth and the Cassinis.

As a matter of record, the Lapland expedition's measurements were not particularly accurate. The flattening they found was much greater than later, more precise, observations showed its true value to be.

---

[10] La Condamine incidentally discovered exactly which type of quinine was the best for treating malaria. Godin got side-tracked into becoming Professor of Mathematics in Lima and only returned to France in 1751 via Rio de Janeiro. For more on these expeditions and their incredible adventures, see the books by Whitaker (2005), Murdin (2009) and Trystram (1979).

[11] A transcript of this lecture is available in English; see Maupertuis *et al.* (1738).

The source of error was almost certainly gravitational anomalies that affected the astronomical latitude determinations.

Survey of the Paris Meridian

The Academy was concerned as to why the new measurements had led to such a different conclusion from the old ones, made within France. Feelings between the parties remained high. They decided that the best way to resolve the issue would be to make a completely new survey of the meridian passing through Paris from the south to the north of the country, that is from Perpignan to Dunkerque.

They assigned this task to Cassini III and La Caille, perhaps feeling that these two young astronomers, who had not obviously taken sides in the dispute, would be neutral arbiters. Their faith in La Caille's competence was justified by various mapping projects he had just completed with Cassini III and Maraldi. They had surveyed parts of the Channel and southern coasts of France as well as the mouth of the Rhône (Brown, 1980). In May 1738 they had mapped the French coast from Nantes to Bayonne. This last expedition had led to Maraldi becoming La Caille's best friend. Ultimately he was to be his scientific executor.

The Paris Meridian survey started in July 1739 and needed around three years to complete. It took the young scientists into some wild and dangerous regions of the country. They were accompanied by the botanist Louis-Guillaume Le Monnier, brother of the astronomer Pierre Le Monnier, who recorded the natural phenomena that they encountered in the south of France.

La Caille often observed by night as well as by day, surveying large triangles between prominent landmarks and setting up baselines to calibrate the distances. Frequently he had to climb mountains, install beacons and light signal bonfires. He had to camp out under all weather conditions and often had little to eat. We learn for example (Cassini de Thury 1740, p. 17): 'In the depth of winter of the year 1740, at a time when the whole earth was covered by snow, and when the roads were almost impassable, he undertook the verification of certain angles in the mountains of Auvergne ...'. On another occasion, while working in the Pyrenees, his horse, with him on it, was swept away by a raging torrent. The horse reappeared without La Caille, leading his companions to think they would never see him again. To their surprise, he turned up a little while later, soaking wet and, after a change of clothes, stoically went back to work.

This hard outdoor life had its good side. His earlier precarious health seemed to have been put behind him and he acquired a hardiness and an adventurous spirit that stood him in good stead later on in Africa.

The survey included an estimate of the earth's radius obtained from two places at the same latitude but different longitudes. Their distance apart was found by detonating a large charge of gunpowder and timing it in terms of the local time at each place. Of course, determining the local time to the required degree of accuracy was a significant task in itself.

The account of the survey, called *The Meridian of the Royal Observatory of Paris Verified. . .*[12] was published under Cassini de Thury's name as a special volume of the *Memoirs of the Royal Academy of Sciences* for 1740, appearing in 1744. In the preface, Cassini acknowledged the work of La Caille. However, the historian of eighteenth-century astronomy, Jean-Baptiste Delambre (1827), stated that when he examined La Caille's manuscripts he found that they contained all the calculations that had gone into the book. This was proof that he was the person that had done all the work! Delambre, who wrote many years afterwards, probably did not know how upset his self-effacing hero had been at the time. However, in presenting a copy of one of his books to James Bradley, Astronomer Royal of England, the Abbé had expressed his frustration quite openly:

> . . . I have also had printed the details of all the geometrical and astronomical operations that I have made with Mr Cassini (the son), to amend the work of his father on the figure of the earth. I would have sent it at the same time if I had not been so shocked by the behaviour of Mr Cassini, who has taken complete possession of this book, to which he has hardly done more than put his name and pay the costs of printing: if it had been on sale I would have bought a copy for you and one for me; but this book is not yet published so far as I know. What I am telling you here is not to complain about Mr Cassini but only to inform you about the author and the work. When you have seen it you can assure yourself of what I have the honour to tell you and can inform yourself of it through those of our academy whom you know. However, you would please me by not revealing to anybody that I have told you about it myself. I ask a thousand excuses for the liberty that I have dared to take with you. But also I beg you to believe that there is nobody more inclined than myself to render all the services in this country that you judge me capable of . . .
>
> If you do me the honour of writing to me, you can do it in English. I understand it quite well.[13]

The conclusion of the 1739–40 survey was that the one conducted by the older Cassinis and their associates was in error; the Newtonian view of an earth flattened at the poles was finally shown to be correct. Cassini de Thury accepted the findings he had reported—he hardly could not. The errors in the work of his father and grandfather had to be admitted.

---

[12] *La Méridienne de l'Observatoire Royal de Paris vérifiée . . .*
[13] La Caille to Bradley, dated Paris, 28 July 1744; see Rigaud (1832) pp. 429–31.

The discrepancy between the old and new surveys was eventually traced to an error of one part in 1000 in the original baseline laid out by Picard in 1668.

It is interesting to note that some fifty years later this survey was fundamental to the provisional definition of the metre. In August 1793, following the French Revolution, a commission of the Royal Academy of Sciences had decided that the new unit should be one ten-millionth of the distance from the equator to the pole. To specify the new unit as accurately as possible in 1791 the National Constituent Assembly commissioned a new and more accurate meridian survey. The task eventually devolved upon Jean-Baptiste-Joseph Delambre and Pierre Méchain, but its completion was delayed by many vicissitudes associated with the unsettled state of the country (see Alder, 2002, and Lequeux, 2008). As a result of the delay, the survey of 1739–40 had to be accepted as the best measurement of the earth's figure for the time being. The final value of the metre, adopted in 1799, was about 0.3 mm shorter than the provisional one.

Professor at the Collège Mazarin

At the outset of the Meridian survey, La Caille was suddenly appointed by Jacques Robbe, the Grand-Master of Collège Mazarin, another of the Paris colleges, to be their professor of Mathematics. This was through the recommendation of the same Grandjean de Fouchy, who had helped previously with the introduction to Cassini II. He was then 25 years old and, though he had no special qualifications, his friends were not particularly surprised, his reputation having spoken for him. He had to interrupt his work on the survey for a short time in November 1739 to return to Paris to take up his new position.

The Collège Mazarin (Fig. 1.3), also known as the Collège des Quatre Nations, where La Caille was based for the rest of his career, was an institution dating from 1661 that had been founded through a bequest from Cardinal Mazarin, the all-powerful Chief Minister of France in the early part of the reign of Louis XIV. It overlooked the Seine and was situated in a magnificent building designed by the classical architect Louis le Vau. Apart from housing the Cardinal's library in one of its wings, its central chapel served in part as his mausoleum. The 'Four Nations' in its alternative name were four protestant territories that had come under the rule of France during the seventeenth century as a result of treaty settlements following the Thirty Years War, a period of bitter religious strife. The college was originally intended as an elite residential one for the impoverished sons of noblemen from these territories but had expanded into a very large institution taking many day scholars (called 'martinets', or swifts) as well, around 1000 when La Caille taught there. Its building still stands today but was appropriated after the Revolution and eventually came to house the Institut de France, the umbrella body of the post-revolutionary French Academies that succeeded their 'Royal' predecessors. The Mazarin library survived the Revolution and the changes it brought.

The Collège had become over time the leading institution in France where mathematical subjects were taught and quite a few of the celebrated scientists of the eighteenth century studied there, such as the mathematicians d'Alembert and Legendre, the physicist Coulomb, the chemist Lavoisier and the economist Condorcet. Even Jacques-Louis David, the famous painter of Napoleonic times, was an alumnus.

The circumstances of La Caille's appointment to the professorship are not known but it seems to have been made in some haste. His predecessor, Léonor Caron, was a Jansenist, a member of a puritanical movement within the Roman Catholic church that was opposed strongly by the Jesuits. He was removed from office by a 'lettre de cachet'[14] on 29 September 1739 during a politico-religious purge. A later Grand Master of the college, Ambroise Riballier, tried to justify this action by stating that Caron was a difficult person who had lacked competence: his idea of teaching mathematics had simply been to regurgitate the Latin lectures of his predecessor. On the other hand, in his favour, d'Alembert, a former student of his at the Collège Mazarin, was grateful to him for his introduction to mathematics. According to Riballier, in spite of his bad reputation, Caron was re-appointed professor at the age of 72 following La Caille's death and re-commenced teaching in his old-fashioned way (see Peiffer 2009). However, if this is true, he must soon have been succeeded by the Abbé Joseph-François Marie,[15] who made use of La Caille's methods and was to be the teacher of several famous mathematicians such as Adrien-Marie Legendre.

The Collège Mazarin Observatory

La Caille could only take up his new post towards the end of the work on the Meridian survey.

Astronomy at the Paris Observatory had been neglected for many years by the Cassinis in favour of geodetic surveying and cartography. Its equipment had become out-dated. Thus, in 1742 La Caille persuaded the administrators of the Collège Mazarin to let him construct a small observatory on the very substantial vaulted roof of the chapel, directly above Cardinal Mazarin's tomb (see Fig. 1.3). Thanks to his almost

[14] *Lettres de cachet* were one of the many abuses of the pre-revolutionary régime: they were documents signed on behalf of the King that were effectively sentences without trial or the possibility of appeal.

[15] Marie died in exile in Memel, Prussia, after the Revolution, probably by suicide.

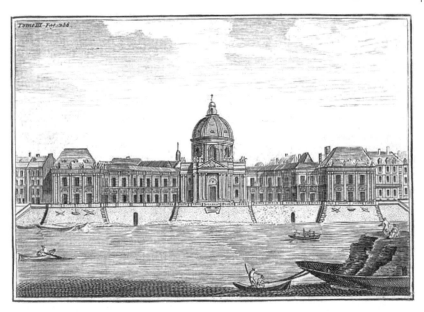

Fig. 1.3 The Collège Mazarin in Paris, where La Caille spent most of his working life. The building faces NNE. The Abbé's first and second observatories were on the roof of the chapel, at the back of the dome and somewhat to its right in this view. Mazarin's tomb is below the same spot. Since 1806 the building has housed the Institut de France. The observatories did not survive the change (seventeenth century woodcut from Brice 1725), courtesy Library, University of Kyoto.

unaided efforts, it soon became the most important observatory in Paris, even if a large part of the sky was obscured by the chapel dome (see Bigourdan, 1919, for details). In October and November 1748 a larger observatory was constructed in a somewhat better position, closer to the NW corner of the building. There were two rooms, one of fourteen by ten feet and the other of fifteen feet square.[16] The smaller room had walls of two and a half feet thick to give good thermal stability. Its ceiling had a circular opening of six feet in diameter with a rotatable conical roof above it. In one of his rare personal letters, he grumbled about the dilatory behaviour of the builders, who were working too slowly.[17] According to Johan III Bernoulli (1771), who visited it in

[16] The expenses in connection with constructing and fitting out this second observatory are listed in the *Abbe Nicolas Louis de La Caille's Working Notebook*, Historical Papers A892–1, William Cullen Library, University of the Witwatersrand, Johannesburg.

[17] La Caille to Madame d'Éstouilly, dated Paris 9 October 1748. Archives of the Academy of Sciences of the Institut de France, Fonds la Condamine, 50J 76. Madame d'Éstouilly was the sister of his colleague and friend in the Academy of Sciences,

1769,[18] even this observatory did not have a clear view towards the horizon and suffered from various other inconveniences. To get there, it was necessary to thread one's way through a dark and dangerous labyrinth in the attics of the college.

To furnish his observatories La Caille acquired a number of well-made instruments. The principal supplier of these was Claude Langlois, who was appointed the official 'Engineer of mathematical instruments' to the Academy in 1740. His products were state-of-the-art at the time and played a crucial role in La Caille's work. According to Cassini de Thury (1740), Langlois 'combined much intelligence with great precision in the execution of the instruments which left his hands'. In the introduction to the *Journal Historique* (La Caille 1776, p. 107), it is stated that La Caille had the instruments made under his own eyes, verifying all the critical parts carefully, and understanding them in complete detail. Nobody else was allowed to come near them. Separate instruments of less importance were made for his students to practice on.

Member of the Academy of Sciences

On 3 May 1741 La Caille was appointed 'Adjoint Astronomer' of the Royal Academy of Sciences (Académie Royale des Sciences), founded in 1666 by Jean-Baptiste Colbert, Minister of Finance under Louis XIV. It enjoyed royal patronage and received a generous budget. Directed in practice by its Perpetual Secretary, it was the official agency for answering scientific questions, almost the equivalent of a modern 'think tank'. Unlike some later Academies, it was a research organisation rather than an honorific one. It exerted great influence and all the leading scientists belonged to it or sought to belong to it. Its professional members were divided into three classes: the Pensioners, who received a salary, the Associates and the Adjoints. In each speciality, such as geometry, astronomy and mechanics, there were just a few members; positions only became available when somebody died or was promoted. La Caille had been elected to fill the Adjoint position previously occupied by Grandjean de Fouchy, who had just been made an Associate. Members were expected to attend the twice-weekly meetings in the Louvre on a fairly regular basis. The minutes (Procès-Verbaux), which have survived, indicate that the attendance was typically about 25.

La Caille received a salary from the Academy only after his return from the Cape. As one of his biographers, the Abbé Carlier, wrote (see La Caille 1776, p. 21), 'The Academies are the orders of chivalry of

---

Charles-Marie de la Condamine. In 1756 La Condamine married her daughter, his niece, Marie-Louise Charlotte Bouzier d'Éstouilly, by special Papal dispensation.

[18] Quoted by Bigourdan (1919).

Fig. 1.4 Jean le Rond d'Alembert, engraving by Hopwood. The original portrait is by De la Tour. Courtesy of University of Cape Town library.

the Republic of Letters. Ordinarily in them one amasses more honour than cash'. La Caille's membership indeed brought him great prestige, unwelcome because of his modest nature, and official recognition. After a few years later he advanced to the level of 'Associate' (5 April 1745), again taking the place of his sponsor Grandjean de Fouchy who had just become Perpetual Secretary of the Academy.

At meetings of the Academy he regularly came into close contact with other leading scientists. Apart from the question of the shape of the earth, the theory of planetary movements was one of the main issues of the time. As mentioned, Newton had 'explained' Kepler's brilliant observational discovery that the planets moved in simple ellipses with the Sun at one focus, dominated by its gravitational attraction. But, as the measurement of celestial motions improved, it was becoming evident that things were less 'simple' than they had at first seemed. It became clear that the basic elliptical orbits of the solar system bodies were being distorted by gravitational interactions between them and that even the slightly non-spherical shape of the earth was causing certain effects. French mathematicians such as Clairaut, Maupertuis, Jean le Rond d'Alembert (Fig. 1.4) and Leonhard Euler, a Swiss, were working on theories that could explain these effects. It soon became clear to them that when more than two celestial objects were involved, simple theories were inadequate. Though the basic orbit of a particular planet around the Sun could be predicted exactly, the much smaller perturbations caused by the other planets could only be treated approximately. The mathematicians thus eagerly awaited the publication of accurate data by La Caille and other observers to test their latest ideas. Following the 'Scientific Method', the relevance of a new theory was judged by the accuracy with which it fitted the facts and by how well it predicted the future movements of the planets. Such was the interest in this question that in 1748 the Academy of Sciences actually offered a prize, won by Euler, for the solution to this problem in 'perturbation theory'.

The Abbé's first contribution to the Academy was not, however, an astronomical one. Instead, it was an exercise in differential calculus, a development of the mathematical work of Roger Cotes, a contemporary of Newton's, who had studied how small errors in measuring angles during a survey affected the overall results. This knowledge was of great importance to him later on in understanding the limitations of the large-scale surveys he was to make in the course of his geodetic work (see La Caille 1741).

La Caille as a teacher ahead of his time

The full course at the Collège Mazarin took nine years and combined elements of modern secondary school and college education (Guerlac 1956). La Caille took his teaching very seriously and during his career wrote several textbooks and study guides on mathematics, optics and astronomy. These were very successful and ran into several editions. He chose to write in French rather than the Latin of academic tradition, believing that mathematics is difficult enough as it is and would be understood more readily in everyday language. Latin obscured meaning instead of making it clearer and wasted the precious time of the students. He paid the printing costs of his books himself so as to keep them affordable. Many were later translated into other languages, even Latin.

These textbooks sometimes reveal his advanced beliefs. It is clear that he was a strong propagandist for Newtonianism, which was still accepted rather reluctantly in France. The old idea of Descartes, that space was permeated by a medium containing vortices that somehow drove the planets, was still to a great extent accepted as canonical. La Caille's position was far in advance of the previous generation of French astronomers, not to mention the church to which he belonged, which still officially denied the truth of Copernicanism. However, the latter at least had made considerable headway thanks to Bernard le Bovier de Fontenelle, later Permanent Secretary of the Royal Academy of Sciences. He had published in 1686 his *Conversations on the Plurality of Worlds*[19] (Fontenelle 1686) which accepted Copernicanism and even

---

[19] *Entretiens sur la pluralité des mondes.*

the idea of extraterrestrial life, but still explained the motions of the planets on Descartes' model. This influential book was a precursor of the 'Enlightenment' that occurred towards the middle of the following century.

The first of La Caille's books was a rather unexceptional *Elementary lessons in mathematics or elements of algebra and of geometry*, published in 1741. It was at the level of a present-day high school text and was intended as a set of notes to help students digest what they had heard in lectures. Nevertheless, it was a runaway best-seller, running into about 30 printings in various languages. The edition of 1758 was the first to include a section on calculus. After La Caille's death it was continued by his successor, Joseph-François Marie.

His *Elementary lessons in geometric and physical astronomy* of 1746 is much more interesting and contains some advanced ideas for his time:

> In regard to the true place of the stars in the Universe, their true distances from the Sun, their nature, their sizes, their number and their uses or the reason God made them, the observer has no established facts to go on ...
>
> But because of the fact that they emit light and are immobile it is possible to make very reasonable conjectures and to suppose that they are all Suns, that is to say, of the same nature and equal to our star in size and luminosity, and are each destined to be the centre and principle of movement of several habitable planets, which turn around each one at different distances ... one can even determine their approximate distances by comparing the intensity of light from each one, which is in inverse proportion to their distances, following the rules of optics.

The notion the Abbé expresses here, though put forward before by Fontenelle, that there are other inhabitable worlds besides our own, was one of the heresies that had been espoused by Giordano Bruno, causing him to be tried and ceremonially burnt by the Italian Inquisition 150 years before! Also, the idea of determining relative distances from apparent brightnesses is one that is of fundamental importance today, though with the recognition that it applies only to certain well-defined classes of stars.

Much of the book concerns the orbits of celestial bodies such as planets, moons and comets and the deviations from perfect ellipses that they show.

He held that all celestial movements could be explained by two simple mechanical ideas: Newton's law of gravitational attraction and something—a 'prime mover'—that had set the system going in the first place. If there was some general principle of physics involved, it had to explain these two things. This 'clockwork' model of the universe was a common point of view once Newton's work had been generally accepted. La Caille saw that there was no sense in quibbling about a physical explanation for gravity—the lack of one was a major objection to the theory. The main thing was to accept that the two ideas could be used to model all known celestial phenomena until such time as the real physical cause was found, or until a new and even more comprehensive law was discovered that included what worked already.

Elementary lessons in optics (1750), was a short but very popular textbook that was reprinted ten times, sometimes in other languages, until 1810, and is a fairly uncomplicated treatment of optics as then known, especially as applied to lenses, mirrors, eye glasses, telescopes and microscopes. Once again La Caille revealed himself to be a good Newtonian, even if classical corpuscles are no longer the whole story today:

> Light is composed of a prodigious quantity of particles of matter or of corpuscles distinguished from each other, of infinitely small size, very elastic but with an extreme velocity so that when they arrive at the organ of our sight they hit with a force proportional to the density of corpuscles, which in virtue of the intimate union of our body with our soul, occasions in our spirit different ideas on the presence of objects from where the corpuscles or luminous atoms departed.

Programme of research

Refining the positions of the stars

In a speech to the academy La Caille (1742) announced a programme that was to take up much of his working life:

> The renewal of astronomy and physics that happened in the last century, occasioned especially by the establishment of scientific academies in France and England, the invention of spy-glasses and a thousand other aids due to the sagacity of modern man, or to the natural progress of the human spirit, could not fail to have influence on the denumeration of stars and the determination of their positions.

The bright stars were to be re-measured in order to make a new catalogue, more precise than any in existence up to that time. This was a necessity not only because of the improvements in instrumentation but also because of the recent discovery of aberration by Bradley. Once such a catalogue was established, the movements of the Sun, planets and comets against the background of the stars could be observed with high precision. An accurate star catalogue would also lead to improvements in navigation, of significance to all sea-faring nations.

The procedure he had in mind was essentially to survey the sky systematically in the way that he was to use later at the Cape. A wide-angle telescope would be kept fixed for a whole night and the positions of all the stars passing through the field of view due to the rotation of the earth would be noted. The telescope would be moved to another position the next night and so on until the whole sky had been covered. The problem was that long spells of clear weather were necessary for success and the idea was not really practicable in the Parisian climate.

'That said, M. l'Abbé de la Caille remarked that what was most likely to put an astronomer off working on a catalogue was the prospect of the immense sea of calculations that would have to be carried out . . . .' However, as he pointed out, it was not really necessary to provide more than the basic position of each star, which would keep the work to a manageable level.

A survey from France could, of course, only cover the northern hemisphere and he already foresaw the need for an expedition to the southern hemisphere to complete the task.

Computation and historical studies

The Abbé was, in fact, an indefatigable calculator and, in the course of his working life, produced three volumes of Ephemerides, or tables of predicted star and planet positions, each covering ten years.

There were other ways in which he could put his phenomenal computational ability to use, such as in the re-reduction of other people's observations and the investigation of historical astronomical events such as eclipses.

Edmond Halley, a generation before La Caille, had discovered that several stars had changed their positions slightly since ancient times. Measurement of their so-called 'proper motions'[20] was becoming an important subject of research. Until a little after the time we are considering, position measurements were simply not accurate enough to notice proper motions over shorter intervals, because their effects are so small. Nevertheless, La Caille's disciple Bailly (1770) mentions having seen in a lost manuscript that he was working on this question in 1750 and had obtained the positions of a number of stars that had been measured many years before by de la Hire. This was just one of the reasons why the Abbé was always interested in old data, provided they were accurate. Another was his desire to monitor long-term changes in the shapes, positions and tilts of the planetary orbits.

The impact of Bradley's discoveries

It was during La Caille's student days that the first of two very important discoveries was made by James Bradley (1728, see Fig. 1.5), the Astronomer Royal of England (from 1742). In trying to determine increasingly more accurate star positions by observing stars close to

---

[20] 'Proper' in this sense means 'own', from the French word 'propre'.

Fig. 1.5 James Bradley, Professor of astronomy at Oxford University and later Astronomer Royal. He made two important discoveries: the aberration of starlight and the nutation of the earth's axis. These led to a new era of precision in star positions. Engraved by Edward Scriven 'From the original picture by Richardson in the possession of the Royal Society'. SAAO collection.

the zenith he had found that the apparent position of a star in the sky is affected by the 'aberration' of light, an annual 'movement' caused by the combination of its velocity with the earth's orbital motion through space.

Around 1737, Bradley made a second important discovery, that the axis of the earth is not exactly fixed in space but describes a small circle on the sky with a period of 18.6 years[21] (referred to as 'nutation'). He was sufficiently diffident about his result that he did not publish at the time, preferring to wait until he had acquired more data. His discovery did become widely known, however, because he had outlined it to Maupertuis, who had informed the Royal Academy of Sciences.

By 1744, La Caille was in correspondence with Bradley, for whom he always had great admiration, but communication was soon to become difficult due to the War of the Austrian Succession, which lasted until 1748. It was only in that year that Bradley (1748) finally published his discovery of nutation and provided the details. La Caille was excited to receive a copy of his paper:

> It was the paper from you that I waited for with the most impatience since the rumour of this discovery spread, that is, since about ten years ago. I have been disgusted to see several of our astronomers quarreling over the glory [of supposedly themselves having made this discovery] . . . ;

---

[21] Apart, that is, from its already well-known precession with a cycle of 25,800 years.

but it and the rules obeyed by the movements should in fact have been ascribed to you . . . Since I received your letter I have made a translation from which I read an extract to our academy, which is happy to have acquired you as one of its members.'[22]

The consequence of Bradley's findings was that, in the most accurate work, corrections of a few seconds of arc have to be made to any measurement of position. These adjustments are dependent on the exact date of the observation. La Caille, because he always scrupulously recorded the date, could take the new discoveries into account without having to repeat his work. Unfortunately, this was not often the case for previous generations of astronomers. Thus it happened that work that was otherwise accurate was sometimes not up to standard.

In applying Bradley's nutation corrections to his own solar observations La Caille greatly annoyed another French astronomer, the irascible Pierre-Charles Le Monnier. He was one of those referred to in La Caille's letter to Bradley, quoted above, who had heard of the unpublished discovery via Maupertuis and had made observations which agreed with Bradley's own. However, La Monnier went a little too far by suggesting in one of his lectures to the Academy that he had been involved in the discovery himself. He was soon forced by his colleagues to acknowledge Bradley's priority. Nevertheless, he came to see himself as the proprietor in France of this knowledge and had the effrontery to accuse La Caille of plagiary and of having stolen his equations! Afterwards there was no love lost between them.

The orbit of the earth

A major lifelong interest of La Caille was the orbit of the earth around the Sun (until *c.* 1900 more conveniently observed as the orbit of the Sun around the earth, following the pre-Copernican viewpoint). Though Kepler had discovered more than a century before that this was basically an ellipse, it had gradually become evident that there are deviations from this ideal curve, as mentioned. These are called 'inequalities' by astronomers, and are caused by the attraction of the other planets. La Caille applied a new method to finding the changes in the position of the orbit. He also made a number of accurate measurements of the tilt of the earth's axis,[23] the familiar ~23½ degrees that gives rise to the seasons, by measuring the altitude of the Sun above the horizon at its highest point in the sky in midsummer and its lowest at midwinter noon. He confirmed a suspected slow but very tiny annual decrease in the value of this quantity. After finding out that a medieval astronomer, Bernhard

---

[22] La Caille to Bradley, dated Paris, 22 August 1748 (see Rigaud, 1832, pp. 454–5). Bradley was made a Foreign Associate of the Royal Academy of Sciences in July 1748.

[23] Known technically as the 'obliquity of the ecliptic'.

Walther of Nuremberg, had produced comparatively accurate values for the tilt in the fifteenth century he could then, using current data, provide a figure for its average annual decrease. Later, theorists were able to show that this change stems from the influence of the other planets and does not go on in the same direction for ever, but is cyclic in nature with a very long period. It may be responsible for the Milanković cycle of climate change (period *c*. 41,000 years).

The axes of the elliptical orbit of the earth also slowly change their directions in space. La Caille was concerned with determining this and also the exact length of the year.

The eccentricity or precise shape of the orbital ellipse he determined by comparing the earth's actual motion to what would have been seen if it were purely circular. This was a difficult measurement which led him into controversy later in his life.

Over the years, he was to publish several papers in the Memoirs of the Academy on his 'solar' researches, each one improving on the last.

Eclipses and occultations

Other interests of La Caille's were the calculation of eclipses of the Sun and Moon. He also predicted the times when stars were due to be occulted[24] by the Moon. Simultaneous observations of these events could be used to find the longitude differences between places on the earth and were especially important before chronometers or radio signals became available.

Cometary orbits

La Caille dug deep into the theory of comets, which had been neglected since Halley's time: 'Animated by so many examples and to make full use of the hours of leisure that bad weather gives only too often to astronomers', he set to work on the cometary records of the Paris Observatory. 'If there is anybody who knew how to fill the hours of unwanted leisure, it was La Caille...there never was an astronomer who could better manage his time' (Delambre 1827). He produced a simplified method for calculating a parabolic orbit from a small number of observations. Such orbits, in effect infinitely long ellipses, would be followed by comets that appear only once.

Historical researches

As a means of introducing accuracy into the dating of historical events, La Caille spent five weeks working fifteen hours per day to calculate all the total and partial eclipses visible in Europe from the beginning of the

---

[24] An occultation occurs when one astronomical body moves in front of another.

Christian era until 1800. These he sent to the Benedictine Charles Clé-mencet, the author with others of a work *L'Art de vérifier les Dates...* (*The art of verifying dates...*, 1750), an immense chronology compiled from ancient writings. La Caille had realised that the Benedictines had uncritically accepted whatever dates they had found, not knowing whether they contained errors. Any eclipses that were mentioned were a sure way of tying them down. He expected nothing in return for this labour of love and was highly embarrassed when they acknowledged his work in their preface. 'Scholars considered him to be a person gifted with superior talents in his field; but the public, always extreme in its judgements, regarded him as a unique genius from whom nothing was hidden that had the least connection with the science that he professed' (Carlier, in La Caille 1776, p. 33).

Growing reputation

Each year, he published his results in the *Memoirs of the Royal Academy of Sciences*. He was very careful to show the details of his observations and how he had come to his conclusions, making estimates of their probable errors. In this he was in advance of his contemporaries, whereas his enemy Le Monnier, at least according to Delambre (1827), was always a bit behind the times!

As Grandjean de Fouchy said later in his éloge,[25] all this work produced in such a sort time would have been sufficient to establish the glorious name of the Abbé. But glory was not his aim; rather it was the progress of astronomy. His reputation spread far and wide, with the result that he was made a corresponding member of many foreign academies—St Petersburg, Berlin, Stockholm, Bologna, Göttingen and the Royal Society of London, to the last of which he was elected in January 1760. Honours had to be thrust upon him as he would never have dreamed of taking the initiative in such matters.

Even before his visit to the Cape, La Caille enjoyed a certain repu-tation with the public:

... some distinguished persons, unenlightened as to the real aim of astronomy, consulted him from time to time in all seriousness about the probable outcome of important trials, others on the likely date of their deaths, on how their children would turn out and whether they would be badly or favourably treated by fate—a kind of insult to his probity, his candour and his deep knowledge.

Though he was a lively and impatient person, especially when asked nonsensical questions, he listened quietly to the doubts and worries that he was consulted about. He varied his responses according to the circumstances and made it a principle to calm people's worries charitably

[25] An éloge is a eulogy or form of obituary.

and sooth their spirits, however crazy they were. The number of those who cannot distinguish astronomy from astrology is even greater than one might think [!] (Carlier, in La Caille 1776, p. 34).

Similarly, his ex-pupil Bailly (1770) mentions:

Mr de La Caille made for himself a kind of solitude in the middle of Paris; not that he closed his doors to anybody, feeling that a scientist who wanted to be useful should never go into hiding. But his face would become dark and would glaze over when he was approached by idlers, depriving them of any desire to return.

The southern hemisphere plan

After some years, La Caille realised that observations made in the southern hemisphere would enable him, especially if supported by simultaneous measurements in the north, to get improved values for several numbers of fundamental importance to astronomy such as the distances of the Sun, Moon and planets, the tilts of the planetary orbits and so on. He could also complete the star catalogues that only covered the northern hemisphere; up to that time, the best southern catalogue available was a comparatively rough one of 341 stars made by Edmond Halley when observing as a young man from St Helena and published in 1678.

It was also important to understand how the apparent positions of the stars were distorted, to however small an extent, by the refraction of light by the earth's atmosphere. This problem remained a particularly difficult one until the advent of observations from space. He saw that it could be solved in part by southern hemisphere observations.

It appears that the Abbé was offered the chance of making a trip to the Cape of Good Hope at fairly short notice through the hydrographer d'Après de Mannevillette (see also Chapter 2). Contacts such as these were common in the relatively small scientific community. He quickly prepared a request for funding[26] during early July 1750 which he sent to the Secretary of State for War, Comte Marc-Pierre de Voyer de Paulmy d'Argenson, outlining a possible scheme and emphasising of course the usefulness of what he proposed to geography and navigation. In spite of being an aristocrat with a high official position, d'Argenson was a leading figure of the enlightenment, a friend of Voltaire and other writers critical of the pre-revolutionary state of affairs in France. The Comte promptly wrote to the Academy[27] to ask their opinion of the plan so that he could present it to the King.

---

[26] Note the absence of book-length proposals and large committees!

[27] D'Argenson to the Academy of Sciences, dated Versailles 3 July 1750. Archives of the Academy of Sciences of the Institut de France, Folio 408.

La Caille's memoir explained in detail the difficulties hitherto experienced in the determination of longitudes at sea by means of Lunar observations. The accuracy of the Sun's and Moon's orbits had to be improved upon by having experienced observers make simultaneous observations with the best instruments from the parts of the earth furthest apart along a north–south line [i.e. a meridian]. Two circumstances, extremely favourable to success, were going to present themselves in the course of the year 1751: an opposition of Mars close to its perihelion and an inferior conjunction of Venus.[28] To profit from such a rare chance, la Caille, emphasising his thirteen years of experience with the most delicate observations, using the most suitable instruments, was asking the Academy to find him the means for spending a year at the Cape of Good Hope. He explained that in every respect it was the most advantageously situated place, being very distant from Paris and at the same time close to the meridian which passes through the middle of Europe: two absolutely essential conditions if he was to hope for reasonable success.

The observations that he proposed were as follows:

(1) To determine the true position of the Cape, about which even the most celebrated geographers differed by about 100 leagues [440 km].
(2) To determine by concerted observations, the parallax[29] of the Moon, the most important element and yet the least known fact about this object.
(3) To observe the parallax [distance] of the Sun, a quantity even more uncertain than the parallax of the Moon; the two rare planetary phenomena mentioned being expected to furnish several sure means of obtaining it.[30]
(4) To complete the catalogue of the principal fixed stars, by the same method and with the same instruments with which he has already established the exact positions of the northern ones.

He claimed, rather optimistically as it turned out, that this project could be executed quite simply. There would be no expenses for the construction of the instruments which already existed; solely travel and

[28] These are the times when Mars and Venus are at their closest to the earth. Mars, further from the Sun than the earth, is in 'opposition' when it is on the opposite side of the earth from the Sun. The perihelion of Mars is the closest it gets to the Sun in its elliptical orbit, so the coincidence of this with its opposition was a particularly favourable opportunity. Venus, closer to the Sun than the earth, is at 'inferior conjunction' when it is between the earth and the Sun.

[29] A solar system object's parallax is related to its distance, and is determined by trigonometry from a baseline on the earth (see Appendix 1).

[30] What he means here is that if we know the distances of the planets Mars and Venus we can use this information together with Kepler's laws of planetary motion to derive the size of the earth's orbit.

subsistence costs would be needed for about a year. No assistant or servant would be required; he would board wherever he was told to as the nature of his observations required only a quiet place to stay where he could set up his instruments.

> The Dutch [having previously allowed the German astronomer Kolbe to do this type of work] cannot reasonably refuse the King [the same for] an astronomer of his Academy, who will stay exactly in the place that he is assigned to, whether in the fort or in the interior of the country. Besides, this project is for the common good of all nations.[31]

It was by no means a simple matter to arrange an expedition of this kind. His plans were facilitated by various people whom he thanked later; for example, Roland-Michel Barrin de La Galissonière, head of the Dèpôt de la Marine, the French Hydrographic Office.

> Scarcely had I presented this project to be approved by the Academy when the Minister undertook to procure all possible facilities to execute it. [In fact, he received a grant of 10,000 French pounds from the Royal Treasury.] The gentlemen of the Compagnie des Indes (French Indies Company) volunteered to transport my instruments; and if one was not already aware of their zeal for the progress of navigation I would not know to what to attribute the care and attention they had for me or how to show my appreciation. (La Caille 1751, p. 521)

Obtaining the support of the Dutch for a prolonged scientific visit to the Cape, which was then a commercial colony operated by the Dutch East India Company, was a somewhat more delicate matter since they had recently been at war with the French. It was necessary to go through the proper diplomatic channels. In August 1750, the Marquis de Puisieulx, Secretary of State for Foreign Affairs, asked the Netherlands Ambassador, Lestevenon van Berckenrode, to approach his government to seek permission for the expedition. He handed him a copy of La Caille's proposal, as previously summarised, to explain why it was worth doing.

A formal request, together with the proposal, was sent by the ambassador to the States-General of the Netherlands, his superiors in The Hague. Through the influential Dutch–British aristocrat Count Willem Bentinck, the Dutch Stadtholder or hereditary head of state, Prince Willem IV of Orange-Nassau, in his capacity of Director General (Opperbewindhebber) of the Dutch East India Company, was also approached directly; a subtle move, since he was known to be interested in scientific matters (Zuidervaart, 2006). The States-General rather

---

[31] Memorandum enclosed by d'Argenson in a letter to the Royal Academy of Sciences, dated Versailles 3 July 1750. Archives of the Academy of Sciences of the Institute de France, Folio 408. A copy of this memorandum was sent a little later to the Dutch authorities and was quoted by Maclear, 1866, p. 58.

grudgingly gave their permission and requested that precautions should be taken to make sure that no improper use was made of it.[32] However, the Stadtholder himself took a more positive line and requested the Governor of the Cape to render whatever assistance was needed. It is rather noticeable that La Caille was referred to as 'Mr' rather than 'Abbé' in this correspondence, probably to avoid the hostility of the Dutch East India Company towards religions other than the official Reformed Church.

Meanwhile, on 5 September 1750, La Caille's proposal was read to the Academy together with a short statement from him, largely paralleling the memoir, but containing the following:

> Being kept here in Paris by the chair that I occupy at the Collège Mazarin, I was only able to wish that some experienced astronomer would undertake a long voyage to put the finishing touches to my work until several favourable circumstances came together to make me consider doing it myself. The rare occasion to determine the parallax of the Sun by the opposition of Mars followed by an inferior conjunction of Venus, the approbation and even the exhortations of several enlightened persons to whom I showed the plan, the obliging offer of Mr D'Après, who is getting ready to leave for the isles of France and Bourbon [Mauritius and Réunion, in the Indian Ocean], the information he has given me on the places I could go to, the confidence I have in the zeal of people who would like to help with the success of this enterprise and finally the desire I have always had to contribute something to the progress of astronomy—all that made me produce a memoir a few weeks ago on the utility and ease of this voyage, and by the care of Mr Duhamel,[33] I have had the satisfaction of seeing that my project has not only been approved by the Minister but further by the Controller-General and that the gentlemen of the Indies Company at once provided the means to carry it out.[34]

Before the voyage, La Caille wrote a printed pamphlet entitled *Advice to Astronomers* (*Avis aux Astronomes*, La Caille, 1750) which he circulated to several colleagues around Europe with details of his proposed programme. They were asked to make observations simultaneously with his own at pre-determined times, when this was necessary. For example, in finding the distances of relatively (astronomically speaking) nearby objects such as the Moon or the planets, two widely separated places on the earth could form the base of a survey triangle. This sort of measurement was best done when a planet was at its nearest to the earth, because then the angle at the apex of the triangle would

---

[32] See further correspondence reproduced in Maclear (1866).

[33] Henri-Louis Duhamel du Monceau, Inspector-General of the Marine.

[34] Read by La Caille to the Royal Academy of Sciences, 5 September 1750; Archive of the Academy of Sciences of the Institut de France, Folio 408.

be at its maximum and any observational errors would have the least effect. The fact that during his stay at the Cape both Mars and Venus were going to be appropriately placed in September and October 1751 respectively was particularly fortunate. He gave detailed instructions as to which dates were important and which objects and comparison stars should be examined on each occasion.

His pamphlet continued in a kind of footnote to blast Halley's idea that the rare phenomenon of the 'Transit of Venus' (passage of Venus across the face of the Sun) expected in 1761 could be expected to yield a very precise value for its distance from the earth. Though he felt obliged to criticise Halley on several occasions, he always expressed his admiration as though to compensate for his temerity:

> In spite of the respect I have for the ideas of this great man, this precision appears to me impossible...I can't believe that [it] would be possible to determine the exact time within two seconds as Halley supposes, because the edges of the Sun when near the horizon are waving about continually...and because the rapid movement of the Sun and Venus in the field of a high-magnification telescope renders it very difficult to tell the exact moment of contact'.

In this he has been proved correct time and time again, since these problems dogged all the observed Transits of Venus in the years 1639, 1761, 1769, 1874 and 1882. Better ways of finding the distance of the Sun are nowadays, of course, available.

According to Carlier, (La Caille 1776, p. 90) the Abbé ensured that the debts of his father were paid off before his departure. He was summoned to visit the Minister a few days before he left and given 200 Louis d'or (4800 French pounds) towards his expenses. He promptly spent them on a magnificent quadrant whose construction he had been supervising. 'This quadrant, with several other instruments, had been ordered by the President of the Academy of St Petersburg, whose decease had reduced the maker to the necessity of keeping it'. He then made it over to the Academy.[35] Travel within France was scary enough; voyaging to foreign parts was so dangerous that he must have wondered if he was ever going to see Paris again.

---

[35] Wolf (1902) traced the subsequent history of this instrument, which he thinks was probably the sextant used at the Cape (see Fig. 2.10) rather than a quadrant. Its date of manufacture (1750) supports his suggestion. After passing through various owners, It was acquired by Admiral Mouchez for the Paris Observatory museum in 1883.

2

The Cape

On 21 October 1750, the Abbé left the comfort of Paris and the Collège Mazarin for the port of Lorient on the south coast of Brittany. Though the distance was only about 450 km, he did not arrive there until 1 November, thanks to the primitive state of land transportation. Lorient was where the French Indies Company (Compagnie des Indes), founded in 1664 and chartered by King Louis XIV, had its shipyards. The Company was then at the height of its influence, controlling extensive territories on the eastern side of the Indian sub-continent.

La Caille embarked that same night on the Company ship on which he was to sail, Le Glorieux, a brand-new frigate not yet quite ready for the sea. It had been launched in St Malo on 26 July 1750 and has been described as being of 500 tons with 14 cannons and a crew of 89.[1] They had to remain in port for a further month.

The crowded conditions aboard eighteenth-century ships on long voyages were extremely insanitary, though they probably did not differ much from one nationality to another or even from conditions at home. Quite a few living animals and birds, brought along to provide fresh meat from time to time, must have added to the general stench and overcrowding. Most of the meat onboard was preserved in salt. Drinking water was scarce and tasted bad, even though a small amount of it could be made from sea-water by distillation on some vessels.

As an honoured guest of the Company, La Caille was probably given a cabin at the stern with the ship's officers. The Captain was a scientist himself: Jean-Baptiste-Nicolas-Denis D'Après de Mannevillette was a noted hydrographer who had worked extensively in the Indian Ocean and was the author of an important hydrographic atlas, Le Neptune Oriental, first published in 1745, as well as being the main advocate in France of using John Hadley's recently developed octant (see Fig. 2.1) for navigation. He was a correspondent of the Royal Academy of Sciences and was later a member of the Académie Royale de Marine (Royal Marine Academy), founded in 1752.

---

[1] See www.memoiredeshommes.sga.defense.gouv.fr/indes/armement/armement/

Fig. 2.1 Octant developed by John Hadley for taking sightings of stars. This was the precursor of the sextant. La Caille had a strong long-term interest in practical navigation (From Hadley, 1731).

Others on board included Julien-Marie Crozet, serving as an officer. Later on he was the navigator and second in command of the expedition that discovered the Crozet Islands. La Caille's technician, Mr Poitevin, described on the personnel manifest as a domestic servant, sailed with him. Unfortunately we know no details of the the latter except that he had been trained in the workshops of Claude Langlois who, as mentioned, had made most of the instruments that the Abbé used. Altogether, there were about 65 people on board in addition to the crew, including a stowaway.

While killing time ashore the Abbé came cross a still-blind newborn puppy that somebody had abandoned in a corner. He picked it up and took it on board as something with which to amuse himself during the voyage. During the months at sea he relieved his boredom and loneliness by teaching it little tricks. He gave the pup the name of 'Grisgris', some say from the grey colour of his coat.[2] He seems to have taken a strange attitude to this creature. According to an anonymous contributor to his life as given in the *Journal Historique* (La Caille 1776, p. 98), he accustomed the dog so much to blows and tricks 'that after a long sleep he wanted to be hit; that was the way to please him! Upon which some people remarked in joking that the dog outdid his master, who fled applause and caresses'. When they got to Rio the animal amused the crew by barking at buildings, stumbling and

---

[2] 'Grisgris' is also the name of a good-luck charm used in Voodoo by the slaves of New Orleans; Lorient was no stranger to the slave trade. The word 'grigri' also refers to a charm.

falling because he had never known anything but life on board ship. He only had sea-legs and had never been on *terra firma*. Later on, at the Cape, he always accompanied his master. He was kept inside during the day, especially when they were far from town, because of the fear that he might be bitten by a snake. Night was for him the time for work and play. Whenever La Caille had an interval of leisure between observations he would play with Grisgris and forget the pain of keeping his head in a constant and tiring position. The anonymous maker of additional remarks in the *Journal Historique* (La Caille 1776, p. 99) asked if 'our Gris-gris didn't deserve more than Sirius to give his name to some constellation or at least to some remarkable southern star'! The dog's name is the same as that of a cape in Mauritius; it is said that Grisgris was lost there during the survey that La Caille made just after he left the Cape of Good Hope.

The day before sailing La Caille wrote to his friend Jean-Dominique Maraldi (Fig. 2.2), asking him to say goodbye to some of his other acquaintances and to take care of a very boring task, the proof-reading of his Ephemerides (tables of planet positions etc.). He ended:

I would ask you to speak sometimes to Mademoiselle Le Jeuneux[3] to let her know my departure is fixed for tomorrow 21 at seven o'clock in the morning, and to carry my farewells to her mother and father. I will not miss any chance to send my news.

I ask you to present my respects to Mr Cassini and his sons and Madame de Thury, his wife, to Mr and Mrs[4] de Breger and Mr de Charmoi.[5] [Then the formal ending followed by:] I am the carrier of a letter from the Stadholder and one from the Chief of the Directors of the Dutch East India Company for the Governor of the Cape. I hope to be well received.[6]

The voyage

They set sail at 7.30 a.m. on 21 November and by 10 a.m. the Abbé was seasick. He remained so for three weeks!

---

[3] Anne-Louise Le Jeuneux was a young artist who La Caille seems to have been fond of (See Chapter 5).

[4] Possibly this was Suzanne Cassini, sister of Cassini III de Thury, who married Philippes Breget in 1729 (see Wolf, 1902).

[5] The wife of Cassini II was born Susanne-Françoise Charpentier de Charmoi, suggesting that Mr de Charmoi was a connection of this family.

[6] La Caille to Maraldi, dated L'Orient, 20 November 1750. Observatoire de Paris ms 1076 (133).

Fig. 2.2 Jean-Dominique (Giovanni Domenico) Maraldi (Maraldi II), La Caille's best friend (private collection, House Maraldi; artist unknown). Photograph courtesy of Marina Musi, Perinaldo.

Navigation at the time, before the invention of the marine chronometer, was very unreliable. Knowledge of the time was essential to finding one's longitude. Though the first chronometers dated from 1762, further development was necessary. Besides, they were so expensive that they did not become common until well into the nineteenth century. This meant that a ship's position was usually uncertain. Dead reckoning with the aid of a magnetic compass could not allow for the effects of winds and ocean currents. Latitude, on the other hand, was easy enough to determine from the altitude of stars above the horizon. The technique that Captain D'Après employed in going to the Cape was to sail southwards in what he hoped was a straight line until the latitude of the Cape Verde Islands was reached, and then to proceed directly west until the islands themselves were sighted. He missed his target but on 13 December La Caille was able to obtain a time, and hence a longitude, from an eclipse of the Moon. They found out that they were already too far to the west to encounter the islands. As a result it was decided to head for Rio, which they reached on 25 January 1751. There they had to careen (beach) a small ship which was part of their expedition in order to repair a serious leak.

During their voyage, La Caille investigated the problem of navigating using the method of Lunar distances[7] to find local times and thereby longitudes. It became obvious to him that the position of the Moon could not, in fact, be predicted with sufficient accuracy:

> In this awkward situation, Mr Halley, the most learned astronomer of his time, and zealous for the the improvement of navigation as well as for the glory of his nation, had made a decision which could be regarded as the last resource in an almost hopeless cause. Knowing that it would never be possible to determine longitudes at sea without having fully calculated the movements of the Moon ... he believed it should be possible to supply them through the use of certain *Empirical Equations* ... This idea of Mr Halley (in the execution of which he worked without cease during the last twenty years of his life) is well enough known to astronomers: it was excellent in Mr Halley's theory; but today [writing eight years later], now that the Theory of the Moon is a solved problem, [his idea] has become as useless as it is inconvenient in the determination of longitudes ... (La Caille 1759, p. 66).

These difficulties encouraged La Caille to look further into the question of the orbit of the Moon and into the construction of Lunar tables. In this he met with considerable success and can be considered the first person to show the practicality of the method of 'Lunars', which, developed further by others, was the most important method of finding longitudes at sea until well into the nineteenth century (see also Chapter 5, Later studies).

From Rio, La Caille wrote a short report on the voyage to Maraldi in Paris.

> Since my departure nothing serious has happened to me or any other members of our company—apart from the three weeks of seasickness that I had because of the bad paint my room was coated with. I have not had a chance to be bored, being in good company and in a good vessel. I have not yet made any particularly important observations. We found here Mr Godin [a member of the Academy of Sciences' expedition to Peru] on his way back to Europe; he has been of great help to us in this country where we do not have too many friends. I have given him this letter to hand over when he gets to Lisbon. I hope you receive it in good health. I will write to you in more detail from the Cape, where I hope to arrive at the end of March. I will let you know how to send your news. In the meantime, I ask you to present my respects to Mr and Mrs Cassini and to be so good as to send this letter on to Mademoiselle Le Jeuneux. The voyage I am making is doing me infinite good. I have learned navigation and can speak of it with some knowledge. Goodbye

---

[7] This involved measuring the distance of the Moon from certain bright stars and comparing these to previously tabulated values.

Fig. 2.3 Table Mountain as viewed from Table Bay with Dutch ships in the roads, *c.* 1770, by Johannes Schumacher, published by J.H. Schneider, Amsterdam. The mountains from left to right are: Devil's Peak, Table Mountain, Lion's Head and Lion's Rump. The Castle is to the left, behind the jetty. La Caille's observatory was close to the shore behind the cluster of small boats. (Library of Parliament, Cape Town, PARL 0023).

my dear friend, love me always a bit, and don't grumble too much about correcting the proofs of the Ephemerides—do it patiently and for the remission of your sins. If you can let it be known at Collège Mazarin that I am well you will oblige me greatly....'[8]

While in Rio La Caille made observations of its longitude and latitude, the strength of gravity and the magnetic declination. In his diary (*Journal Historique*; La Caille (1776)) he took note of the beautiful churches and numerous religious statues. He also commented on the amount of debauchery, even among clergy and monks, as well as 'excesses of disorders and superstition'. He was rather disgusted when lunching with the Governor, who gave him and Mr D'Après small napkins that were creased and dirty, showing signs that they had been used before. 'For all that, he is a wealthy gentleman who prides himself on knowing how to live.' A meal with a local Dutchman was more civilised—coffee was served to his visitors by his wife, something that would not have occurred in a normal carioco household, where wives were then kept in a kind of purdah.

They set sail again on 22 February 1751 but were halted for several weeks by unfavourable winds close to their destination. At last, on 18 April, following a thick fog, they sighted land. That night, a rainstorm accompanied by heavy seas kept them from approaching closer. The next day was beautiful and they anchored in the roads[9] of the Cape at one o'clock (Fig. 2.3). There they had to stay as Table Bay had no harbour; merely a jetty. Loading and unloading required the use of small lighters that carried passengers and freight between ship and shore.

---

[8] La Caille to Maraldi, dated Rio, 19 February 1751. Observatoire de Paris ms 1076 (135).

[9] Anchoring place.

Arrival at the Cape

On 20 April 1751 La Caille and D'Après stepped ashore at 10 a.m. to pay a first visit to the Governor and his officials. The Abbé presented his letters of credence, one of which read as follows:

> At Het Loo, 17th October, 1750
>
> To the Honourable, worshipful and pious, Our beloved and trustworthy Governor of the Cape of Good Hope:
>
> Mr de la Caille, Member of the Royal Academy of Sciences of Paris, whose intention it is to make a trip to the Cape for some time to pursue his astronomical observations, has sought the necessary permission of their High Mightynesses [The Lords Seventeen, directors of the East India Company], and, not wishing to deny him, we having decided to defer to this request, and hereby recommend him to you, trusting that you will extend to him all possible assistance that he may require during his stay.
>
> Honourable, worshipful and pious, Our loved and trustworthy, we commend you to God's holy protection
> Your well-wishing friend
> Prince of Orange and Nassau (signed)
> By order of his Highness
> in the absence of his Private Secretary
> J.D. Horst[10]

Other letters were from the Dutch East India Company itself and Count Bentinck, the Anglo-Dutch aristocrat who had helped arrange Dutch permission in the first place.

The Governor happily complied with His Majesty's request and told La Caille that he was welcome to remain at the Cape with full freedom to do as he wanted. In general the Abbé was to find himself treated very courteously by the Company's officials.

The Cape, as the town itself was then called, was then home to about 5500 people of European origin and about 6300 slaves. There were also a small number of freed slaves. About a third of the European population were employees of the Dutch East India Company, officially in Dutch, the Vereenigde Oost-Indische Compagnie,[11] whose initials VOC appeared as a monogram on all its properties. In the nearby countryside were perhaps another 15,000 Europeans. Almost all the surviving indigenous people of the area, the pastoralists at one time called 'hottentots' (more correctly referred to as Khoina), lived outside the parts occupied by the Europeans and the 'wild bushmen' (a different group, the Sonqua, who did not farm either crops or animals) were

---

[10] See Maclear, 1866, pp. 60–61.
[11] United East India Company.

found far to the north. The slaves came from many places such as Madagascar and various territories bordering the Indian Ocean. They did most of the manual work but, contrary to popular belief, were seldom badly treated, being their owners' most valuable possessions and, in some cases, almost 'part of the family'. Many were owned by the VOC itself. The laws in the eighteenth century were generally very harsh but particularly towards those slaves who showed signs of rebellion. It was not completely unknown for Europeans to marry slaves who they had freed, though prejudice against inter-racial marriages occurred even then. Generally, manumission (freeing from slave status) was possible but expensive and therefore rare (see also Chapter 4).

The Company, the VOC, existed in the years from 1602 to 1798 and was the first multi-national corporation as well as the first company to issue stock. Its headquarters were in Amsterdam and its operations covered most of the Far East. It was virtually a sovereign state, having the right to wage war, make treaties, found colonies and issue money. It had tens of thousands of employees worldwide, many of them stationed in the East. Apart from purely cargo vessels, it operated armed merchantmen and maintained a large private army. It was far larger than the India Companies of the other European countries.

The VOC colony at the Cape was founded in 1652 to re-supply ships on the long voyage to the Indies. Arriving vessels often contained sick passengers and crew suffering from scurvy (vitamin C deficiency), who recovered quickly once they ate fresh food. Though at first all the Europeans at the Cape were company employees, a permanent settlement of free citizens or 'burghers' very quickly developed. The Company tried to control the lives of individual colonists in strict fashion, though with varying degrees of success. For example, they set the prices of all commodities, annoying the locals by buying cheap and selling dear, and generally tried to keep all trading activities under their own control. A partial result was that most commercial activity was underground and there was a great deal of smuggling.

La Caille was fortunate in that Ryk Tulbagh, the governor of the time, was one of the best of the Dutch East India Company's servants. He had just been appointed, on 22 February 1751, and had taken office on 15 April, five days before his interview with La Caille. Born in Utrecht in 1699, he attended the Latin School of Bergen-op-Zoom and seems also to have known French. He had initially been apprenticed at the age of 16 to the Company, for five years. After his arrival at the Cape in 1716, his hard-working and studious demeanour led quickly to a series of promotions. In 1739 he was appointed to be 'Secunde' or second in command at the Cape, and was given the rank of Senior Merchant (a title of honour rather than a trading position). His wife was Elizabeth Swellengrebel, the sister of the previous governor. They had had two children but both died young. Tulbagh took a benevolent interest in the inhabitants of the colony, who referred to him as 'Father Tulbagh'. He had a lively mind and was interested in the flora and fauna of the Cape, encouraging the investigations of visiting botanists and corresponding in Latin with the botanists Adriaan and David van Royen of Leiden and the Swede Linnaeus. In April 1761 he was to welcome the English astronomers Charles Mason and Jeremiah Dixon who observed the Transit of Venus of that year from Cape Town on the 6th of June.[12] Visiting the Cape in 1771, the French novelist Bernardin de Saint-Pierre (1773) wrote 'He often invites strangers to his table. Although aged eighty[13] his conversation is lively: he knows our intellectual works and likes them. Of all the Frenchmen that he has met, the one he misses most is the Abbé de La Caille. He had built an observatory for him. He appreciated his learning, his modesty, his disinterestedness, his social graces.'

Jan Lourens Bestbier

The day after they first set foot ashore, La Caille and D'Après again went to see Tulbagh and were invited to dine with him (dinner at the time was usually from 12 noon to 2 p.m.). Later on, the Abbé was able to arrange accommodation with a certain Jan Lourens Bestbier in his private house. It was then customary for the better class of visitors to stay in private homes as the more public hostelries were aimed at sailors who were apt to be raucous and uncouth. In fact, quite prosperous burghers such as Bestbier were only too happy to make money in this way.

This Jan Lourens Bestbier, whose help proved to be almost essential to La Caille's success, was born Johann Lorenz Bestbier in Oppenheim around 1715–18, in the Rhineland-Palatinate of Germany. He arrived at the Cape as the bookkeeper on the ship Karssenhof and was to become the founder (stammvater) of the Bestbier family in South Africa. According to La Caille, he was one of the most esteemed people at the Cape for probity and disinterestedness. Though the Cape was nominally a Dutch colony, Germans were almost as numerous as Dutch. In fact, the Dutch often had trouble finding suitable people of their own nationality to serve there. The somewhat higher Dutch standard of living was however attractive to many Germans, especially the young and adventurous. Bestbier had already served with the French before arriving at the Cape as an adjutant in the army of the Company. As a result, he could speak French and could thus be of tremendous assis-

---

[12] The 'Mason–Dixon Line' between parts of the borders of Pennsylvania, Maryland, Delaware, and West Virginia and the traditional division between the northern and southern states of the USA was surveyed by them a few years later.

[13] Actually about 72!

Fig. 2.4 No. 2 Strand Street (right), the early eighteenth-century house where La Caille resided and had his observatory, photographed in the late nineteenth century when the street was no longer a fashionable one (W. Cape Archives & Record Service E4051).

tance to the Abbé, who admitted that none of his observations could have been made without his aid. Bestbier must have become prosperous with exceptional rapidity (if the dates associated with him are correct),[14] since he married and acquired his house in 1737. A year later he was made a Burger or full citizen and he served on the board of the Orphan Chamber, which had wide powers in the administration of deceased estates, dealing with intestacy, orphans etc., and was very prestigious to belong to. As a member of the Burger Council and Court of Justice, he was about as influential as a non-company man could be. He was also a Captain in the Burger Militia. The latter was a body, meeting for training each year, that defended the countryside from rebellious native peoples, particularly the 'bushmen', who frequently caused trouble in the frontier areas and were still capable of mounting serious campaigns against would-be farmers.

Bestbier held a contract to supply meat to the Company, a position which would have led automatically to some wealth. Such contracts

---

[14] Several people at the Cape became wealthy quite rapidly during the eighteenth century through marrying rich widows.

were auctioned and he is mentioned as having obtained one for one year in 1748 and another for five years in 1749.[15] The contractors had free and exclusive use of an area called 'Slagtersveld'[16] between the west coast and the hilly area called Groene Kloof (near the present-day Darling). Each butcher was lent a farm as a base where animals and herdsmen could stay safely at night. La Caille visited this area with Bestbier on several occasions during his geodetic survey work.

Bestbier's commodious house was at No. 2 Strand Street (see Fig. 2.4), then the closest street to the sea of the Cape Town grid, and originally called Zeestraat. It ran parallel to the shoreline of Rogge Bay. The latter was a small bay within Table Bay proper. The back yards of the houses on the sea side of the street reached almost to the shoreline. Its site is now well inland thanks to land reclamation. The rear boundary of the property was about 50 metres from the shore. La Caille noted that the difference between high and low tide was only about a metre and that during north-westerly hurricanes the streets were sometimes covered by waves which broke against the houses.

La Caille's observatory

Two days after landing he made plans to erect a small observatory in Bestbier's back yard. Once his instruments had been brought ashore, he set them out in his room just as they would be when in use and designed a suitable little building to house them (see Fig. 2.5). The Governor generously offered the services of Company workmen and the use of its materials for the construction of the Observatory.

On the 24th Mr de Ruyter, described by La Caille as the Port Captain,[17] came to check the site and plan, telling him that the workmen would arrive on the 29th.

The building took just under a month to construct. Its dimensions were about $5\,m \times 5\,m \times 5\,m$, forming a cube. The roof was sloped and constructed like a floor. It was waterproofed by a tarpaulin thrown over it. The instruments, from front to back, as seen in Fig. 2.5, were a sextant, a quadrant and a zenith sector, each of which had its own

---

[15] In the latter case, for example, he was paid 11 duiten per pound for butchered mutton and beef and 2 rijksdalers each for live sheep.

[16] Butchers' land.

[17] Mentzel **1**, p. 152 (1785) declared that this person was more likely to have been the Captain of the Militia, whose job included supervising the artisans employed by the VOC. In fact, Hendrik de Ruijter is referred to as 'Equipagemeester' in *Resolutions of the Council of Policy of the Cape of Good Hope* Cape Town Archives Repository, Reference Code C130, pp. 227–237. The Equipagemeester's job was to see to the equipping of the VOC ships.

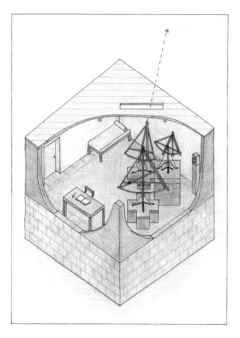

Fig. 2.5 Cut-away reconstruction of La Caille's observatory in Bestbier's back yard on the Cape Town foreshore, based on his plan and textual description. The right corner in this view pointed to the north. ©I.S. Glass

special purpose, even though they resembled each other in many ways. To avoid vibrations they were mounted on solid pedestals, each with its own foundation.

During the period of construction, La Caille was at relative leisure. He prepared lists of observations to be made and checked that his instruments had not suffered or been distorted during transportation. He was invited to visit the Governor again. He also walked along the Table Bay shoreline, went up to the foot of Table Mountain and to the Lion's Rump (Signal Hill). He visited the Company's garden which was founded to supply ships with fresh vegetables and which still exists in part as a city park, finding it to be 996 by 261 paces.

In a letter to Maraldi he expressed his frustration at the time the VOC workmen were taking to build the Observatory, but otherwise he felt very well, happy and at ease with himself. He went on:

> I wish from all my heart that we were here together. It would be for you more agreeable than staying in Paris…For the rest you would find it to your taste…I expect that from time to time you see Mr and Mrs Le Jeuneux. If they show any interest in me please give them my regards…

Fig. 2.6 The eighteenth-century (1790) shoreline of Table Bay (or strictly, the part of it called Rogge Bay, looking from the north; part of a painting by Samuel Davis), showing the location of La Caille's Observatory, or a building on the same spot, behind No. 2, Strand Street. The dark structure at the left was the workshop of the VOC, which La Caille used as a landmark when taking bearings from far to the north (W. Cape Archives & Record Service M799).

> I beg you to make my compliments to Messrs De L'Isle, Buache, Camus, Bourdelin and Guettard [all scientific friends from the Academy].[18]

La Caille's observatory, being in Bestbier's backyard, overlooked Rogge Bay (see Fig. 2.6). Unlike a modern observatory, this one did not have a dome or a sliding roof. A series of trapdoors could be opened to allow just a small part of the sky to be viewed. This had the advantage that the instruments were protected from wind-shake and the observer was kept more comfortable. Most of La Caille's measurements were made on or close to the meridian (the line passing overhead that divides the eastern from the western sky). The interior of the observatory may have been painted black like his observatory on the roof of the Collège Mazarin in order to spare his night vision.

The three main instruments of the Observatory, a zenith sector, a giant sextant and a quadrant, will be described in the next section. Besides these, there were two pendulum clocks, by the famous Paris makers Julien Le Roy and Antoine Thiout. He could measure the time within ½ second. A work table and a bed completed the furnishing. The clocks were necessary for timing when the stars crossed the meridian. They were set to sidereal[19] time by observing a bright star such as Sirius at the start of every evening. At that time, pendulums did not usually have compensation for changes in temperature, which could be a significant source of error if comparing observations made during a hot day with those made during a cool night.

---

[18] La Caille to Maraldi, dated Cape, 13 June 1751. Observatoire de Paris ms 1076 (134).

[19] Whereas ordinary time relates to the rotation of the earth under the Sun, sidereal time relates to the rotation of the earth under the stars. The sidereal day is shorter than the solar day by about four minutes thanks to the revolution of the earth around the Sun.

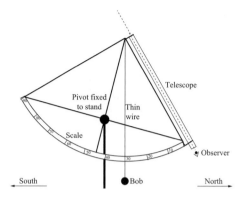

Fig. 2.7 Principle of instruments used by La Caille. The frame was usually aligned north–south and could be swung around the pivot so that the observer could view a particular star as it crossed from east to west. The time it passed the centre of the reticle in the eypiece gave its Right Ascension and the position of the wire against the scale yielded its Zenith Angle and from this its Declination. ©I.S. Glass.

There seems to have been a small workshop where La Caille and Poitevin could work on and even manufacture instruments. Mention is made of constructing a barometer and some thermometers and there was also some sort of facility for dividing and checking the angles marked on his scales. While waiting for the observatory to be finished they constructed a quadrant of about 30 cm radius.

The instruments

The three main instruments were rather similar. Each one was aligned with its frame running north–south and perpendicular to the ground. They all depended on knowing the direction of the zenith (the point straight up). This was achieved by a plumb line consisting of a thin silver wire connected to the top of the frame (see Fig. 2.7). It had to be enclosed in a tube to prevent disturbance arising from air currents. A spherical copper bob on the lower end was immersed in water to help dampen down vibrations. The position of the wire against the scale could be read under a strong magnifying glass and there was a lamp arranged for illumination under night-time conditions.

When observing a single star, the whole instrument was swung by the observer so that the star was on the crosswire of the telescope as it passed the meridian, and its angle from the zenith could then be read from where the vertical wire crossed the large curved scale. Figure 3.3 shows the sector in actual use, with one person looking through the telescope and another reading off the scale behind the plumb line to get the declination. All three instruments were used in the same way.

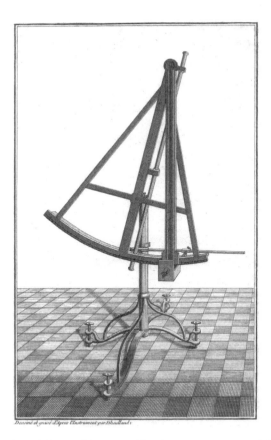

Dessiné et gravé d'après l'instrument par Dheulland.

Fig. 2.8 La Caille's 1.9 m zenith sector. This instrument was used for finding the latitude of a station by observing stars near the zenith (straight up). The heavy box-section hanging straight down enclosed a plumb line consisting of a fine silver wire and a spherical copper weight about 22.6 mm in diameter, suspended in front of the scale. The reading was taken with the aid of a lamp, to give the angle of the star from the zenith. Drawn and engraved by Dheulland. From Cassini de Thury, 1740.

The illustration shows the same sector in use by La Caille and Cassini a decade before in France (Cassini de Thury 1740).

The *zenith sector* (see Fig. 2.8), with a scale of 1.9 m radius, was intended for finding the latitude from the stars. The telescope was fixed centrally to the frame and the length of the measuring scale was 51°, allowing the instrument to be swung only up to 22½° north or south of the zenith. The observer centred the star through the telescope and its declination was read from the enclosed plumb line. The sector was built in 1738 for the survey that La Caille undertook with Cassini de Thury within France. It is the one shown in use in Fig. 3.3.

The *quadrant* (see Fig. 2.9), La Caille's favourite instrument since 1743, was smaller, with a scale of 98 cm radius and slightly lower

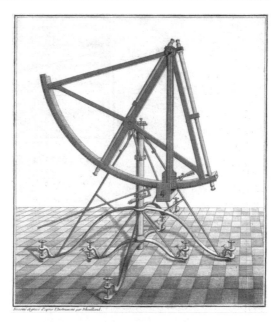

Drawn & grave d'après l'instrument par Dheulland.

Fig. 2.9 A 'portable' quadrant of 98 cm of about the same period as La Caille's. Drawn and engraved by Dheulland. From Cassini de Thury, 1740.

accuracy. It was however more general in its capabilities. Its main use was in the sky survey, which will be described later, for the mass production of star positions. As with the two other main instruments it featured a plumb line for determining the vertical.

The quadrant could also be mounted nearly horizontally to measure the angles between beacons, perhaps with the aid of an auxiliary telescope. If the beacons were not at the same altitude, a correction had to be made to get the horizontal angle.[20]

The 1.9 m *sextant* (see Fig. 2.10) was used for measuring the positions of a small number of bright reference stars with very high accuracy. These were used later on to calibrate the less precise but much more numerous positions obtained during the sky survey. The scale of the sextant covered 64°. A telescope of 1.9 m focal length was fixed to the frame at the zero point of the scale. This sextant still exists and is on display in the museum of the Paris Observatory. It also carried a second telescope at right angles to the first one so that stars could be observed down to the horizon. Each telescope had a micrometer eyepiece.

---

[20] The modern theodolite, developed at the end of the eighteenth century, has a horizontal azimuthal circle and a tiltable telescope. Thus it can directly measure the horizontal angles between beacons at different altitudes.

Fig. 2.10 La Caille's 1.9 m sextant, The frame of the instrument had to be set up vertically and north–south. This instrument still exists and is in the old Paris Observatory, though some of the small parts are missing. The scale bears the words 'Fait par Langlois Ingenieur du Roi Paris aux Galleries du Louvre 1750' ©Bibliothèque de l'Observatoire de Paris.

As well as the main instruments he had some telescopes of various diameters, including a 'really good one' of 14 feet focal length, with which he observed the moons of Jupiter. The achromatic telescope had not yet been invented and the images must have been fringed with colours, making their outlines hard to define.

Before starting work, he reduced the length of the tube of his telescope on the quadrant from five French feet to three and a half. He did not mention the reason for this but it was probably to increase the field, (amount of sky) that he could see at one time. He was aided in this work, as in his other endeavours, by Mr Poitevin.

Once the Observatory was ready, the first order of business was to get on with measuring the positions of the brighter southern stars with the same precision that he had already reached for the northern ones. But first he had to make sure that the instruments had not suffered any distortion in all the manhandling they had endured on the way from Paris.

For example, he had to carry out a check on the precision of the divisions of the scales. He did this by setting up a precisely measured angle 'on the plain at the foot of the Lion mountain, on the sandy part between the savannah and the seashore', presumably Green Point Common today, and checking how well the various parts of the scale gave the same angular measurements, making at the same time a table of the deviations he found.

> Those who know what it is to make such delicate measurements will readily understand that though I often found small deviations it was almost impossible to attribute these to faults in the division; thus after writing all of them down in my notebook I had to neglect those below 3 seconds; this was to pose only a small problem.

These deviations from perfection were in fact quite small by the standards of the time, varying from 3 to 5 arcsec.

The sky survey

La Caille's southern survey was the first really systematic one ever to have been made in either hemisphere.[21] Every part of the sky south of the Tropic of Capricorn was examined in turn in the course of his work.

In organising his survey, La Caille divided the 66½ degrees between the tropic of Capricorn (at 23½ degrees south) and the south pole (at 90 degrees south) into 25 equal zones just less than three degrees wide. The survey telescope had an objective lens of 71 cm focal length and was attached parallel to the normal telescope of the quadrant. Its aperture was a mere 13.5 mm. The eyepiece had a focal length of 88 mm, giving an overall magnification of about 8 times and meeting the field requirement of about 3° in diameter. In modern terms, this could be described as an 8 × 13.5 power monocular. In practice, neither high power nor a large aperture were necessary for observing what were

---

[21] The first systematic survey in the north was that of William Herschel in the 1780s and the next one in the south was that of John Herschel in 1835–8. The Herschels, by using much larger telescopes, were able to include much fainter objects but they were interested mainly in surveying double stars and nebulae and did not measure precise positions.

actually naked-eye stars. The bottom end of the tube, just above the eyepiece, had a square box attached into which he could fit special reticles for measuring the position of an object within the 3° field.

Although he had expected that many nights would be clear at the Cape, what came as an unpleasant surprise was the terrible 'seeing' or unsteadiness of the images caused by the prevailing south east wind. Instead of the stars being minute points that would be easy to measure, they were often fuzzy blobs of light. To alleviate this problem, the box behind the eyepiece usually contained a diamond-shaped mask at its focus so that each star could be timed twice, as it entered the diamond and as it left. In this way, systematic errors in the estimates were reduced. The Right Ascension (equivalent to longitude) of the star was obtained from the average of the two measured times and the declination (equivalent to latitude) came from the time difference between the two (in conjunction with the known declination of the centre of the graticule and whether the star was above or below it).

The quadrant was always set on the meridian (exactly north–south) and its telescope was pointed at a fixed angle from the south pole for a night, so that all the stars in a particular zone had to pass through the eyepiece because of the earth's rotation. Of course, only about one third of a zone passed through between dusk and dawn on a particular date, so that two or three more nights had to be employed several months apart to measure the other two thirds. La Caille estimated in advance that 100 clear nights uninterrupted for at least six hours were going to be required. This was quite feasible in the weather conditions at the Cape but a similar programme in the northern hemisphere would have been impossible to conduct in Paris. William Herschel, working later in England on his surveys, reckoned that a year with 90 to 100 good hours was a very productive one (Herschel, 1800)! Carlier (see La Caille 1776, p. 51) states that La Caille's survey actually took 17 full nights and 110 other sessions of eight hours each.

As mentioned, to calibrate his survey, he made separate precision observations of a number of bright stars in each three-degree zone using his six-foot sextant. According to Evans (1992), who compared the positions of 24 of these bright stars to their modern values, La Caille's accuracy was usually within 5 arcsec in declination and 15 arcsec in Right Ascension.

The survey started on 6 August 1751 and ended on 18 July 1752.

In November 1751 he wrote a progress report to the Academy of Sciences. He had already observed the Moon, Mars and Venus and had done work on finding the latitude of his observatory. He had observed five eclipses of the first satellite of Jupiter (Io), to get a time for finding his longitude compared to Paris and had made gravity measurements with a pendulum. He had measured the height of Table Mountain by triangulation and had made observations of temperature and barometric pressure. By this time he had already observed the positions of 2900 stars, of which only 100 occurred in previous lists.

The workman that I brought with me and who I am very happy with for his diligence and zeal has made it possible for me to have all kinds of reticles made for the micrometers of the telescopes without any expense, having brought here all the materials and tools necessary. I am only annoyed with myself for not having made better provision because everything here sells for four times as much, if one has the good luck to find it. The host whose house I stay in takes so much care that I lack for nothing, and to put me at my ease that I think I have not taken enough advantage of the favourable circumstances in which I find myself.[22]

He ended by sending greetings to Cassini, Bouguer, Camus, de Mairan (for whom he was keeping quite a few birds), de Jussieu and de la Condamine, all colleagues in the Royal Academy of Sciences.

By 21 February 1752, he could report to Grandjean de Fouchy at the Academy:

The general catalogue of all [the stars] between the South Pole and the Tropic of Capricorn is advancing with the season. I have done more than 3/5 of it and because I am always prepared to profit from clear nights, I am sure to have finished it by the end of June, assuming the weather is no worse than last year, and that my health always keeps up. It is very arduous work, which requires around 150 complete nights of observation, my head almost always tipped back, however, the more I advance, the more I am content to have undertaken to do it, because the furious southeaster prohibits any other kind of observation when it blows and because the sky is then of admirable clarity. I have seen double stars and the most singular nebulae, all worth being studied. As soon as the work is finished I will put it all in order and I will send a copy before I leave; there will probably be no fewer than 10000 stars.

Because Jupiter is low down and we are in the windy season I was only able to observe four emersions of the first satellite...

The temperature on the 16th of this month was 31½ degrees [39.4°C] and on the 17th 33½ degrees [41.9 C]. It was calm on these two days and a very serene evening. On the 17th at midnight the thermometer descended to 15 degrees [18.8°C] and a humid fog came up and from the following day everybody was seized with a high fever and inflammation of the lungs among those who neglected it....'[23]

Some idea of how tedious the survey work was can be obtained from the following description of the Abbé at work by his former

[22] La Caille to the Academy, dated Cape, 18 Nov 1751. Archives of the Academy of Sciences of the Institut de France, Folio 333.
[23] La Caille to Grandjean de Fouchy, dated Cape, 21 March 1752; via Du Hamel de Monceau, Inspecteur General de la Marine de France, received 17 June 1752. Archives de de l'Académie des Sciences de l'Institut de France, Folio 333.

student Jean-Sylvain Bailly, to whom he must have confided his reminiscences:

> Think of a man who spends seven to eight hours each night with his eye
> continuously pressed to a telescope where he observes all the stars that
> can be seen, sometimes standing, sometimes lying down when observing
> the zenith, always fighting sleep... His original plan was to observe only
> those stars brighter than magnitude four[24] but since they were not so very
> numerous his eyes grew heavy with sleep between them; so he decided
> to observe all the [fainter] ones to be always busy...
>
> He was often in an inconvenient position for so long that he had a
> support made in the shape of a fork on which he laid his head. As well
> as observing, he had to count the ticks of the clock and write at the same
> time without interrupting his viewing. The clock face was illuminated
> by a dim lantern so faint that it would not affect his adaptation to the
> dark. To further preserve his sensitivity, he closed his right eye when not
> looking through the telescope, such as when making notes.[25]
>
> When the night was over, he hardly allowed himself three or four
> hours of sleep before getting up again to observe the altitude of the Sun.
> This was followed by another task; the reduction of the observations that
> he had made during the night. His meal was sometimes interrupted by
> the arrival of the time for taking [more] altitudes, sending him back to
> his instrument.
>
> At last, his walk, the sole relaxation that he permitted himself,
> offered him something else to research. He took note of the plants, the
> animals unknown in our climate, the direction of the wind, the meteors,
> the temperature and pressure of the air, the magnetic declination,[26] the
> length of the pendulum[27] and the duration of dusk. That was how he
> assembled the physical knowledge of this climate, like stones which will
> one day support the edifice of nature.
>
> He would return to finish the day by preparing for the night that
> followed. Work and fatigue started again when night delivered rest
> to the remainder of humanity. However he also made all the other
> observations that are the aim of astronomy, eclipses of the Moon and
> the satellites of Jupiter, the occultations of stars, the obliquity of the
> ecliptic etc. The forced work, the night-time vigils, together with the
> warmth of the climate overheated his blood so much that he had
> to have recourse to repeated blood-lettings to prevent inflammation
> (Bailly 1770).

[24] The stars visible to the naked eye are divided into magnitudes from −1 to +6;
from the brightest to the faintest.

[25] It takes about half an hour for the eye to reach its greatest sensitivity after being
exposed to a bright light.

[26] The magnetic declination he found to be 19° west of true north.

[27] He did not, however, discuss the value of gravity.

Life was hard but La Caille was in his element. He wrote to Maraldi:

...Though I work here much more than I ever worked I am always fine. My spirit is tranquil and every day I feel grateful for the many agreeable actions of my host. After the month of June I will have more leisure and will walk around a bit.

I am obliged to you for the trouble you have taken informing me what my friends are doing in my regard. I wrote to them by the same vessel so as not to importune you more.

I am so tied to the house here that I do not know the [?] of the Cape streets. I cannot make a large collection of seeds or of plants, but perhaps the leisure that I will have after this winter will allow me to take advantage of it for the naturalists, at the risk of doing nothing worthwhile.

I hope that you are always well and that you keep for me that friendship of which I remember the effects. When I return I will be a bit more docile towards your exhortations and having sacrificed my best days to astronomy I will put its interests back into younger hands than mine.[28]

Finally, on 6 August 1752 he could record with a sigh of relief that he had slept in his room on a clear night for the first time since 23 May 1751! 'Up till now I have observed on all clear nights, sleeping on a little bed in the observatory during the time when there was nothing to observe'.

He had been ill on two occasions, one of them in February 1752, when he caught a fever that he ascribed to the thick and unhealthy fog mentioned in his letter to Grandjean de Fouchy quoted earlier. He was treated by two episodes of bleeding, the standard (but useless) eighteenth-century remedy, and fortunately recovered. Later, in September 1753, while in Mauritius, he was attacked by a violent dysentery but this did not affect his work and he was back to normal after a strict fast of fifty hours.

For the two following months he turned to another project which we will discuss in the next chapter. Then, in October 1752, he began to consider what he had achieved so far.

The new constellations and La Caille's planisphere

The first fruit of the survey was a set of 1942 star positions published in the Memoirs of the Royal Academy of Sciences (La Caille 1752, p. 529). These were selected from his whole list of 9766 stars and were

---

[28] La Caille to Maraldi, dated Cape, 14 April 1752. Observatoire de Paris ms 1076 (136).

worked up during the last two months of 1752 and the first two of 1753, following his geodetic expedition described in the next chapter. Even so, the positions were not corrected for the small effects of aberration and nutation, though the dates on which they were made were given so that readers could calculate these for themselves.

> I applied myself especially to the construction of a planisphere (see Figs. 2.11 and 2.12), as complete as possible, of the southern part of the sky included between the pole and the tropic of Capricorn. To do this, I first constructed a catalogue of 1930 stars chosen from the 9800 that I had observed. I placed them on a chart and compared this chart with the sky to see if I had not omitted from my catalogue any that could be seen by eye because I proposed to designate each one by a letter from the Greek and Roman alphabets, in the same manner as in planispheres that represent the stars visible in Europe. On the same chart I traced in their places the southern constellations described by the ancient Greek and Roman astronomers and those which were formed around the pole by the first Portugese navigators. I still had between the constellations large spaces which, though filled with fully visible stars, were absolutely empty on our charts, because it has only been possible to mark up to now the approximately 300 stars that had been observed before. I could only designate the new stars that filled the voids by introducing new constellations, but instead of using, like the Portugese did in imitation of the ancients, figures of animals unknown in Europe and which are consequently represented ridiculously on our celestial charts, I drew the shapes of the principal instruments of the fine arts ... (La Caille 1751, pp. 531–2).

The instruments were, of course, those in use in the mid eighteenth century. The telescope (Telescopium or Le Telescope)[29] was typical of long-focus refractors of the time, mounted on a pole and presumably very awkward to use. The clock (Horologium or l'Horloge) was a simple type with an unenclosed pendulum and a secondary weight, possibly part of an alarm mechanism. The air pump (Antlia or La Machine Pneumatique) was of a type popular for demonstrations at the time and the furnace (Fornax or La Fourneaux) with its still also appears antique.

After his return, La Caille presented the Academy with a planisphere, of six feet (1.95 m) diameter. This rather dark picture painted by his artist friend, Mademoiselle Anne-Louise Le Jeuneux (see Chapter 5) in 1755, hangs today in the Paris Observatory. Unlike on the printed planisphere, the constellation figures are painted as proper pictures rather than as outlines. The stars are picked out in gold on a dark blue

[29] The French names are mentioned here for convenience in finding these figures in Figs. 2.11 and 2.12.

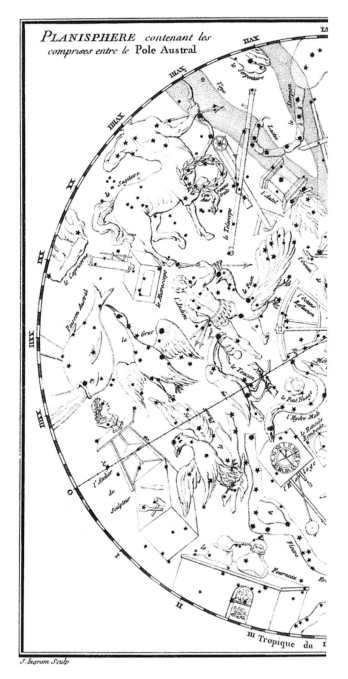

Fig. 2.11 La Caille's planisphere. From La Caille (1752) Plate 20.

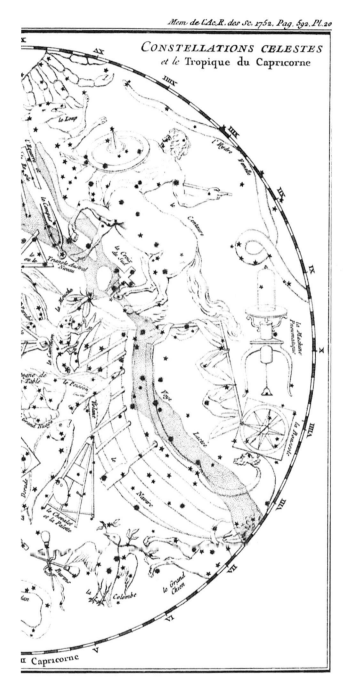

Mem. de l'Ac. R. des Sc. 1752. Pag. 592. Pl. 20

CONSTELLATIONS CELESTES
et le Tropique du Capricorne

Fig. 2.12 La Caille's planisphere. From La Caille (1752) Plate 20.

background. Delambre (1827) remembered seeing it on the wall of the lecture room of the Academy of Sciences but it had been moved to the Observatory by the time he wrote.

The planisphere was first printed in the Memoirs of the Academy of Sciences in La Caille (1752), p. 592, Plate 20. It was engraved by John Ingram, an Englishman who was resident engraver at the Academy in the years 1754–5. The constellation names are given in French and the star designations were not marked. Another version, with the names in Latin, was published in La Caille's posthumous *Coelum Australe* of 1763.

In his 1752 paper, he listed the new constellations in order of Right Ascension:

1. [Sculptor] the *Sculptor's studio*: it is composed of a pedestal carrying a model and a block of marble on which a mallet and chisel have been put.
2. [Fornax] The chemical *Furnace* with its still and receiver.
3. [Horologium] The pendulum *Clock*, reading seconds.
4. [Reticulum] The rhomboidal *Reticle*, a small astronomical instrument which served to construct this catalogue: it is made from the intersection of four lines drawn from each corner of a square to the middle of the two opposite sides.
5. [Caelum] The engraver's *Burin*: The figure is composed of crossed burins tied together by a ribbon.
6. [Pictor] The *Painter's easel*, to which a palette is attached.
7. [Pyxis][30] The *Mariner's compass*.
8. [Antlia] The *Air pump* with its reservoir, representing experimental physics[!].
9. The *Octant* or reflecting quadrant, the principal instrument that navigators use to measure the height of the pole, &c.
10. [Circinus] The geometrical compass.
11. [Norma] The *Square* and ruler of the Architect: I have also delineated the southern triangle in the form of a level.
12. [Telescopium] The *Telescope* or the large instrument suspended from a mast.
13. [Microscopium] The *Microscope*: according to the usual image it is a tube placed above a square box.
14. [(Mons) Mensa] Finally, I have placed above the Large Cloud the *Table Mountain* (see Fig. 2.13), celebrated at the Cape of Good Hope because of its table-like appearance, and principally for a white cloud which covers it at the approach of a violent south-easter; also what most navigators call the Cape Clouds and what we call the Magellanic Clouds or the Large & Small Cloud (La Caille 1752, pp. 588–9).

---

[30] Literally a little box or casket.

Fig. 2.13 Region of Mons Mensa (Latin for Table Mountain) from La Caille's plani-sphere. This rather inconspicuous constellation is the only one named after a terrestrial feature. The Large Magellanic Cloud (Nubecula Major) is in the position of the 'table-cloth' of cloud often seen above the actual mountain (the lettering of the original is inverted). From La Caille, *Coelum* . . . , (1763).

Reorganisation of Argo

The constellation Argo Navis being composed of 160 stars very easy to distinguish by eye, I have distributed Greek letters to all the brightest stars of which it is composed; I have then divided it into three parts; that is the Poop (Puppis), the Hull (Carina) and the sails (Vela). The poop is separated from the body of the vessel by the wheel and I have called the sail everything outside the vessel, between the side of the ship and the horizontal mast or yard on which the sail is folded...(La Caille 1752, p. 590).

The end of Charles's Oak

You will not find there the new constellation which Mr Halley inserted in his planisphere of 1677, under the name of *Robur Carolinum*,[31] because I have given to the Ship [Argo Navis] the bright stars that this astronomer, then aged twenty-one, detached from it to court the king of England. However praiseworthy this motive may have been, I cannot approve of the fashion in which Mr Halley took them to make up his constellation; because he so much shortened the Ship to make it appear isolated that he left out some bright stars between the Ship and his tree; and to make out that the stars making up his tree are new ones, or had never before

---

[31] Charles's Oak, named after the tree in which the future Charles II is supposed to have hidden during the English Civil War.

been observed, he did not compare their positions with those of previous catalogues, which he had always done in regard to the stars of other constellations; however, of the twelve stars which make up Mr Halley's tree, nine are in previous catalogues and are designated by particular letters on Bayer's planispheres, in the constellation of the Ship. Finally, one cannot doubt that in the fifteenth and sixteenth centuries those who observed the southern stars to place them in constellations had attributed to the ship all the stars that Mr Halley's constellation is composed of; otherwise how can one believe that they were formed from the constellations of the Flying Fish[32] and of the Chamaeleon, which are so close to the Ship, and whose brightest stars are of the fifth magnitude, while, between the Centaur and the ship, there is a large space left without a constellation and filled with stars of the first, second and third magnitudes, unless they are grouped with those of the Ship (La Caille 1752, pp. 591–2).

The general acceptance of La Caille's scheme of constellations probably owes itself to the thoroughness of his work. Only about a century later was his survey of stars improved upon though, as mentioned, the southern nebulae were catalogued by John Herschel in the 1830s.

The Coelum Australe Stelliferum

The main publication of the survey was entitled *Coelum Australe Stelliferum; seu Observationes ad Construendum Stellarum Australium Catalogum Institutae, in Africa ad Caput Bonae-Spei* (*The Southern Starry Sky; or Observations Instituted for the Construction of a Southern Star Catalogue*), La Caille, 1763, see Fig. 2.14. As with La Caille's other books, it was printed by H.-L. Guérin and his son-in-law L.-F. Delatour. Since the Abbé died before the printing was complete, it was finished off by G.-D. Maraldi as a last labour of love for his departed friend.

The *Coelum* commenced with a Latin life of La Caille by Gabriel Brotier, a Jesuit who had lost his position as librarian of the famous Parisian school Louis-le-Grand following the suppression of his order in 1762. He had been given a place to live by the Delatour family and had presumably been commissioned to write this piece.

The body of the book was written in both Latin and French. It also included a detailed description of the observational techniques that had been employed.

Full reductions including the effects of precession, aberration and nutation for the epoch of 1750 January 1 were presented for 1952 stars. For the remainder, raw data were given.

---

[32] Originally called Piscis Volans but now called Volans.

Nineteenth century reduction of La Caille's Catalogue

The British Association for the Advancement of Science felt even as late as 1838 that La Caille's complete observations of 9766 southern stars should be fully reduced. The idea was to look for stars with large proper motions by comparing his observations with later ones.

The actual computations were largely carried out in Edinburgh by Thomas Henderson, Astronomer Royal for Scotland. Following his death, the final catalogue was prepared by Francis Baily (1847) (not to be confused with Jean-Sylvain Bailly) one of the principal founders of the Royal Astronomical Society in London. An interesting person in himself, Baily, after an adventurous youth had made a fortune as an actuary and stockbroker before turning to astronomy.

The individual errors in this large catalogue are of the order of $\pm 30''$, considerably greater than for the calibration stars but in line with La Caille's own estimate, given in the introduction to the *Coelum Australe Stelliferum*. In addition, Baily noted a number of cases where La Caille had erred, typically by writing down the wrong minute. Given the circumstances under which he worked, such mistakes are perhaps not too surprising.

Nebulous (cloud-like) objects

In the course of his sky survey La Caille found quite a number of nebulous objects. Before his survey, only about 20 of these were known and indeed, nobody showed much interest in them. They included things we now know to be galaxies, the dominant preoccupation of many present-day astronomers. It should be remembered that he was observing on all possible nights and it is quite likely that he missed some of these extended low-brightness objects when the Moon was bright. Nevertheless, he realised that he was onto something interesting and could only regret that his equipment was inadequate for following up what he had seen:

> The stars that one calls nebulous offer to the eyes of observers such a varied spectacle that their description could occupy an astronomer for a long time and allow scientists to make a great number of curious reflections...I would very much like to have given something more detailed and instructive in this article, apart from the fact that the ordinary telescopes of 15 to 18 feet focal length, such as I had at the Cape of Good Hope, are not sufficient or convenient enough for this sort of research; those who take the trouble to examine what occupied me during my stay in that country, will see that I did not have enough time to make these sorts of observations (La Caille 1755 p. 194).

He divided the nebulous objects into three classes, each containing 14 objects:

CŒLUM AUSTRALE

STELLIFERUM;

SEU

OBSERVATIONES AD CONSTRUENDUM

STELLARUM AUSTRALIUM

C A T A L O G U M

INSTITUTÆ,

In Africa ad Caput Bonæ-Spei,

A NICOLAO-LUDOVICO DE LA CAILLE ; *in alma Studiorum Univerſitate Pariſienſi Matheſeon Profeſſore, Regiæ Scientiarum Academiæ Aſtronomo, & earum quæ Petropoli, Berolini, Holmiæ & Bononiæ florent, Academiarum Socio.*

Laudate Dominum . . . . qui numerat multitudinem Stellarum, & omnibus eis nomina vocat.

Pſal. 146. ℣. 4.

P A R I S I I S,

Sumptibus Hipp. Lud. Guerin & Lud. Fr. Delatour, viâ Jacobeâ, ſub ſigno Sancti Thomæ Aquinatis.

M. DCC. LXIII.

Cum Privilegio Regis.

Fig. 2.14 The title page of La Caille's Catalogue of 1763, *The Southern Starry Sky; Observations Instituted for the Construction of a Southern Star Catalogue*, published after his death. The quotation is from Psalm 146 (Vulgate numbering): 'Praise the Lord . . . who counts the multitude of stars and calls each one by name' (SAAO).

(1) White region, no clear edge, often very irregular in shape, resembling the nucleus of a faint, tailless, comet.
(2) Nebula composed of a cluster of small stars which can be distinguished in the telescope.
(3) Stars accompanied or surrounded by a white patch of type 1.

Finally, he commented that the white patches called the Magellanic Clouds seemed to be of the same nature as the Milky Way.

A version of La Caille's (1755) table with modern identifications was given by Gingerich (1960) in an article in the popular magazine *Sky and Telescope*. According to him, at least eight objects were purely asterisms (chance clusters of stars).

Some of his objects will be familiar to people who have at least a basic idea of the southern sky and have looked through a small telescope (bear in mind that La Caille's telescope had less than a hundredth of the light-gathering power of many modern amateur telescopes). The first class includes the globular clusters 47 Tucanae and Omega Centauri, spherical clusters with of order a million stars, not distinguishable from each other in a small telescope, the Tarantula Nebula, a bright gaseous nebula in the Large Magellanic Cloud, and M83, one of the brightest southern galaxies.

The second class includes many 'open clusters' such as the famous 'Jewel Box' (Kappa Crucis), a group of youngish stars.

The third includes the nebula surrounding the very luminous star Eta Carinae and other bright stars. Eta, probably an unstable supergiant star, was to become extremely bright during John Herschel's stay at the Cape in 1835–8.

It was only in the early twentieth century that the true nature of many nebulae began to be understood. The Magellanic Clouds are the nearest galaxies outside our own Milky Way. The globular cluster 47 Tuc is an almost primeval feature of our own galaxy and most of the true nebulae (that are formed of gas and dust and are not simply unresolved stars) are regions where stars are still being formed.

The first person to specialise in nebulous objects was Charles Messier, another French astronomer, who was mainly interested in making sure that comet hunters were not confused by them. Even today, many of the brightest such objects are known by their 'M' or Messier numbers. Later, William Herschel (*c.* 1780) and his son John (1835–8) surveyed the northern and southern skies respectively, finding thousands of nebulae.

Other observations

Latitude and longitude of the Cape

La Caille did not explain very clearly how he obtained the latitude of the Cape ($-33°\ 55'\ 15''$), which was dependent on his estimates of the refraction by the earth's atmosphere (La Caille 1751, p. 412).

The longitude was found by an observation of the Right Ascension of the Moon at a certain time. This could be compared to the time tabulated by Halley for when it would be at the same Right Ascension at Greenwich. He got for the position of his observatory longitude 1^h 12^m 13^s east of Greenwich, whereas the modern value would be about 1^h 10^m 41^s, or about one and a half minutes of time different (*Journal Historique* 1763, entry for 11 May 1751).[33]

The effect of the earth's atmosphere (refraction)

One of the things observers of star positions must allow for is the bending of light rays by the earth's atmosphere, which acts as a prism. Rays away from the vertical are bent as they enter the atmosphere and the colours are slightly spread out. However, the eye is mainly sensitive to green light when viewing faint objects, so that the dispersion is not usually very noticeable. The main effect is that an object's apparent position in the sky is shifted by an amount ranging from negligible when it is directly overhead to several minutes of arc when it is lower down. Straight up there is no problem, because the star's rays enter the atmosphere perpendicularly. But the light from stars to the north, south, east or west enters obliquely.

Because the Right Ascension of a star is simply the exact time, measured by a suitable clock, when it goes from the eastern side of the sky to the western side, it can be measured without having to make any correction. But its precise angle north or south of the equator, the declination, analogous to latitude, is more tricky. In this case, the atmospheric bending must be allowed for by means of a pre-calculated table, and even the effects of temperature and barometric pressure must be taken into consideration.

To make such a correction table is very difficult and liable to involve circular arguments, because one first has to have a large number of stars whose true declinations are somehow known. La Caille was able to use some convenient facts about the latitude of Cape Town to make good estimates of the corrections for some particular angles and to make approximations for the others. Even so, his corrections, particularly for a star very low down in the sky, were over-estimated. In 1787, the Astronomer Royal in England, Nevil Maskelyne, suggested through a careful analysis that his problem was due to small inaccuracies in the sextant that he had used for all his calibrations and indeed this was verified afterwards by Delambre (see also Chapter 5, Interaction with Tobias Mayer).

In spite of the problems with corrections that La Caille encountered, comparisons with modern data show that his catalogue of the bright

---

[33] In the Evans (1992) translation but not in the French published version of 1776.

stars was very accurate for his time. This seems to have been because he had used his sextant both for his work on refraction and for measuring the bright stars. The inaccuracies in the refraction had, in effect, cancelled themselves out. Further, most of his stars were high in the sky so that both the corrections and their uncertainties were minimal.

His positions, in fact, were not improved on until the 1830s, when the Royal Observatory, Cape of Good Hope was established with a new generation of more precise instruments.

Critical technical discussions of La Caille's approach to this issue can be found in Delambre (1827) and Evans (1992).

Observations of the Sun, Moon and planets

While at the Cape, as he had proposed, La Caille made observations that contributed to the determination of the distances of the Sun, Moon and planets. These being essentially trigonometrical, they depended on nearly simultaneous observations in Europe, at Stockholm, Berlin, Greenwich, Paris and Bologna (see Fig. 2.15). His final result for the distance of the Sun was published in La Caille (1760); see also Chapter 5, More on the Cape data.

Lalande observed the Moon from the northern hemisphere (Berlin, at 53 °N) and La Caille from the Cape at 34 °S.

La Caille's discussions of his results from this work occupied several papers and tended to be revised as improved methods of reduction came to hand. His final work on the subject is discussed in Chapter 5.

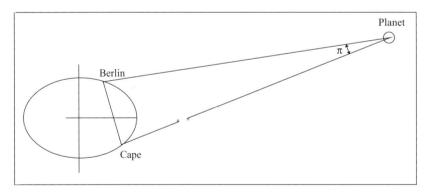

Fig. 2.15 Measuring the distance to the Moon or a planet from Berlin and Cape Town by triangulation. The base length Berlin–Cape can be derived from the latitudes if the shape of the earth is known. The angles to the target can be measured from each city. The very small included angle π, here much exaggerated, is obtained from simultaneous observations against the very distant background stars from the two positions on the earth. It will be at its largest when the target is at its nearest approach to the earth ©I.S. Glass.

The triangle used to get the distance has a base which is a straight line drawn from Cape Town to, for example, Berlin. To calculate this accurately, the shape of the earth has to be known. It was assumed to follow theoretical expectations and to be ellipsoidal with flattening towards the poles to the extent of one part in 200.[34]

Allowances had to be made for two further effects. The observatories at the Cape and in Europe were never quite at the same longitudes, i.e. not along the same north–south line. Further, the times of observation were not exactly the same, so that the motion of the Moon had to be allowed for.

The final results of this work were published in La Caille (1761, p. 1).

---

[34] The modern value is close to one part in 300.

3
The shape of the earth

To return to August 1752, the Abbé found that he had time on his hands when he had completed his survey. He had expected his observations of the southern stars to take a year to carry out. However, a number of things had caused delays. Firstly, there had been the need to carry out repairs at Rio de Janeiro, then he had been becalmed as he approached the Cape. Finally the construction of the observatory cost another month of his time. Thus, he had not been able to finish his programme before winter set in. By then it was too late to leave the Cape, since shipping came to a halt every June. Many disastrous experiences had shown that the second half of the year was unsafe for sailing ships. Indeed the terrible winter storms had caused the fifteenth-century explorer Bartolomeu Dias to give the area its original name of 'Cabo Tormentosa' or 'Cape of Storms'.

Thus there were at least five months to kill before he could hope to return to France. He had done all that he could for the southern stars, as he put it, but the special treatment from the Governor that his letters of recommendation had brought led him to think he might be able to get support for another large project, that of measuring a degree of the meridian[1] in order to see if the earth was similar in both hemispheres.

Measuring the earth

To understand what La Caille now had in mind it is necessary to explain how the radius of the earth is measured. In the seventeenth century, during Newton's lifetime, the French astronomer and geodesist Jean-Felix Picard developed the method. There were three steps involved:

(1) find the latitudes of two beacons along a north–south line by astronomical means.
(2) measure the land distance between them using land-survey techniques.
(3) calculate the radius of the earth from the previous two.

[1] A meridian is a north–south line on the surface of the earth or in the sky.

The second step has itself two main requirements:

(1) precision measurement of the angles between the beacons and the ends of a designated baseline.
(2) making a precise measurement of the length of the baseline using standard rods or chains.

Although the principle of the method had been suggested in the early seventeenth century by, for example, the Dutchman Willebord Snell, Picard saw that he could make much better angular measurements than his predecessors by improving his survey instruments. Instead of using the unaided eye to sight objects, he fitted telescopes to them and designed eyepieces that contained cross-hairs. He also added micrometer screws to be able to make finer adjustments. Using his new techniques, he laid out a precise baseline about 11 km long (which eventually turned out to be in error by about 0.1%) near Paris, against which survey triangles could be calibrated.

Ultimately, Picard's work led to the survey already referred to along a line from northern to southern France (Dunkerque to Perpignan), intermittently between 1700 and 1718, by the leading French astronomer of that time, Jean-Dominique Cassini (known as Cassini I), his son Jacques Cassini (Cassini II) and others. As mentioned, the conclusion had been that the earth must be a spheroid that bulged towards the poles, resembling an egg or a rugby ball. Cassini II continued to maintain until he died that the available evidence supported this conclusion.

This was in spite of the fact that another French astronomer, Jean Richer, had found from pendulum measurements in the 1670s that gravity is less near the equator, specifically at Cayenne, French Guiana, than it is in France. This result supported Newton's view that the earth was fatter at the equator because, according to his theory, gravity should fall off the further one goes from the centre of the earth. Of course, this information was not then relevant because Newton's theory had yet to be published!

La Caille, in reviewing the earlier measurements, said '...little errors, neglected a little too much, have already led more than once to a conclusion contrary to what physics requires; the finding that the earth is elongated [towards the poles].' Delambre (1827, p. 501), in quoting this, says 'La Caille had to be cautious [not to offend] in referring to the publication of 1718. [However], not having the same motives for sweetening an inconvenient truth, [I] point out in *La Mesure de la Terre*[2] other neglected items which appear to have been designed to arrive at this conclusion so contrary to physics and which were adopted in advance for the most futile reasons'. What Delambre was hinting at

---

[2] *The History of the Measurement of the Earth*, a book that seems not to have been published before his death.

here was that La Caille, out of gratitude to his teacher Cassini II, had not wanted to criticise him explicitly.

As described in Chapter 1, newer data had overturned the early conclusions. By the 1740s, measurements had been made in the northern hemisphere at a low latitude (Peru), in the middling latitudes of France and at high latitudes, in Lapland. Taken together, these were all consistent with an ellipsoidal earth, flattened at the poles.

No measurement had as yet been made in the southern hemisphere. It therefore became one of La Caille's aims during his visit to the Cape to determine the earth's curvature there. A further reason was that the shape of the earth had a bearing on another of his interests: making trigonometric measurements of the distances of the Sun, Moon and planets. This was because the baselines of the necessary survey triangles stretched across widely separated points on the planet (see Fig. 2.15). Their lengths could not be measured directly but depended on knowing the latitudes of the end points as well as the size and shape of the earth.

The expedition to the Swartland

The idea of measuring an arc of meridian while at the Cape had obviously occurred to La Caille quite early in his stay. In April 1751 he had written to the Minister of War, seeking his permission for an expedition:

> Having arrived here after a longer voyage than I had counted on, my first care was to conform to your orders. It is possible to measure here an arc of meridian. I have assured myself that the thing is very easy because of the position of the west coast of Africa which runs from south to north. It has a wide plain and a beach of sand and is terminated by high mountains, detached from each other but visible from one to the other over great distances, in such a way that one can measure a space of more than forty leagues [~180 km] with a very small number of triangles. The travelling is very easy and almost without expense. I have all the necessary instruments, but I await your order to undertake it. You know better than anybody all the advantages of this measurement.[3]

As with La Caille's original proposal, d'Argenson forwarded this letter to Le Monnier 'Director of the Academy of Sciences' for their opinion.[4] Whether or not he was going to receive permission, La Caille could not afford to wait. On 6 September 1751, while in the middle of his sky survey, the Abbé made a short trip northward from Cape

[3] La Caille to d'Argenson, dated Cape, 27 April 1751, Archives de l'Académie des Sciences de l'Institut de France, Folio 51.

[4] D'Argenson to Le Monnier, dated Versailles, 26 January 1752, Archives de l'Académie des Sciences de l'Institut de France, Folio 51.

Town with Bestbier, visiting his farm in the Mamre area, then called Groene Kloof. It was an opportunity to explore the possibilities. The settlement there was a military outpost of the VOC and the surrounding hilly farmland was made available because of its relative lushness to cattle suppliers such as Bestbier. It was also the place where ox-wagons travelling to the north could 'outspan' to allow the animals to rest and feed. Near it is the mountain called Kapokberg[5] and some way east is Kasteelberg, an isolated peak rising above the plain near the present town of Riebeek Kasteel. These two mountains were well placed to form the bases of two large triangles, one of them with his observatory in Cape Town at the apex and the other with an apex in the mountains at Klipfontein (near the present-day village of Aurora) that he could see about 20 leagues (89 km) further to the north (see Fig. 3.1). What was more, between the two mountains and just to the north of them was a vast sandy plain where he could lay out a baseline to calibrate the large triangles.

On the morning of the 7th he climbed Kapokberg and noted that he could see all the way from Hout Bay on the Cape Peninsula to Saldanha Bay. That afternoon he also climbed the nearby Contreberg. He concluded his visit by spending three days shooting birds and gathering wild flowers, it being springtime and the season for the latter.

He prepared a proposal which he gave to Tulbagh, part of which reads as follows:

> Situated in the part of Africa closest to the south pole, counting on the protection of the Dutch Nation, of which I have been assured by an infinity of tokens, and especially by the enthusiasm with which the Governor of this Colony has procured for me all that could contribute to the success of my mission, I cannot avoid, following the intention of the Academy, looking for the means of carrying out this last measurement. I had to profit from the good luck of finding myself in such favourable circumstances, besides which it seemed as if the locations had been set up expressly to make the operations most simple and by consequence the most suitable for precision work (La Caille 1776, p. 191).

He also reported to the Academy on this proposal:

> Having made a short trip of 50 leagues [~220 km] towards the north, I found the terrain so suitable for measuring more than sixty thousand toises [117 km] in two triangles in the direction that I wanted that I immediately presented a project to the Governor to measure the 34th degree of southern latitude: he not only approved but even promised me all resources possible for its execution. Because it costs nothing here to

---

[5] Kapokberg is so named from the kapok bush *Eriocephalus Ericoides* which is common there.

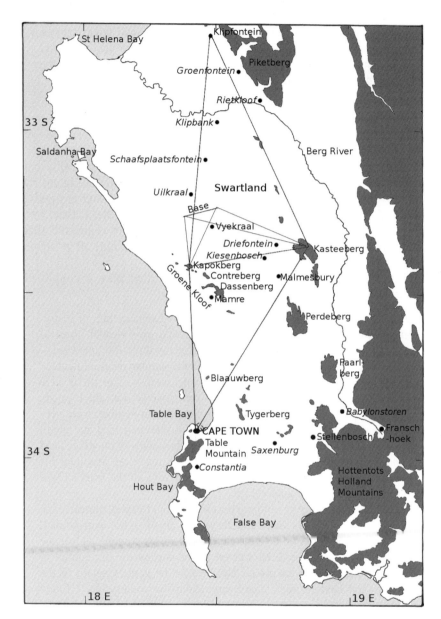

Fig. 3.1 Map of the region covered by La Caille's map of 1752 (see page Fig. 5.1). Land above 300 m altitude is shaded. The base in the centre of the area called the Swartland was used to measure the sides of the large triangles joining his stations at Klipfontein and Cape Town via the mountains Kapokberg and Kasteelberg. Farms that he visited during his expeditions are shown in italics ©I.S. Glass.

travel to any place I am counting on the expenses being very little. The biggest of them consist of presents for those who will help me. My host will furnish me a cart, twelve most vigorous oxen and three negroes, because there is no other way to travel here and one can easily make 12 or 15 leagues [50–60 km] a day even across the loose sand that covers the plains of this country ....[6]

Since Governor Tulbagh had duly given the nod, La Caille decided to go ahead whether d'Argenson approved or not. However, he admitted (La Caille, 1751, p. 529) that he was taking a chance; he also did not yet know if the Academy had sanctioned the project.

Only in August of the following year (1752) could La Caille get ready for the expedition. He was greatly helped by a letter signed by the Governor giving him all the necessary permissions and assigning Mr Muller, 'Artillery Captain and officer in charge of the Castle',[7] to be a witness to his operations. The Governor further requested that all inhabitants approached by the Abbé should give him all possible help.

But travelling in a place that had been settled only a couple of generations before was not for the faint-hearted:

The countryside I had to traverse with a large baggage-train of instruments, the places where I had to go to make my celestial observations, the mountains up which I had to carry my three-foot quadrant— a much heavier one than had been used for similar measurements— the plain where the baseline was to be measured—all of these were almost complete deserts, without water and covered with thick brush. The inhabitants one might come across were few in number, were very poor, and hardly had the wherewithal to cultivate their land and guard their herds. It would be useless to give here the details of the other local conditions which could have stopped me and made me abandon this enterprise, even though I had been provided with all the wagons (see Fig. 3.2) and everything necessary.

Mr Bestbier, the ever-obliging host with whom I stayed, informed me of all these difficulties and I saw they were anything but exaggerated; but at the same time he offered me the use of his wagons and of the slaves that I would need: he wanted to accompany me throughout to serve as a guide and interpreter and because he is the Captain of the Militia, and held in high regard throughout the countryside, I found myself throughout my trip as at ease and as free as if I had been in the best province of France (La Caille 1751, p. 529).

[6] La Caille to the Academy, dated Cape, 21 Feb 1752, Archives of the Academy of Sciences of the Institut de France, Folio 333.
[7] Mentzel **1**, p. 152 says that Müller was Kampanjemeester but he is clearly referred to as 'Captn der Artillerij' in *Resolutions of the Council of Policy of Cape of Good Hope*, Cape Town Archives Repository, Ref, Code C130, pp. 304–311.

Fig. 3.2 An ox-wagon seen crossing the Parade Ground (very close to where La Caille lived) in Cape Town in 1762, as drawn by Johannes Rach. Often as many as twelve oxen were used to pull one wagon. Such wagons were of simple construction and well-suited to the very rough country tracks and the streams that had to be forded. They stayed in use until the early twentieth century (W. Cape Archives & Record Service M163).

Serious reconnaissance

Before the end of the month he made a second trip to the Swartland to formulate detailed plans for a full-scale expedition. He again had the company of Bestbier and was joined by a French-speaking bombardier as an interpreter. A compass was the only instrument carried on this occasion.

On the 9th of August the reconnoitering expedition set out for Groene Kloof. On the 10th he put a marker on the Kapokberg. This was at a 'nearly cylindrical rock, the easternmost of those that are on the western extremity of the mountain of *Groene-Kloof* called Capocberg' (La Caille 1751, p. 427). In his *Journal Historique* (1763), p. 173, he added further detail:

> The place of this beacon is a large rock propped up by a smaller one to the north. This rock is towards the western extremity of the summit of the mountain, which is very flat. It faces Cape Town and there is another bigger but less high one a few paces away towards the north-north-west.[8]

The following day he rode out to find a suitable place to set up a baseline and chose for the south-western end a hillock near the present-day railway halt of Kiekoesvlei that looked like it was made of white marble.

On the 12th he headed east to the Kasteelberg, dining at Driefontein, the home of Mr 'Claas Waltere' (Nicolaas Walters), before heading to another farm, Keesenbosch (Kiesenbosch), which he noted had a lovely

---

[8] The last rock mentioned supports the present Trigonometrical beacon.

view. (These farm names still appear on the Trigonometrical Survey maps.) Surprise guests were always welcome at remote farms and their hospitality was depended on by travellers. Often, the hosts would take no money for their pains but wine or brandy were usually offered in thanks.

On the 13th he climbed the Kasteelberg mountain (see also Chapter 4), accompanied by six slaves, to put a marker on the second peak from the northern end. He had all the trees in the vicinity felled to improve the sight lines. He mentions the baboons, which still inhabit the mountain, and also visited the less suitable main peak some distance away. The terrain of this mountain of 966 m, which is not a popular place to hike even today, is quite rough and covered by small prickly bushes.

Then it was back to Groene Kloof for a break. On the 15th they went north again via Uylekraal (Uilkraal)[9] and were guided by a son of the house to Schaafplaatsfontein, where they spent the night. The following day they pushed on, to a farm called Klipbank, near the Berg River, which turned out to be further south than expected from the available maps. La Caille decided that to have a full degree of latitude difference he would have to establish his northern station on the other side of the river, in the Piketberg region. At this point the reconnaissance expedition returned to Groene Kloof where they were detained by bad weather for several days before they could get back to the Cape.

The expedition proper

The last few days of August were spent in preparing for the full expedition, except for time taken off to celebrate the proclamation of Jacob Mossel as the Governor General of Batavia (he was the VOC official senior to all the Company's other Governors). A grand dinner was given to the military officers and principal citizens. La Caille proudly noted that he was the only foreigner to participate.

The main expedition left the Cape on 9 September 1752 and went first to the Contre Berg homestead at Groene Kloof. La Caille climbed the Kapokberg again to select a place for a signal fire visible from the north.

Eventually the whole expedition, consisting of two wagons, one drawn by six horses and the other by ten oxen, set off. Progress was slow since, according to Mentzel, (**3**, p. 70), an ox-wagon could only travel for seven or eight hours per day, at about 4 km per hour, because of the need for the oxen to graze and rest frequently. There were eight slaves to drive the wagons and carry the instruments when needed.

[9] Owned by the Smidt family.

They followed the previously described route north, dining again at
Uilkraal and sleeping at Schaafplaatsfontein. On the morning of 12th
they crossed the Berg River at Rietkloof, using a canoe nine or ten feet
long and two and a half feet wide. The river was 'very deep, though
less than sixty paces wide'. They had to unpack everything and take
their cases and parcels across one by one. The wagons were floated
across, pulled by the oxen. The whole operation took only two and a
half hours, 'because we had enough people'. There they dined at the
farm and afterwards carried on for a good hour to Groenfontein in the
foothills of the Piketberg range.

The next morning they went straight to the proposed northern end
of the measurement. This was a farm called Klipfontein,[10] situated at
the foot of an anonymous mountain behind the Piketberg and almost
directly north of the Observatory in Strand Street.

> [13 September] The countryside is absolutely dry along the whole of
> this route and almost completely uncultivated, covered in bushes and
> high woody plants; the ground is sandy and rocky in some places. In
> general, the aspect is not pleasing and the ground is of no value.
> [14 September] I spent the whole day mounting my instruments and
> arranging them in place.[11] That of the sector was at the northern
> extremity of the barn of this homestead. The support area was about 7
> feet square, with the direction of the meridian along the diagonal.
> I had made an opening about three feet by one foot in the roof,
> which was thatched with thick reeds. This was covered except during
> observations with a heavy tarpaulin, measuring 12 feet by 8½, fixed
> in the middle to the ridge of the roof and staked overhead on the other
> side so as to make a kind of roof.
>
> The place where Mr Bestbier, Mr Poitevin and I slept was the site of
> the same barn, six feet long and seven feet wide, separated from that in
> which the sector was by a cloth which formed a sort of partition: we put
> there the two mattresses of my camp bed, one beside the other, on bags
> half filled with straw. Beyond this place was another small one where the
> slaves slept.
>
> In general, this homestead, though very small, furnished us with
> all we had need of. It is situated in the corner of a large sandy plain
> between the Berg river, the Piketberg and the sea, at the place where
> the anonymous mountain, of which I spoke, is closest to the Piketberg.

[10] Though not stated by La Caille, Klipfontein was then owned by Cornelis Coetsee
whose son, Jacobus Coetsee, was in 1761–2 a leading member of the expedition that
first penetrated the region north of the Orange River. Cornelis's grandson was the Jerrit
or Gerrit Coetzee who, then aged 76, was interviewed by Maclear around 1838 (see
Maclear 1840 and Maclear 1866).

[11] This paragraph is not in the printed *Journal Historique* and is taken from Evans
(1992). Clearly, it could not have been available to either Everest or Maclear who
investigated the site later.

Fig. 3.3 Using the sector to find the latitude during the verification of the Paris Meridian a few years before La Caille's expedition to the Cape. According to Delambre (1827, p. 279) this picture shows La Caille on his back, pointing the instrument towards a star and Cassini III de Thury at the plumb line reading off its declination. This sector was used by La Caille at his observatory in Cape Town and at the Klipfontein farm (Cassini de Thury 1740).

This farm appears to be a plane because one climbs there almost without noticing, but one sees from there the whole chain of mountains to the east of Cape Town, as far as the place called Hottentots Holland Kloof, east-south-east of Cape Town. One sees from there the mountains of Groene Kloof, the Table, and the mountains that border the sea. In general, one sees all that can be seen from the top of the Piketberg, or from the neighbouring mountain; that is why I have not placed beacons on these mountains to terminate my triangles, but have marked instead a point taken 36 toises [70 m] to the west of my observatory, so as to make fires there to form my last triangle.

[15 September] Worked at defining a meridian with a cord, in which to put the sector.[12]

The sector in its barn was carefully orientated north–south using a wire stretched along the meridian (see Fig. 3.3). For six nights La Caille concentrated on determining the latitude.[13] He was fortunate enough

---

[12] Also not in *Journal Historique*.

[13] La Caille's notebook of these observations is in the library of the University of the Witwatersrand where the catalogue entry reads: 'Lacaille's working notebook 1746–54 (Ref. A892). Contains observations made at the Cape from 1751 April 19 to 1753 March 8. Also observations made elsewhere and a list of expenses in connection with his observatory at St Martin (Paris) in 1748'.

Fig. 3.4 The rock on the summit of the Kapokberg identified by Maclear's team as that used as a beacon by La Caille. Sketch by William Mann and Charles Piazzi Smyth. Table Mountain is seen faintly in the background (Warner, 1989, by permission).

to have mostly clear skies and good seeing. On the 16, 18 and 19 September he observed eight stars to the north of the zenith with the face of the sector to the east; on the 22, 23 and 24 he observed eight others with the sector facing west. The results of the measurements had to wait until he returned to the Cape to be reduced. In combination with similar observations from his observatory on the foreshore he found that the latitude difference between the two ends of his arc was $1°$ $13'$ $17''\frac{1}{3}$.[14] He concluded the write-up of the latitude determinations with the few blunt words 'That is the result of the astronomical part of this measurement'.

The next thing to do was to to measure the angles between the two mountains in the Swartland plain and the two end stations. For this work, the quadrant was used in a horizontal position.

He sent a message to the Groene Kloof farm to have a fire lit on the Kapokberg (see Fig. 3.4) and sent Poitevin to light another on the second peak from the northern end of Kasteelberg. Observations were successful during the period 22–24 September. In the case of the Kapokberg he also made use of the 'nearly cylindrical' rock beacon.

On the 25th, he packed up and left for Groene Kloof, sleeping at the Berg River crossing. It took all the following day to cross the swollen river and reach Schaafplaatsfontein. A day later they were back in Groene Kloof.

---

[14] After re-reducing his data much later, La Caille, in his *Astronomiae Fundamenta* (1757), p. 184, gave the last figure as $17''.5$, according to Henderson (see Maclear (1866), p. 111).

Measuring the baseline

To obtain the absolute distance from his observatory to the Klip-fontein station, it was first necessary to find the distance between the Kapokberg and the Kasteelberg, which formed the bases of the two largest triangles. This was done by a secondary survey involving the setting up of a precisely measured baseline and triangulating between it and the two mountains (see again Fig. 5.1).

On 29 September he set out to find a better direction for his baseline than that he had found on August 11. He stated that the new line ran over very smooth ground except for small bumps which he took care to level.[15] In some places it was encumbered by bushes, which is why he says it took him seven days to do the work, as much because of the laying out as for the actual measurement. He would like to have made a much longer baseline but, especially towards the western end, the bushes were too dense. But he was satisfied with what he was able to do.

Today, most of the length of the base is across wheat fields. Growing relatively bulky grain crops only became possible after the advent of railways, because before then the farmers had no means of getting their produce to market. Thus they concentrated on raising animals that were left to graze on the uncultivated scrubland and whatever grass they could find.

The ends of the baseline were beacons placed on hillocks that were slightly elevated from the plain. Unlike Maclear, who repeated his work in the following century using a slightly different baseline, he did not erect permanent markers.

From 30 September to 2 October he and Bestbier laid out the proposed base. The first night they slept at Vygekraal (probably the present Vyekraal), about 6.7 km south of where they had got to. The second night they observed angles and slept at the farm of a Mr Slabber, presumably towards the east end. Then they returned by wagon to the west end to make further observations. An advantage of ox-wagons was that they were not dependent on finding a road!

On 4 October they headed for the Kasteelberg again, via Kiesen-bosch and Driefontein, the latter being where Bestbier stayed. The following day they climbed the mountain with seven slaves, who carried the quadrant with other instruments and provisions. They encountered bad weather and could not see the signal fire at Klipfontein. The fact that La Caille at first used an incorrect azimuth for Klipfontein did not help. He found that he had been out by nearly a degree by observing the rising Sun on the 12th. His stay on the mountain was to last 9 days and nights, through rain, hail and mist. He complained 'the smoke, cold and wet greatly upset me, as I had neither tent, covering nor mattress'.

---

[15] This was not strictly true, according to Everest (1821).

Bestbier had to leave at that point for militia duties and was replaced by Captain Muller at their effective base of Driefontein. On the 13th La Caille went down the mountain as his assistants (slaves?) were required to help with barley harvesting. However, on the 14th, as luck would have it, the weather at last cleared and he had to go up again. On the way he met the slaves bringing down the instruments. He had to persuade them to go back up! That evening, he was able to make measurements of the direction of the signal fire at Klipfontein. Looking towards the Cape, he could distinguish the whitewashed corner of the block containing his observatory clearly against the black wall of the Company's workshop in the next block.

Not wishing to waste any time, they descended the mountain 'in faint moonlight' and loaded the instruments onto the wagon. They walked all night to get to Groene Kloof [about 35 km], changed the oxen for fresh ones and sent the equipment to the top of the Kapokberg. The next day he measured from there the azimuths of the ends of the base and the fire at Klipfontein but had to return to Groene Kloof to get some sleep! Finally, on the 16th he was able to finish the observations with the quadrant.

The same afternoon he set off with his wagons, bringing Muller, Poitevin and eleven slaves to measure the baseline.

The measurement of the base took from 17 to 21 October, starting from the eastern terminal. They slept on the ground each night, 'under four sticks leaning against the wagon, over which was stretched a cloth to keep the dew off.'

La Caille used four rods of pine 18 French feet (~5.85 m) long with iron ends. He had brought with him from Paris a standard iron toise (1.949 m) which had been calibrated in the workshops of the instrument maker Langlois, as had the standards for all the other geodetic baselines. He also carried with him a secondary standard which was always kept in a wooden case and never exposed to the Sun.

This kind of work was second nature to him because of his years of similar measurements in France. As everything depended on the accuracy of his baseline he explained each day's programme in detail. First he checked the length of his poles. Then he measured 100 to 700 toises (1169–1385 m) according to how easy the terrain was to cover. He personally checked the abutting of each pole. Each time a pole was carried, he gave a token to the person at the head of the poles and after every 10 carryings he planted a small marker in the earth (see Fig. 3.5). Then he returned to the starting point for the day, measuring a second time, always counting his tokens and making sure he found his markers. Back at the start, he noted the difference between his two measures and once again checked the length of his rods. That was the morning's work.

Then he transported the rods, his bed and his provisions 1200–1300 toises (2339–2534 m) further on, to the place where he expected to end the day's work. There, after eating and taking a little rest, he checked his

Fig. 3.5 La Caille measuring a survey baseline in France using standard rods or poles. He is probably the one checking that the rods abut properly. He used the same method in the Cape Swartland in 1752 (Cassini de Thury 1740).

rods again and measured back to where the morning's work had ended. Then he returned to camp, measuring again, and checked the poles on his return.

On the 22nd, their task completed, they slept at Groene Kloof. The next day they rode back to Cape Town and the instruments began their return journey by ox-wagon, arriving a week later.

Calculating the length of the arc

From his surveying he came to the conclusion that his base measured 6467¼ toises or 12604.7 metres, after making some corrections for unevenness of the ground.

Before the start of the expedition he had made observations of the Sun to determine the exact deviation from the north–south direction of the line from his observatory to the beacon on the Kapokberg. This was necessary to correct for the fact that the Klipfontein station was not precisely north of his observatory.

He was then able to calibrate his distances and calculate that the length of one degree of the terrestrial meridian passing through 33° 18'½ south latitude was 57,037 toises or 111,165 m.[16] From the length

---

[16] In 1872, the pioneering science fiction writer Jules Verne wrote a novel about a geodetic expedition: *Aventures de 3 Russes et de 3 Anglais dans l'Afrique australe (Adventures of 3 Russians and 3 English in southern Africa), Verne (1872)*. The scientists on this expedition obtained exactly the same result as La Caille had, namely 57,037 toises per degree!

Table 3.1 Length of a degree and the apparent radius of earth according to various 18th-century measures.

Latitude (degrees)	Length of 1°		Place	Radius of earth (km)
	toises	metres		
0	56,749	110,604	Peru	6337
45	57,074	111,237	France	6373
66	57,438	111,947	Lapland	6414
−33	57,037	111,165	Cape	6369

Note. The Peruvian measure is from Maupertuis, as quoted by Murdin (2009). The other three are taken from Everest (1821).

of a degree, the apparent radius of the earth at that place can easily be calculated by dividing by one degree expressed in radians, or 0.01745329.

Including his, the French expeditions in the eighteenth century had thus given the results shown in Table 3.1, with their conversions into modern units:

He was surprised and very worried to find that the length of one degree along his meridian arc at 33° south latitude was so large, almost equal to what he and Cassini de Thury had found in France between 42° and 45° north latitude. In other words, the earth seemed to be more heavily flattened in the south than in the north! But, facts are facts and have to be respected. As he remarked at the time, 'An observer is only responsible for the accuracy of his measurement and not for the actual number found'.

The previous results had shown that the shape of the earth, at least in the northern hemisphere, was consistent with its being an 'oblate spheroid', that is, a sphere flattened towards the poles. In other words, its radius of curvature along a line of longitude is least at the pole and greatest at the equator. This was in general accord with Newton's prediction from centrifugal force. This is why he was said to have found a pear-shaped planet (see Fig. 3.6).

He pondered the details that had led to his conclusion—the observations of the stars, the measurements of the angles of the triangles and the measurement of the baseline. If there had been an error, it could not have been due to the stellar observations—long experience and a thorough knowledge of all the precautions ensured that they were as precise as was possible with a sector of 1.9 m radius. Besides, the internal agreement of the measurements left nothing to be desired.

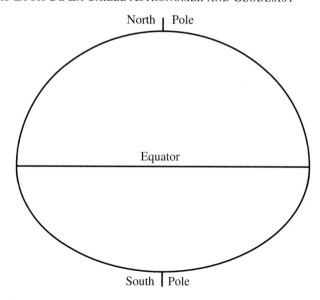

Fig. 3.6 The 'pear-shaped' earth that La Caille's Swartland measurement seemed to be leading to, here greatly exaggerated. His measurement showed that the earth was as flattened at 33 degrees south as it was at 45 degrees north ©I.S. Glass.

Could it have been the measurements of the angles of the survey triangles? The solidity and the accuracy of the scales of the quadrant as used over ten years, the small number of angles and the fact that those for each triangle added up very closely to 180 degrees did not allow for any significant error.

Thus, if there had been an error, it could only have been in the measurement of the baseline. Perhaps he or Mr Muller had mis-counted somewhere. But the first count had always agreed with the second. Just to be sure that he had not deceived himself, La Caille went back to Cape Town to check his calculations in peace on 23rd October. The results turned out just as before. Though he had no personal doubts about the base measurement, he decided to anticipate any criticisms by checking it again.

On the 2nd of November, he rode back to the base with a rope 30 toises (58.47 m) long, divided into sections of 3 toises. The alignment could still be followed and he found the marker pegs again, except for three, but he was always able to find the following ones in these cases. That is how he could say that there was no error in the distance of 6467¼ toises (12,604.7 m) from one end of the base to the other.

It is rather curious that the Abbé left his anomalous conclusion as it stood and does not seem to have referred to it in later life. This in spite of the fact that Pierre Bouguer and Charles-Marie de La Condamine, both of whom he knew very well, had actually tried to measure the effect on a plumb line of the mountain Chimboraçao while in Peru. Perhaps he was privately uncertain as to what his result really meant or even had some inkling himself of the eventual explanation that Table Mountain and the Piketberg had deflected the plumb lines of his zenith sector. He must have taken the attitude that he had explained quite clearly everything that he had done and that he had taken the utmost care. In the end he may have taken refuge in his previously quoted words: 'An observer is only responsible for the accuracy of his measurement and not for the actual number found'.

4
Notes about the Cape

Remarks about the Cape

During La Caille's geodetic operations in the south of France with Cassini de Thury, the Academy of Sciences had sent along a botanist to record not only the new plants they encountered but also all kinds of other natural phenomena. However, his expedition to the Cape was not so favoured. He therefore took it upon himself to record the physical and even the human environment that he found. Few literate travellers before him had spent enough time at the Cape to form a realistic idea of the local peoples and their customs. Those who wrote about the area had usually been more interested in the 'savage' native peoples than in the lives of the colonists. They tended to exaggerate what they saw in the hope of selling their books. The illustrations and maps that they used were often unrealistic and it is obvious that the artists involved had sometimes never seen what they were portraying. It was common to re-use illustrations from earlier works. For this reason, the sophisticated Abbé's sober remarks must be regarded as particularly valuable.

La Caille made the following statement in his *Abridged Account of the Voyage Made by Order of the King to the Cape of Good Hope* (La Caille 1751, p. 532), the text of a lecture he gave to the Academy after his return to France:

> You may have expected that I would make here a description of this famous Cape of Good Hope, that I would expatiate on the customs of the natives of the country known as *Hottentots*, that I would speak of the particular products of the land and of the adjacent seas but, as you can judge from what I have said, I have not had the leisure to research these things; I must confess that my knowledge is too limited to satisfy the curious and the scientists about this part of natural history.

In the *Journal Historique* (La Caille 1763), the editor Claude Carlier included a set of the Abbé's considered *Remarks* about matters other than astronomy, which may or may not have been intended to be the basis for a general description of the Cape. In it there is also a series of critical *Notes and Reflections* on the work of a previous traveller, Peter

Kolbe, which in fact contain a number of original observations on the Cape scene in the form of corrections to the latter's opinions.

Later in this chapter, some opinions about the *Journal Historique*, both critical and informative, are mentioned. They were expressed by Otto Friedrich Mentzel, a knowledgeable but little known German writer on the Cape who had read the *Journal Historique* before penning his own reminiscences.

Extracts from La Caille's *Journal Historique*

The first section of this chapter comprises descriptions from La Caille's *Journal Historique* or diary proper, with dates and page numbers from the second edition (La Caille 1776).

TABLE MOUNTAIN

[11 May 1751]   I went for a walk this evening at the foot of Table Mountain. It is a space more than 400 toises [780 m] long and 600 [1169 m] wide, completely covered with stones thrown around in confusion, and like debris from a part of the north of the mountain that has collapsed. In fact, on 11 November a large rock located where the mountain becomes sheer, somewhat towards the middle, collapsed with a huge noise and brought down a prodigious quantity of stones to the valley. Its track has remained visible for a long time from the town, which is a league [4.4 km] away. Beyond these stones, towards the Town, the ground is so soaked with spring water that one cannot get to the mountain with dry feet (p. 142).

[15 September 1751]   Table Mountain, though very steep, is not difficult to climb via a large crack [Platteklip Gorge] which is somewhat west of the middle. I got there from town in less than three hours. Its foot, up to about a third of its height, is stony and covered with plants and bushes; the remainder is nothing but a heap of stones placed in exactly horizontal beds up to the summit. The crack is very deep; it starts around two fifths of the way up and is 50–60 paces wide and narrows in proportion as one approaches the summit, where it is no wider than five or six paces. It is covered in the same way with stones, earth and bushes right to the top. One finds at the top several very flat grassy areas, resembling meadows; these areas are separated by rocks, of which several are flat and placed level, but most are like the back of an ass, placed horizontally: its edge, which is towards Cape Town, is not a straight line but makes a slight arc, concave towards the town. On the platform at the summit are somewhat elevated beds of stones that are not visible from town, so that from the latter one does not see the [true] summit of the mountain.

Though the summit extends from east to west, trending about nine degrees towards the north, there is however a branch that starts towards the middle of the mountain and stretches southwest to end near Hout Bay. One finds water in the hollows of the rocks and towards the eastern part that faces False Bay there is an abundant spring from which a fairly large stream flows. The view extends into the distance on all sides except to the east where it is limited by a chain of mountains [the Hottentots' Holland range] at a distance of 15 to 18 leagues [67–80 km]. The sea is to be seen to the south in all directions but in the north one only sees the horizon at 22 degrees from north in direction west. I was easily able to recognise the mountain that I intend will form the end of my measured degree [Piketberg] (pp. 148–150).

BLAAUWBERG

[11 Sep 1751]   We returned to the Cape [Cape Town] at dinner time; I climbed the mountain called Blaauwberg West, where I saw at the same time Table Bay & False Bay, with the coast from Hout Bay as far as Saldanha (p. 146).

HOUT BAY

[4 June 1752]   I have been at Hout Bay to make a map at the request of the Governor. This bay, properly speaking, is only 600 toises [1169 m] wide and 700 [1364 m] or 800 [1559 m] in depth. It is completely surrounded by rocks and mountains, full of reefs and unapproachable except at the inner end, where there is a sandbank, but all that a longboat can do is to run aground there. There is in the valley that ends here a really beautiful farm [Kronendal; still extant] belonging to Mr le Sueur, a former clergyman at the Cape (p. 171).

KASTEELBERG

[13 August 1752]   (see also Chapter 3, Serious reconnaissance) I climbed Riebeek Kasteel [Kasteelberg] accompanied by six blacks to make a beacon there: this mountain is quite high and long. Its summit is accessible from the west, it runs approximately north–south, its crest is very steep on the east side. It is very overgrown. One finds all over it a large number of quite large trees, but of a very spongy wood. I placed a signal beacon on the second peak, counting from the north. I had all the surrounding trees cut down. I visited the fourth peak, which is towards the middle of the mountain and is the highest; but the rock which forms it is almost inaccessible: and having climbed it with a certain amount of trouble, I was for a long time unable to descend or to find the way by which I had come up. This mountain is full of baboons and marmots [dassies]; it is said there are still wild horses (zebra), but I did not see any.

Though it is rather arid and though one sees no spring that forms a stream, it is however surrounded by nine or ten farms, of which several are very good, according to the large quantity of corn that is reaped: there are sources of water at some distance from this mountain, that serve to provide water to the dwellings (p. 175).

RONDEBOSCH

[26 November 1752] I have been at Rond-Bosch [Rondebosch], invited by the Governor: he took me to see the garden of Newlands, with the pleasure-house that he had built for himself last year. I returned on 3rd December: I saw a large number of aloes of different species that are cultivated [there], out of curiosity. Newlands is a large garden where vegetables are grown for the refreshment of the Company's vessels. It was rather disordered when I was there; but it is to be worked on to make it one of the most beautiful round about (p. 186).

Newlands House still stands in spite of having undergone numerous alterations and a reconstruction following a fire.

INLAND TRAVELS

[27 October 1751] In the afternoon I went to a house or farmstead called Saxenbourg, six leagues [27 km] to the east of Cape Town [The Saxenburg farm dates from the late seventeenth century and is still extant].

[1 November 1751] I have been to Stellenbosch, where there was a review of the Militias of the districts of Stellenbosch and of Drak- enstein. Stellenbosch is a village composed of thirty houses and a church. There are two principal streets, bordered by large oaks which give very good shade. There is also a river that traverses the village.

This village is in a wide valley completely surrounded by very high mountains except for the side where the view extends to False Bay, but because these mountains are at a reasonable distance the place is most agreeable (p. 154).

[19 May 1752] I have been to Drakenstein. First we crossed the Tygerberg by the valley in its middle, going from north-west to south-east, and from there we crossed fairly even ground to arrive at Drakenstein. This is a very long and broad valley running from the south towards north-north-west, enclosed by Swartberg [Paarlberg today?] to the west and the chain of large mountains that runs from False Bay to the far north. This valley is bordered on both sides by a large number of farms mainly given over to vines. They are all watered by the streams that descend from the mountains towards a river that goes down the middle of the valley, namely the Berg river. It leaves this chain of mountains near Piketberg. Thereafter it heads westwards towards St Helena Bay. The church[1] is a little southeast

---

[1] He is probably referring here to the first church at Paarl, on the site of the Strooidak Church which dates from the early nineteenth century.

of the middle of the valley; it is not much to look at. To the southeast of this large valley there is another smaller one, enclosed between high mountains, called Franschhoek, that is to say French Corner. It is there that the refugees were established in the beginning and where they cultivated the vines.

Regarding these refugees, they kept the French language and taught it to their children but the latter were obliged to speak Dutch, as much because they did business with the Dutch and Germans who spoke Dutch as because they are married or allied with Germans or Dutch. They have not taught French to their children so that, there being none of the former refugees from 1680 to 1690, only their children spoke French and these are all old. I have never met any person younger than 40 who spoke French, at least who had not come from France. I cannot however be sure that this is absolutely always the case, but I have been assured by those who speak French that within 20 years there will be nobody who can speak French (pp. 169–171).

[29 January 1753]   I have been to Constantia (see Fig. 4.1): this famous vineyard is composed of two farms; one ancient and constructed by one of the Van der Stels, Governor of the Cape; the other is more modern and in the taste of ordinary habitations; both are in a hollow but the first is more elevated than the other; it has a bit of a view over a part of False Bay, the other has none at all. Both have plenty of water and the gardens and orchards are very fertile. Each one belongs to a particular individual (p. 194).[2]

BOTANY AND ZOOLOGY

[8, 9, 10 August 1751, around Mamre] I amused myself shooting some birds and collecting some local flowers (p. 146).

He sent to the King's Garden (later the Jardin des Plantes) a great number of bulbs, plants, seeds and roots unknown in Europe. The late Mr Jussieu [Antoine de Jussieu] has several times rendered public thanks to him for having enriched the Royal Garden with precious treasures.

He took the trouble to have dried out some rare and unusual birds, both as to body shape and plumage, and sent a box of them from the Cape to Mr de Réaumur. This case was lost in transit from the Cape to Holland. He sent from the Cape a great number of shells and unusual stones as well as the skin of a wild ass [zebra?] which can be seen in the display at the Royal Garden (Carlier, in La Caille 1776, p. 63).

---

[2] At the time of La Caille's visit, Groot Constantia was owned by Carl Georg Wieser. The other farm referred to was probably the present Hoop Op Constantia, belonging then to Johanna Appel (the widow Colyn). See also La Caille's remarks, later in this chapter for a comment on Constantia wine production.

Fig. 4.1 Groot Constantia as pictured in 1741 by J.W. Heydt. The present single storey house, dates from the end of the eighteenth century but was partially reconstructed in the 1920s following a fire, using the same foundations. The two buildings in the foreground, one rectangular and the other U-shaped, are probably parts of the existing outbuildings (W. Cape Archives & Record Service M148).

[22 October 1751]   A boat left for Middleburg; I sent by it a packet addressed to Count Bentinck, containing birds for Mr de Réaumur and seeds and shells for Mr Duhamel (p. 151).[3]

[15 August 1751]   I was shown a fish taken in Hout Bay (see Fig. 4.2). It was dried; its natural colour appeared to have been an eel-like blue. It had no scales; its length from the tip of its tail to the end of its beak was seven inches and a half; that of its head around two inches, including the beak: the thickness of its head one inch, about like the body of a fish, as far as one can judge from its state: here is a drawing as exactly as I can make it. Its tail is held horizontal: it only has one small flipper on its back and two on the upper part of its breast.

What is most peculiar about this animal is its neck and elevated head, which is very like a plucked bird; its beak is in the form of an isosceles triangle, whose angle is 36 to 40 degrees: here is its front view (see Fig. 4.3) (p. 148).

In a letter to Grandjean de Fouchy at the Academy of Sciences, written on 21 February 1752, La Caille described the difficulties of collecting:

---

[3] These two had the typical wide-ranging interests of eighteenth-century scientists. René Antoine Ferchault de Réaumur originated a widely used temperature scale with 0 as the freezing point of water and 80 as the boiling point. Henri-Louis Duhamel du Monceau was a physician, naval engineer and botanist.

Fig. 4.2 Fish, side view. According to Raven-Hart (1976), the fisheries department (South Africa) suggested it may have been a foetal dolphin (From La Caille 1763).

Fig. 4.3 Fish, front view (From La Caille 1763).

I await from day to day the arrival of Mr D'Après [on his way back to France]. I sent him the copies of the observations of the Moon, Mars and Venus, and of the principal stars. I included some dried plants between leaves of paper, some seeds, some buffalo and eland horns and some birds for Mr de Réaumur. The seeds are confusingly mixed because I only got them by giving some escalons [?] to the blacks who guard the herds of Mr Bestbier, my host. I could make here a collection of natural curiosities if I could give some piastres to the same. This is not because they are sold but because of carriage expenses which mount up a lot because of the distance of the places where the interesting animals are common and the deficiency of the roads which break the carts, which are very dear and carry only a little. I have given 64 florins for the carriage of a hippopotamus head and a pair of rhino horns that came from a distance of about a hundred leagues [440 km]. Though horses are extremely common, they do not know how to make them carry loads. At the same time wine is in such great abundance at the Cape that they don't know what to do with it, however the rich inhabitants at 40 leagues [~180 km] from here are obliged to do without because a cart is wrecked after 4 or 5 trips.

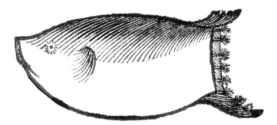

Fig. 4.4 'Sea-sun' fish. This picture was printed upside-down in the *Journal Historique*. From the image and its size it is probably a Slender Sunfish (*Ranzania Levis*), of the Molidae family. These are still washed up from time to time on the Cape beaches (From La Caille 1763).

I expect to make a trip in the countryside during September and October. I will collect there as many plants as I can and I will not neglect the seeds and will send them all as soon as possible . . . .[4]

[23 April 1752] I found on the shore a fish that had been thrown up there; I had already seen a stuffed one kept as a curiosity by Mr Reinius,[5] Captain of the Garrison. This one was full of maggots, which is why I did not bring it back. I have made an exact drawing of its shape. From the mouth to the tail it was 19 inches and a half long, not including a kind of cartilage which forms the tail. It was ten and a half inches at its broadest; the width of its tail was seven and three quarter inches. Its mouth is vertical, it had only four fins, two at the extremities of its tail and one on each side about where the gills would have been. Its tail is a cartilage composed of bony fibres reinforced at intervals and ending like a feather; it was not [as much as] an inch thick; its skin is very hard, and resembles that of polished sharkskin; it is white towards the belly and in all the part of the drawing that is not shaded, and covered with grey patches on the back. The thickness of this fish is two and a half inches. I have seen others since that have black rays between the eyes, curving towards the belly. They are called here Sea-suns (Fig. 4.4) (pp. 167–169).[6]

[7 October 1752] The same day they brought us a stink-badger; it had been taken by dogs and was pulled behind the wagon. Here I give a description of the exterior of this animal as exactly as I can.

---

[4] La Caille to Fouchy, dated Cape, 21 March 1752; via Du Hamel de Monceau, Inspecteur General de la Marine de France, received 17 June 1752. Archives de l'Académie des Sciences, de l'Institut de France, Folio 333.

[5] Possibly Johannes Tobias Rhenius, a retired Captain of the Garrison, mentioned by Mentzel.

[6] Erroneously labelled 28 April in the French printed version.

He was male and seemed old. He had the shape of a middling basset hound, being exactly two feet (65 cm) from the tip of the muzzle to the base of the tail. His hair was about 30 mm long, black under his belly and on his paws. The middle of his back was covered in grey-white hair, from his eyes to the middle of his tail, whose end was black. Two stripes of white hair separated the grey-white band of hair from the black hair of his belly; these were an inch or an inch and a half (4 cm) wide. The head and muzzle of this animal more-or-less resembled those of a dog; the muzzle was short and a bit pointed. This animal does not have exterior ears; it has two oblong holes or slits perpendicular to the opening of his mouth, into which the skin re-enters. His tail was about 8 inches (22 cm), the paws short, the front ones armed with claws sticking out about an inch (27 mm), the back ones having very short claws like those of dogs. This animal when chased by the dogs emitted extremely smelly winds but which were exhausted finally. When I saw it alive it did not stink at all. It was killed an hour after it was brought to the house; because this was done in my absence it was too damaged to take away the skin (pp. 182–184).[7]

FOOD

[7 January 1752]   I have eaten some quite ripe white grapes from a trellis. Also on 23 December of the same year (p. 165).

[17 Jan 1752]   I have eaten a penguin's egg. They are big—about twice the size of a hen's egg and rounder: the white is the same. When the egg is boiled, it is a transparent blue and like a gel; it is really nice to eat and without comparison better than a hen's egg; but the yellow tastes of the swamp; the shell is perfectly white; some are bluish in parts (p. 165).[8]

ANTHROPOLOGY

[31 July 1751]   I have measured the height of a bushman aged about 25 years: it was six feet seven inches and ten lines (2.16 m); he was barefoot and bare-headed; he came from the countryside running in front of a wagon pulled by oxen to drive it; he was fat in proportion to his height (p. 143).

---

[7] This animal has been identified as a Honey Badger or Ratel (*Mellivora Capensis*) by Dr Graham Avery, Curator/Scientist: Quaternary Collections, Iziko Museums, Cape Town. It is very tough and fierce creature, willing to attack much larger enemies. See Fig. 4.5.

[8] [Original footnote] The penguin is a species of bird that stands upright on its feet, has wings without feathers, hanging from them like crossed sleeves, and have white stripes. They never fly but they live in corners without mixing with other birds. They have a little of man, bird and fish.

Fig. 4.5 A Honey Badger (*Mellivora Capensis*) or Ratel was seen by La Caille in 1752 near Kasteelberg and decribed quite accurately by him (From Lydekker 1894, Vol II, p. 81).

[1 January 1753]   Today I saw played an instrument used among the Caffres.[9] It is composed of 12 rectangular boards, each of length 18 to 20 inches. From the first, which is about six inches wide, their width diminishes towards the last, which is only about two and a half inches. These planks are assembled one next to the other on two triangles of wood to which they are attached by thongs, so that the whole instrument forms a kind of table four feet long and twenty inches wide. Underneath each plank is a piece of calabash, to which it is attached to make a resonator. A man carries this instrument in front of him rather in the way our Parisian women carry their goods; they play by striking the top with two wooden mallets, whose shape and size are like a plumber's iron tools. This instrument is passably sonorous and one can play a large number of tunes on it (pp. 192–193).[10]

La Caille's *Remarks*

According to Carlier, but perhaps not quite true, La Caille had decided just before he died to write his own book about the customs and ways of the inhabitants of the Cape and the Khoina. Before leaving the Cape he

[9] By 'Caffres' La Caille means the bantu people to the east of the colonial frontier. During his time they were a rarity at the Cape and the term itself was descriptive rather than pejorative.

[10] This was probably what is called today an African Gourd Xylophone.

had made a series of random notes. Supposedly, in spite of the urging of his friends, he had declined up to then to get busy on this work, telling them that he had neither the stylistic ability nor the materials to write a travelogue, and that besides such works were written just to satisfy idle curiosity, more to amuse than to provide solid information. He was not a travel writer, he said, but an astronomer.

Carlier in his edited version of the *Journal Historique* included La Caille's *Remarks* preceded by an introduction of his own, mainly about Khoina, which seems to have been composed from the reports of previous travellers and which contains little that is original.

The full title of the section containing La Caille's genuine remarks reads: *Remarks of the Abbé de la Caille on the customs and manners of the inhabitants of the Cape of Good Hope and on those of the Khoina.* He introduces the remarks himself, with the words: 'Lacking the time and opportunity to put together a proper memoir for making a complete history of the Cape I will put down here my reflections and the certain facts that have come to my attention, not according to any particular order but solely as they occurred to me.' It is hard to believe that he could have constructed a whole book out of such a flimsy set of notes. In fact, in this section he makes almost no remarks about the Khoina at all.

The *Remarks* are given in this section in their entirety. Sub-titles have however been added for convenience.

1. On the soil of the Cape

The soil of the Cape is in general not excellent. The abundance that is found there is due to choosing the best ground, to a climate such that there is no need to fear frost or hail except on the mountains, to the fertilising of the land by the large numbers of sheep and to the newness of the soil which is not yet tired and is allowed to lie fallow at least as often as in France.

2. Cape winds

Table Mountain and Devil's Peak being quite steep along their whole lengths, a strange thing happens; namely that the houses at the north end of the mountains which should be protected from the SE winds are however those which suffer the most, whilst those that are at the south end, and which by consequence are the most exposed to the SE wind are hardly affected at all. [In the original he wrote north instead of south and *vice versa*.] I have often seen that when the SE wind is terrible in town one feels nothing in Constantia or in the part of Rondebosch towards the north and more at the foot of the mountain, as Newlands and Paradise are. On the other hand, when the NE winds are blowing furiously, it is impossible to remain in Newlands or Paradise. This proves that the violent winds are stopped at the foot of these mountains, that they then rise towards the summits and, piling up there with those that pass close to the mountain, they find a kind of precipice that engulfs them as they fall from the top of the mountain. This is confirmed by the movement of the cloud that covers the Table during the fury of the SE wind. One sees it falling from the summit of the mountain, perpendicularly along it, but dissipating as it descends so that it is invisible by the time it arrives at one third the height of the mountain.

3. On the meat

As a good Frenchman, it is not surprising that the Abbé was particular about what he ate:

Though fresh meat and fish are very abundant at the Cape, the inhabitants only feast on salted and smoked meat and fish that they eat lightly grilled and heavily peppered and bread soaked in warm water. The ladies are extremely fond of all kinds of achars, which are salted vegetables or fruits preserved in vinegar without sparing the spices. I have been at several ceremonial meals where the main dishes were hard and yellow stockfish and half-rotten ham from Europe with yellow and rancid fat. They take care not to eat the fresh meat which is served there truly in quantity, but only to make up numbers. A lady (Mrs Lanu)[11] who lived at the foot of the mountain called Babylontoren came to spend a few days in Cape Town, staying at Bestbier's house. She returned a little out of sorts and died a few days later. She attributed her illness to having eaten nothing but fresh meat at Bestbier's house. Finally, the best presents that ships' captains can give when stopping at the Cape are pieces of meat salted in Europe and intended for feeding the crews—the blacker they are the more they are to the taste of the locals.

The spicy 'achars' are sauces that feature in Cape Malay cuisine today. This group of people is descended from East Indian political exiles and slaves sent to the Cape in VOC times.

4. Vegetables and fruits

Most of the vegetables are as good as I have eaten in France, with the exception of asparagus which is no better than that grown in winter in Parisian cellars, and the celery which is small and shrivelled. In recompense, the carrots are excellent even when raw and all kinds of cabbage are very good there. As far as fruit is concerned, I only found peaches and apricots to be as good as one can find in France; but there is no good plum, some passable apples (the Reinette and the Calville); no good pear except the Bergamote, which is passable; the figs are mediocre; the oranges are much less good than the Portugese ones; though there are almost all varieties here I have not tasted one that pleased me. The

---

[11] 'Lanu' is probably a misprint for Louw. The proprietor of the farm Bablylontoren at that time was Johannes Louw Jacobzoon, the will of whose wife (born Elizabeth Morkel) was dated 1752.

strawberries are good and most raisins exquisite. There are few cherries as sweet as the French ones and almost no gooseberries.[12] There are nuts in enough quantity but I have not eaten the green walnuts—they go bad in no time. Melons are only good in the first and second year after the seed has come from Europe, they degenerate in the third. So far as the fruits of the Indies or the warm countries are concerned, one finds the watermelon which is said to be passable, the guava, a sort of pomegranate, is good there. All the fruits and vegetables are imports and there is nothing particular or native to the country except some bulbs that are sweet enough, the Hottentot fig, the Hottentot raisin and some other berries that the blacks eat when they find them.

Though the fruits and vegetables of the Cape are abundant they are very dear; the best prices one can find for a bunch of the most common ones, even in season, for example, carrots, are two local sous, which is four French ones; even the bunches themselves are small and scarcely sufficient for a small dish.

Many of the fruits such as apples that La Caille complained of are not suited to the immediate neighbourhood of Cape Town but are grown successfully today in nearby places at higher altitudes.

5. Cape weather

One can say that winter is the fine season at the Cape because apart from the fact that it never gets cold enough to require heating one often has six, seven or eight days without wind or unpleasant heat like the most beautiful September days in France. It is also true that one sometimes gets wind, rain or fog and covered skies for five or six days together but this sort of variation not being sudden as in France, i.e. the weather stays fairly constant for several days at a time, sometimes good, sometimes bad—one can say that the bad is compensated for by the good: whereas in the summer, there is a strong and cold wind that keeps one from going out, which obliges one to close the doors and windows, and keeps you closed up; or else there is an uncomfortable warmth that does not allow you to take the air until late in the evening. Winter doesn't bother anyone in the Cape except for travellers, because of the rivers.

The Cape Town climate is characterised by southeast winds and clear skies in summer. The rain mostly occurs during northeast storms in winter but these are interspersed with calm, clear days. Nowadays the summer climate at the Cape is preferred by most people, though even in Victorian times the hot season was considered intolerable by many European visitors.

In his paper *Diverses Observations...*, La Caille (1751 pp. 438–446) gave a lengthy summary of his daily weather observations between 1 July 1751 and 1 July 1752. He noted the directions of the winds and their

---

[12] La Caille is probably referring to European gooseberries, not the Physalis Peruviana that is the present-day Cape Gooseberry.

correlation with cloud cover and precipitation. He also listed the days when the temperatures were at their most extreme. Although he could record wind direction, he could not give quantitative values for its strength.

6. Economy of farming

The income of the inhabitants of the Cape who are settled deep in the country comes from the sale of their cattle and butter. Those who are at 60 or 80 leagues [267–356 km] go to town two or three times a year. They bring a large [vessel] full of salted butter that they sell to have money to buy provisions. Salted butter is usually worth a shilling a pound: that is, about 12 French sols; but fresh butter is much dearer, I have seen it sold at 32 French sols at the time of year good for pasturage: salted butter from Holland is sold in the Company stores for two shillings: one can hardly believe that in a country where the principal wealth is in the form of cattle that butter and milk should be so dear. Some not-too-good cheese is made from whey or buttermilk [*sic*]; the rich eat their salted butter covered with Dutch cheese which removes the rather rancid taste. It has to be said that the cows are less easy to milk than in Europe and the custom of leaving this to the slaves makes milk uncommon in country houses rich in cattle: besides the cattle have less of it than in Europe. I have stayed several days at a farm in Groene Kloof where there were more than 200 horned cattle and where somebody had to be sent half a league every morning to find milk for morning coffee. At the Cape, infants are fed on soup and not pap.

7. Wine making

The Cape inhabitants do not yet know how to get good productivity from their land; when the colony started they made experiments to find the proper time at which to work the lands, to manure them and to sow; but they are satisfied with having succeeded in this and have neglected the way to make and conserve wine. The ordinary wine harvested here would be as good as our Muscat de Frontignan[13] or Lunel[14] if they did not fertilise their vines so often and if they knew how to make and treat it. They are obliged to preserve it by sulphuring it to the point where it is not only sharp but unpleasant to drink. General Imhoff[15] imported a certain Serrurier from Frankfurt who he thought would be very suitable for carrying out the necessary research on wine conservation but this man, who was only conversant with the way of making Rhine wine, after having been paid by the Burger treasury for five years, found a rich widow who he married and became a wine merchant, without looking for any other method than that which was in use locally.

[13] Called Hanepoot in South Africa.
[14] Muscadel in South Africa.
[15] Imhoff, Governor General of the VOC colony in the East Indies, visited the Cape in 1743 and made a number of administrative changes.

Winemaking technique was revolutionised in the early twentieth century by the advent of artificial cooling, which enabled the fermentation process to be controlled and allowed the production of delicate dry wines.

8. Transportation

The custom in this country is to carry everything on wagons that are not very long or very wide; it is true that there is no lack of oxen or even of horses to pull them; but the price of these wagons makes this mode of transport very costly. A wagon hardly costs less than 120 Dutch écus [gulden]; sometimes more than 140, and when those who use them live far from the town, beyond the high mountains, a wagon can hardly be used for transport because of the jolting caused by the large numbers of rocks and because of the speed with which the oxen often pull the wagons.

9. Corn

It is however necessary to make large numbers of trips at the Cape, above all to deliver goods to God-forsaken places and that is why distant farms are so unprofitable and why beyond a certain distance habitations are only built for animals. However, most inhabitants raise large numbers of horses who graze in large herds throughout the year and have no other function than to tread the grain after harvest and sometimes to pull the harrow after planting seed. Nobody has thought or dared to load them with sacks of corn for sending to the town; it would not cost much and would save the wagons. Also the sacks in use here are hardly supportive of this idea because they are too short and too wide.

10. Cape bread

With the best wheat in the world most of the inhabitants of the countryside make very bad bread; it is partly the fault of their mills, whether hand, wind or water operated; they only half grind the grain, several hardly husking it. They barely separate the bran from the flour; as well as that, they hardly make the bread properly, so that it is black, heavy and fatty and in several places one can count the grains of which it is composed. Masters and slaves eat the same bread. There are however some country people who make good bread for their table.

11. Wild animals

At present, the wild beasts dwell far from the Cape. In the whole space enclosed by the chain of mountains from the east side of False Bay to St Helena Bay there is nothing to be found but some game. There are no elephants, lions, moose, asses or wild goats. Sometimes however during the months of December and January some elephants come as far as the Berg River, because the Cape west coast is then extremely dry. A lion in the area I have mentioned would cause general alarm.

The wild animals in the areas most distant from the Dutch possessions attack nobody and even flee at the sight of man provided they are not surprised; to avoid this happening travellers who arrive at a river bank (the ordinary habitat of these animals as much because of water as because the banks are covered with trees and tall bushes) stop before approaching the water, crack their long whips or let off a few shots. Then, if there are any lions, tigers [leopards?, cheetah?] or elephants in the area, they wake up and move off. There are not many large tigers but a large number of very small ones which are mostly tiger-cats [lynx?]. The animals which do harm to the inhabitants are wolves [hyenas?], tigers, wild dogs and the foxes called jackals. When a wolf enters a sheep enclosure these animals become so frightened that they crowd into a corner, one on top of the other, so that for one sheep that is killed by the wolf 30 or 40 others are suffocated. It is the same with tigers. The jackals hardly ever attack sheep but the wild dogs are only around in the daytime. If they encounter a flock of sheep and the shepherd is asleep or does not see and chase them, they throw themselves onto the poor beasts and in a few minutes they strangle a large number. The wolves sometimes attack calves and foals. It often happens they grab a good part of the tail of an ox but unless the ox is young or weakened by the lack of grazing that the land provides in the months of January and February, the wolf rarely kills them. As for the lion, he has the habit of creeping along the ground between the bushes and quietly approaching an ox until he is within range, killing it with a blow of his paw and then carrying it off on his back without anything dragging on the ground. Sometimes they jump into the kraals and throw an ox over the walls.

12. Game

The most common game in the region of the Cape are, besides the different species of sea birds and water birds, the deer, which differ from those of Europe in that the horns are not branched, they are less high and curved towards the back, a great number of buck or roebuck, among which the most common are steenbock and reebock, the aardvarks, the porcupines and the hares, of which there are two or three kinds. In birds, there are the ostriches, who are very numerous, the korhaans and the pheasants, the partridges, the quails; but all these creatures are only suited to the pot: the wild pigeons that are best roasted, peacocks, geese and wild ducks. The marmots [dassies?] that cover the mountains are also eaten but, in general, with the exception of the steenbock, the game is not tasty. It is the same with the fish of which there are only four good kinds, among which the best is the steenbras. Besides, few are caught in the Bay of the Cape [Table Bay].

13. Baboons

In the region of the Cape there are no parrots; but there is a species of monkey called baboons that are very common and numerous in the mountains. They do not let one approach in any way and if they see somebody approaching their mountains they set up a general cry which lasts one or two minutes, after which one does not see them again or hear them any more. During the nine days that I spent on Kasteelberg I never saw one or heard it cry except when I got there. However, the whole mountain is covered in them; they are never to be found in the plains and away from their rocks; from this one can decide what to think of Kolbe's story of baboons which appear cleverly to steal the provisions of travellers.[16] I have heard it said also that they sometimes come in troops to pillage the gardens at the foot of the mountains, that they put out sentries and that they throw the fruits that they take from one to the other; but even if that is exactly true, the other marvellous details that get added are pure imagination: for the rest, they are normally very big, and when standing on their hind legs they can reach the height of an average sized man. Some country people keep one chained up to a post; but they never release them; when you give them something to eat like bread, fruits or vegetables suitable for salads, they seize it with extraordinary greed and, having broken it with their front paws, without chewing it they put it between their molars and their cheeks which then swell and act as a reservoir: as soon as they have amassed as much as they want, they quietly start to chew what they have just stored up; and to get this food out of their pockets or cheeks they press them with a paw or push their cheeks against the neighbouring shoulder.

14. Wine

The Constantia wine, of which so much is drunk in Europe, must be well-adulterated. There are only two habitations in Constantia where the true wine grows, and in the best years these two places cannot supply more than 60 leagers[17] of red and 80 or 90 of white. The leager holds about 600 Paris pints; in a typical year one counts about 120 leagers.

On 14 April 1752 La Caille wrote to La Condamine...

a letter of advice on the subject of two small barrels of Constantia wine of about 80 to 82 bottles each, one of white and the other of red...The white wine has cost 17 piastres 7/9 and the red 28 piastres 4/9, which is in total in French money 242 pounds and 10 sous. It is up to you to quickly arrange their transport from L'Orient.[18]

---

[16] There is no question today that baboons living in the Cape Peninsula are expert thieves!

[17] One leager is about 575 litres (Raven-Hart 1976).

[18] La Caille to La Condamine, dated Cape Town, 14 April 1752; received 8 August 1752. Archive of the Academy of Sciences of the Institut de France, Fonds La Condamine 50J, 77.

The old Constantia wine is generally agreed to have been a sweet natural (non-fortified) one. It was very popular in Europe.

15. Molerats

One of the great nuisances of the Cape for those who want to hunt on horseback or cross the plains off the roads are the long underground galleries that the moles make in the sand. Your horse sinks every moment, sometimes with one foot, then the other and sometimes both, up to the knees; if on foot one falls just the same: these moles are very big and of the size of a four-month old cat, whereas in France they are the size of a newborn one. Greyhounds are useless in this country.

Molerat holes are still a scourge when hiking along the west coast!

16. Hunting elands

What one finds in Kolbe or in the extracts or translations on the subject about the way of catching [Elands?] is true. As far as the steenboks that often come between the vines is concerned, this animal is hardly bigger than an ordinary fox: but the eland is normally larger than the largest Friesland horses; it weighs 8 to 900 pounds; it is easy to kill because it does not defend itself. A well-mounted horseman pursues it for a quarter or a half hour; then it is so tired that it stops and lets itself be approached; then one fires a shot into its head at close range. The ball ought to be of two or three ounces, half lead and half tin. The strongest man cannot pierce it with an excellent sword, so hard is its skin.

Elands are no longer found outside game parks. Wild steenbok, because they are small and can penetrate fences, still manage to survive in some areas.

17. Hospitality for travellers

To travel with some comfort around the parts to the north of the Cape and in the places beyond the large chains of mountains that go from False Bay northwards, it is necessary to have a good stock of wine, and never to spare it in the houses you go to for dinner or to stay; then you will always be welcome; you will be lent horses, cattle, wagons, guides, etc.: without that, you will have little cheer and unhappy faces: wine, brandy, arrack and tobacco are here the best passports that you can have.

18. Butter

The Europeans of the Cape are naturally lazy, they don't take the trouble to make butter the European way: once the cows are milked they put the milk in a big churn; they wait two or three days until the churn is about half full; then they churn without doing anything else: also the best Cape butter is not valued as much as that which comes from Europe.

19. Cape beer

The beer made at the Cape is very bad, whether from ignorance, laziness or the fact that they employ poor hops because they only use those that come from Holland. The rich inhabitants buy Dutch beer at thirty écus for a barrel of 180 medium bottles, coming to sixteen French sous per bottle.

It is the custom here and perhaps in Holland, that with good meals you are served with beer after the first two or three glasses of wine that you have drunk.

20. Vineyards

Here the vines are planted in the valleys and the corn on the heights, when the farmhouses are nearby.

21. Land rentals

When this colony was established people were given farms for nothing; they comprised about a square league (about 20 sq km) of land. The government then decided to sell them, even at rather a high price, and it was ruled that those who took the new farms must pay the Company one écu per month and that for those who wished to establish some pasturage for their animals the land would be theirs for six months at one écu per month, or for a year at 12 écus. At present the rule is that a person who wants to establish a new farm must pay the Company 24 écus per year, which are mortgaged on the farm itself, and those who sell a farm or house must give the Company a fortieth of the agreed price.

22. Anthills

Anthills are extremely common at the Cape, especially in the Swartland; you cannot go ten steps without finding one; some of them are really large; I have even seen ones that are a good four feet at the base, and more than two high: they are more-or-less hemispherical in shape; often enough they have the shape of an elongated hemisphere. Though they may be made in very loose sand, they are so hard that they cannot be broken without a lot of effort, and a loaded wagon cannot destroy them. You see no activity. At the end of October and the beginning of November the ants add another layer, sometimes at the summit and sometimes at the sides; to do this they pierce several holes and cover them up with a new layer made in the form of galleries; this layer takes a long time to harden like the remainder; it is about an inch thick. Having broken several of these antheaps in the month of October I have found a prodigious quantity of still-white ants, black ones and some bigger ones with very long white wings. The ant-eaters make holes about eight inches diameter and six inches deep in one of the sides of the anthills; when they have de-populated an anthill in this way it normally stays abandoned; but sometimes the ants repair it.

Such termite mounds are still common in uncultivated areas.

23. Administrative districts

The Cape Colony consists at the moment of three judicial districts and six parishes; the first judicial district is that of Cape Town which has only one parish and the Council of Justice decides and judges on appeal: the second is that of Stellenbosch and Drakenstein, where there is a Landrost and councillors who meet in the village of Stellenbosch; there are four parishes under them, that of Stellenbosch, that of Drakenstein, and that which is beyond the mountains of red sand [Roodezand = Tulbagh]. The third jurisdiction covers the whole country beyond the great chain of mountains that goes from south to north. It is called Swellendam, from the name of Mr Swellengrebel,[19] the governor that preceded Mr Tulbagh, who established a parish and a council composed of a landrost and several councillors.

24. Complaints of the colonists

The complaints of the inhabitants of the Cape against the government are: 1. That they are not allowed to sell their crops to foreigners. 2. That they are not allowed to arm a few coastal vessels to trade in the neighbourhood, and especially to look for timber suitable for carpentry and joinery. 3. That the interest on money that they borrow for their needs is at six per cent with two good securities: that the costs of these loans are considerable because of the stamped paper and the Council taxes, that the lenders have nevertheless the right to retrieve their money at three months' notice. 4. That two thirds of the inhabitants are Lutherans who are not permitted to have ministers of this religion even though they have offered to support them at their own expense.[20] 5. That they suffer from the Chinese banished from Batavia who live off thefts committed by slaves; they buy the stolen goods and re-sell them.

The so-called 'Chinese' were probably people from the Dutch East Indies such as Malays.

25. Upbringing of slaves

The inhabitants of the Cape make no effort to educate their slaves, who are a mixture of pagans, Mohammedans and a few Christians. They are never spoken to about religion, and those who were born in the country have no idea of it except that they see their masters assemble in churches. Also, all the slaves are completely abandoned to all sorts of vices; the girls especially are very brazen; they don't want to marry but, after having been the toys of the whites in their first youth, they abandon themselves to all sorts of people whom they

[19] Swellendam is a composite of the names of Hendrik Swellengrebel and his wife Helena Willemina Ten Damme.

[20] The Lutheran church in Cape Town was allowed to operate from 1780.

accost publicly in the streets; this disorder causes a great number of assaults and even assassinations caused by jealousy. Combined with the abundance of wine, of arrack and brandy, this means that there are few houses without disturbances occurring nearly every day. When some master wants to emancipate a slave, he is baptised and received as a citizen; but this hardly ever happens because the master is then obliged to donate 500 écus to the Church for the support of the black in case he can't earn an income. The reason they give for not inspiring their slaves with religious feeling is that those belonging to the Company are instructed in catechism at certain times and on certain days; however they are worse scoundrels than the slaves of the citizens. But if one pays attention to the manner in which this instruction is given and to the fact that the children are afterwards sent to stay with their mothers who live in the most frightful disorder, in a continuous debauch with soldiers, sailors and other blacks and that the price of the best-looking is only two shillings, you can judge that the best intentions of the Company are not carried out and that there is no desire to instruct the children of the blacks better then those of the burgers, and that their only inspiration is fear of the whip.

The Cape today has a substantial minority of Muslims among the descendants of the slaves and political exiles from the Dutch East Indies.

Remarks on Kolbe

Long before La Caille arrived at the Cape, Peter Kolbe (1719) had written a book called *Caput Bonae Spei Hodiernum* or *Cape of Good Hope Today* in German, in spite of its Latin title. Kolbe, a German, was an astronomer of sorts, having been sent to the Cape in 1705 by a Prussian Privy Councillor, Baron von Krosigk, to make astronomical observations on his behalf. He did almost nothing in this line but, according to information collected by La Caille, spent his time drinking and smoking. After some time he became involved in politics and worked towards the recall of the corrupt Governor, Willem Adriaan van der Stel, at least according to Carlier (La Caille 1776, pp. 317–8). Although he later became a Company servant, namely Secretary to the Landrost of Stellenbosch, he was dismissed and sent to Holland in 1713. His book about the Cape was published in 1719 in Nuremberg and relied almost completely on second-hand information that he never examined critically.

Kolbe's original German work was a runaway success as a travel book, and was translated into Dutch and re-published in 1727 in Amsterdam. An English edition appeared in 1731. A French translation of the Dutch version by a publisher named Catuffe went into two editions, dated 1741 and 1742.

Before departing for the Cape the Abbé, La Caille, had bought the 1742 French edition of Kolbe in the hope of using it as a guide book, but on arrival he found it to be nothing but a 'Roman tissue of fables' as the editor of his *Journal Historique* put it. As 'a lover of truth', he felt that something had to be done about it.

La Caille's severe 'frankness' led him to try to find out more about what kind of person Kolbe was and why he made so many errors.

In his *Journal Historique* for 20 November 1751 he mentions:

> Mr Grevenbrock[21], Secretary of the Council of Justice at the Cape at the beginning of this century,[22] a farouche and extraordinary man, had done some research on the habits and customs of the Hottentots: after his death his papers were sent to Kolbe, who plagiarised them without discernment and judgement, according to what is said unanimously by the most judicious people here, namely the Governor, Mr Grand-Pré and Mr Dessin.[23]

Joachim Nikolaus von Dessin was a native of Rostock who arrived at the Cape in the service of the VOC in 1727 and three years later married well. He knew several languages and accumulated a collection of nearly 4000 books and manuscripts, besides mathematical instruments and other items, which he left to the Church to found a public library. This later became part of the National Library of South Africa.

Josephus de Grand-Preez arrived at the Cape in 1722. He achieved the VOC rank of 'Merchant' and was Secretary to the highest body of government, the Council of Policy. He died in 1761. It can be assumed that both he and von Dessin were reasonably well educated before leaving Europe.

Some parts of La Caille's remarks and criticisms of Kolbe are given in the following sections. In general, only those that contain some original observation by La Caille are included here. Sometimes he corrected errors that Kolbe never made but that had been introduced by his translators. Only in the course of his anti-Kolbe remarks did La Caille say much about Khoina.

On the Khoina

> Kolbe never learned the hottentot tongue; he admits it himself; nor did he make any trip among the Hottentots outside the Colony. He had not

[21] Johannes Gulielmus Grevenbroek was born in the Netherlands about 1644 and served as Secretary of the Council of Policy at the Cape from 1684 to 1694. He died about 1726. There is in existence a manuscript concerning the Khoina dated 1695 but never published. See Dapper, ten Rhyne and de Grevenbroek (1933).

[22] Actually, the end of the previous century.

[23] The alleged plagiarism by Kolbe was disputed in Dapper, ten Rhyne and de Grevenbroek (1933). Among other things, it was pointed out that Grevenbroeck died in the same year as Kolbe.

even travelled the whole extent of the Colony; all his trips were limited to Cape Town, to the parishes of Stellenbosch and Drakenstein, and a trip to the Warm-waters,[24] which are a bit beyond the district called *Hottentots-Holland* (p. 321).

(This was criticised in turn by Raven-Hart (1976) who points out that there were many Khoina kraals inside the colony before the small-pox epidemic of 1713 wiped them out. Kolbe was at the Cape before that time.)

Everything that Kolbe said ... is taken from the notes of a certain Greven-broek, Secretary of the Council [of Policy] of the Cape, who wrote down what those Hottentots he had seen replied to his questions. One can easily believe that knowledge got in this way of the manners and customs of these peoples must be very equivocal. These Hottentots have learned to their cost not to trust newcomers; their responses can hardly have been sincere. Kolbe, who never got to know these people, was even less competent than Grevenbroek to verify their responses (pp. 322–324).

The language of the Hottentots is not a kind of monster amongst tongues: it seemed to me to have only two vowels more than those of Europe: these two vowels are expressed by a clicking of the tongue and by a friction of the air between the tongue and the palate; that is all I was able to extract from a hottentot who I interrogated and got to speak to a few times (p. 324).

The Hottentots scattered through the colony are not better than the negro slaves: the Hottentot girls often escape from their parents' homes to work as servants in European houses: they help with cooking and serve to amuse the blacks; these girls are not natural thieves; however it is necessary to lock up the wine and brandy, of which they are extremely fond (pp. 324–325).

It is certain that to the east-north-east of the Cape at about 150 leagues (667 km) there exists a nation that can be called white in compar-ison to the neighbouring peoples; they have long hair and are not more tanned than the Chinese exiles from Batavia that one sees at the Cape; it is this that caused the Europeans at the Cape to call them little Chinese (pp. 324–325).

According to Mentzel (3, p. 95) these people were a little lighter and yellower than other Hottentots. They lived originally in the Camdeboo region of the Klein Karoo but later moved to an area between the Great and Little Fish rivers.

The Hottentots who are in the service of Europeans only keep the clothes of their own country until they are given others. They like to be covered with rags of blue colours in addition to their sheepskins: those women

---

[24] At the present-day town of Caledon.

who can have a scarf to cover their heads as the slaves do are very happy (p. 326).

The most beautiful fringes [?] are glass beads on a string attached at one end; it is not so long since we adopted this hottentot fashion, and in this way we share the taste of the Hottentots. The ornaments of the Hottentots, for example their bracelets and collars and the thongs on women's legs, are crudely made and fitted. One has to avoid hyperboles in this matter [?trans] (p. 327).

The Hottentot nations that were named [by Kolbe] could have existed in Grevenbroeck's time: the multiplication of the European colonists has driven away a large number: a furious epidemic wiped out almost all the Hottentots near Cape Town in 1713, as well as a great number of negro slaves and even many whites. Since this time no Hottentot nation has made a corps or had a regular government in the whole of the colony; those one finds are in the service of Europeans or are of a few families that the Europeans allow to stay on their land. So the names [of the tribes] are almost unknown at present in Cape Town, with a few exceptions ... All the country to the north of Cape Town, as far as St Helena Bay, is dry, sandy and almost uninhabitable, except for a very small area called in Dutch Groene Kloof [present-day Mamre]. How therefore could nine or ten hottentot nations live and subsist there? In view of the knowledge that I have of these places it seems to me to be impossible unless each of these nations is reduced to a simple kraal or village (pp. 327–329).

The bushmen are mostly those Hottentots whose beasts have been removed by the Europeans. The Hottentots that work for the Europeans sometimes conspire with them to help them steal from the whites (p. 329).

The ordinary causes of wars are to get hold of better land or to pursue a murderer and pillage his flocks. Their wars are nothing more than raids (p. 329).

It appears to be the case, according to the unanimous report of those who know the Hottentots well, that they do not recognise any god who they must worship. They have no idea of prayers, they only fear certain evil powers to whom they attribute all the misfortunes that happen to them and who they believe to be in communication with sorcerers. It appears strongly that their extreme indolence has caused them to forget their ancestral tradition in this matter. Because for a Hottentot the sovereign good is to do nothing, even to think of nothing (p. 330).

What Kolbe says about the insect called the Hottentot God [preying mantis] is not founded on any truth. It is only known that this insect is regarded by the Hottentots as a bad omen: it is quite rare in the countryside but is found in the gardens of the Europeans ... (p. 331).

The Hottentots make an infusion in water of a root that they gather in the months of November and December. They put in it honey which they collect in the rocks during these months. They become drunk on this liquor and, while it lasts, they are absolutely incapable of any action whatever. No sooner do they return from the stupefaction that this drink has caused than they drink it again. When the supply is exhausted they stay sick for a long time. Their forced abstinence cures them (p. 333).

Roofing

The houses of the Cape are covered with strong thick reeds, something like those that grow in our swamps or are [?] made of two layers of brick and lime (p. 336).

Topography

I have found 3353 Rhineland feet for the height of Table Mountain at the western end, which is not as high as the middle. In the cleft of the mountain [Platteklip Gorge] one finds only a few stunted trees. This cleft is not formed by running water, because the mountain slopes towards the south and because this cleft is covered by bushes; there is only a stream running down it. What are called Paradise [near Newlands] and Hell [in Constantia] are not two caves [as claimed in the French edition of Kolbe] but are two rather deep valleys towards the south of the mountain and covered in forests that are reserved for Company use. The difficulty of looking for wood in one of these is why it is called the Hell[25] and the ease of getting it in the other is why it is called Paradise. At the entrance to the latter, the Company has a garden and a house (pp. 337–338).

The two adventures of [Kolbe, on his way to Caledon] I am very suspicious of, especially that about meeting eleven lions. It would not take any more numerous a troop to cause the whole region to be deserted. The rumour of a lion in the neighbourhood puts everybody on alert (pp. 342–343).

Farming

What [Kolbe] says about the tails of the sheep is exaggerated. They are normally triangular and flat, the fat extending to the right and left along the vertebrae of the tail. Their ordinary weight is three to four pounds, at the most five or six...(p. 343).

That seeds from Europe degenerate is not true in most cases. On the contrary, the seeds that are brought from the Cape to our islands [i.e. Mauritius and Réunion] are more highly regarded than those from Europe (pp. 343–344).

---

[25] The name 'Hell' probably comes in fact from the Dutch word 'helling', meaning a slope.

At the Cape there are very few of the fruits of the Indies. The most common is the guava. The bananas are worthless, as are the pineapples. Of European fruits there are only the peach, the apricot, the fig, the quince and the grape which are excellent; the others such as apples, pears, plums, nuts and oranges are not worth much (p. 344).

[About the Company Garden] what one can say in general is that it is a fine enough vegetable garden, about a thousand paces long and 260 wide, divided into 44 squares surrounded by a high hedge of oak or laurel. Of these squares, two are kept as flower beds for the governor's residence and another is filled with three covered walks of chestnut trees. The remainder contain vegetables and a few fruit trees. This garden is only watered by a few ditches of running water and one or two furrows within it (pp. 344–345).

The locals

What [Kolbe] says about eye disease being common at the Cape is no longer true, if it ever was. It is true that he suffered a lot from it, supposedly because he drank too much [!] (pp. 345–346).

Gout is very common at the Cape, as are the stone and gravel [kidney diseases].

The inhabitants of Cape Town eat out with each other very rarely or not at all. Their custom is to gather every evening between five and nine o'clock to smoke, gamble and drink without eating (p. 346).

Mining

So far no rich mines have been found at the Cape. A lot was expended on what was hoped to be gold on the mountain called Simonsberg, which separates Stellenbosch from Drakenstein, but this went up in smoke (pp. 346–347).

Animals

Horses brought up for riding are very expensive, for example 400 to 600 pounds (livres), in proportion to their strength and height. Only those used for threshing grain are sold cheaply (p. 348).

The tooth of the largest hippopotamus hardly weighs three pounds (p. 349).

The stink badger is more like a dog than a ferret. It does not stink when it is dead, at least if it is not decomposing (p. 350, see also Extracts from La Caille's *Journal Historique*, earlier in this chapter).

Land tortoises are not eaten at the Cape except in the case of desperate need. They rarely weigh more than three pounds—in comparison with those of the island of Rodrigues which are excellent and weigh 30 to 40 pounds or even 50. I have seen one that weighed more than 100 pounds (pp. 350–351).[26]

I never saw any herrings at the Cape except those dried ones imported from Europe which are greatly appreciated (p. 351).

Poultry is not cheap in comparison to butcher's meat. One gets four hens or chickens for 102 sols and for the same sum one has 17 pounds of meat at the butcher's, sometimes even 36 pounds (p. 352).

The Knorhaan is a sort of grouse which usually sings during its heavy flight. Its cry does not cause other birds to flee. Its meat is good enough for soup (p. 353).

The Cape larks are of a species that differs from ours. They rise perpendicularly to ten or twelve feet, making a lot of noise with their wings, then they fall suddenly making a little cry. They never stay in the air. (pp. 352–353).

Remarks of Mentzel about La Caille

A third traveller to the Cape, who had been present for seven and a half years between Kolbe's visit and La Caille's, was Otto Friedrich Mentzel. This young Prussian spent from 5 July 1733 to 3 January 1741 at the Cape, that is, he arrived 18 years before La Caille's arrival and departed eight years after that. He was born in Berlin (Prussia) in 1709 to a father who was a Hofrat (court councillor; a kind of honorific status for civil servants) and court physician and had attended a Gymnasium or academic high school there. The circumstances of his coming to the Cape are unknown but he served first as a soldier and later was at various times a tutor and a clerk with the VOC. He left the Cape by accident when visiting a ship that was ready to sail. Eventually he returned to Prussia where he became a civil servant and wound up in Silesia, then part of Prussia, as a police chief. Many years later, in old age, he published *Beschreibung des Vorgebirges der Guten Hoffnung* (1785–1787) or *Description of the Cape of Good Hope*, in the town of Glogau, where he was then living. This may have been inspired by seeing La Caille's book.

He agreed with many of his strictures about the writings of Peter Kolbe but felt he had sometimes been too harsh. In fact, he pointed out that La Caille' himself had perpetrated further inaccuracies. He was sure that the Abbé had been led astray by believing too many of the tall stories that he had been told by local people. It should be remembered, however, that the edition of Kolbe that La Caille was criticising was a French translation of a Dutch translation of the original German, and that it had undergone considerable distortion in the process.

---

[26] The Rodrigues giant tortoises became extinct around 1800.

Mentzel was a person of a happy and unambitious temperament and curious about everything that came his way. His book is by far the best and most detailed account of government, finance, nature and people at the Cape in the eighteenth century. Because it was published in an obscure part of Prussia it did not become well known until it was translated in the twentieth century and re-published by the van Riebeek Society.

In his work, Mentzel refers quite frequently to La Caille's *Journal Historique* and, though he has a high regard for the Abbé, he does not hesitate to point out mistakes and errors in his comments regarding Kolbe. Nevertheless, he does not spare the latter.

> He [La Caille] had intended to give a topographical description of the Cape according to the three kingdoms of Nature. As soon as he found an opportunity to undertake this work along with his astronomical observations he was dumbfounded by Kolbe's blunders, and, as he discovered more and more of them, his annoyance became so vehement that in the description of his voyage that he issued in France he pictures Kolbe as a drunkard, constantly smoking tobacco and swilling wine. It is quite true that, even in my day, Kolbe had left no good name behind him at the Cape. Yet I do not know who is the more contemptible, the accused who cannot defend himself after his death and refute the accusation, or the accuser, who divulges an odious vice of a long-deceased person, and which he is in no position to prove or authenticate. If all who smoked tobacco and drank wine were to be called drunkards few sober people would be found at the Cape.
>
> Be that as it may, the Abbé really discovered gross blunders in Kolbe's description. He made a list of these and yet missed several. At the same time he imputed a number of which Kolbe was not guilty and which probably crept into the French translation through misunderstanding of the text of the German original. Kolbe was quite liable to err; he was eager to write much, in fact he is too verbose, and he trusted implicitly the stories of his friends and acquaintances. M. de La Caille fell into the same error. Without wishing to find fault with or criticise so eminent an academician, I must inform the public, as a tribute to truth, that great and learned men are also liable to err when they travel through a foreign country and write a description thereof. In proof of this I will mention a few errors made by the Abbé when he showed too much credulity and confided too implicitly in the stories of his friends, who were really rallying him (Mentzel **1**, pp. 21–22).

He then goes on to ridicule at length an absurd story about elephant hunting that La Caille's editor, not La Caille himself, had inserted in the printed *Journal Historique* for 6 December 1751.

He also criticises a description that La Caille gave of a rhinoceros horn that he had seen at Mr Dessin's house. Though this horn was an exceptionally large one, it does not seem to have been particularly strange. He goes on to explain that Dessin had been at school with him in 1720, at the Joachim Gymnasium in Berlin. 'I will be more explicit and state that the latter was quite capable and even inclined to impose upon a French visitor.'

Mentzel mentions with incredulity La Caille's having said that he had ascended Table Mountain in under three hours. It had taken him and his friends three and three quarter hours to do the same, starting from some way up. He fails to allow for the fact that La Caille was an energetic man who was quite accustomed to climbing mountains. His time to ascend Table Mountain, even starting from where he lived on Strand Street, does not seem extraordinary for such a person.

La Caille's complaints about the food he regards as exaggerated:

> It is not surprising therefore that the Cape inhabitant eagerly welcomes the salted or smoked product of Holland in preference to the fresh mutton of everyday life. The Abbé de la Caille is not of the same opinion. He complains that at various parties which he attended the principal dishes consisted of dry dirty-looking stockfish, and yellow evil-smelling cured pork. This statement . . . is a gross exaggeration. It cannot possibly apply to the hams and pork that the Company supplies, and which form a staple item of diet aboard ship . . . (Mentzel **3**, p. 102).
>
> . . . I think I can explain the Abbé's point of view. We must remember that Monsieur is a Frenchman whose palate has been tickled with fricassées, ragoûts and roasts. How could he be expected to enjoy such barbarous courses as salted, smoked or pickled meats? M. de la Caille continues: 'the Cape inhabitants value no gift more more highly than a piece of meat that has been salted in Europe to feed the crews; the darker the meat has been smoked, the more do they enjoy it.' We can read between the lines the Frenchman's disgust for such low tastes. He does not take the trouble to understand quite what he is talking about. He confuses corned beef with smoked ham . . . (Mentzel **3**, p. 103).
>
> The learned Abbé writes 'Most of the farmers of the interior bake a very inferior bread from the best corn in the world.' . . . But what are the facts? I maintain that boer bread is tastier and more nourishing than the rye-bread of Amsterdam. No doubt a Frenchman who was used to the superfine and delicately flavoured Parisian rolls found some of the bread baked by the farmers unpalatable. M. de la Caille was in no position to judge Cape bread on its merits . . . The Abbé was not competent to write of 'most farmers,' as he had not seen 1/50 part of the country. Criticism should be well balanced . . . ' (Mentzel **2**, p. 143)

Unfortunately, in spite of its excellence, Mentzel's work did not circulate widely, probably because it was published in such an obscure place. He died in 1801.

5
Later years

Journey to Mauritius and Réunion

On 23 October 1752, not long before the time when he had expected to leave the Cape for his return to France, La Caille unexpectedly received royal orders to go to the Isles of France (Mauritius) and Bourbon (Réunion) to find their precise latitudes and longitudes. This was at the request of the French Indies Company, for which Mauritius was an important stopping point on the way to the East. Mauritius was then a comparatively recent French possession, having been abandoned by its previous owners, the Dutch, in 1710. It was taken over by France in 1715 and after 1721 was under the control of the Compagnie des Indes.

La Caille could not help being dismayed at this development: it appeared as though the extra trip would be a waste of his time and effort because he knew that D'Après de Mannevillette had already made the necessary observations, though this information had not yet reached Paris. With only a few months left before he had to leave, communications were too slow to have the order revoked. He felt he had no option but to comply.

The day of his departure from the Cape was a festive one:

[8 March 1753] 'At six in the morning I left the Cape on Mr de Ruyter's boat to embark on the Puisieulx [400 tons, 26 cannons] to go to the Isles of France and Bourbon [Mauritius and Réunion], not having had a countermanding order since the letters I received on 23rd October; none of my friends, or of those who wrote to me from France, seemed to know about the orders that I had received.

At midday the guns of the Castle, the batteries [small forts along the beach] and all the vessels that were in the roads fired a salvo of cannon in honour of the birthday of the young Prince Stadtholder.[1] At half past twelve we got under way and fired seven cannon shots, which were replied to with only three. I became seasick at 3pm.

[1] William V of Orange, born in 1748, was the last Stadtholder of the United Provinces. William IV, his father, had died in 1751.

Once again he spent his time at sea in investigating the best method for finding positions. It was clear that the sophisticated methods used by astronomers would be too complicated for ordinary sailors to use. He researched different schemes that would allow them to avoid the major part of the calculations and decided that the best approach would be to prepare tables in advance for getting time and longitude using the distances of certain stars from the Moon (see also Later studies, this chapter). Though this idea had been discussed in the past, predictions of the Moon's position were not accurate enough for it to be useful. As they went along, he taught the ship's officers how to make the necessary observations and computations. They had aimed to arrive at the latitude of Rodrigues, an island 560 km east of Mauritius, and then to sail west until they got to their destination. The lunar observations, such as they were, showed that they were much farther off than planned, in fact a whole 180 leagues [1000 km] to the east, which they duly found out to be the case (Anon, 1751).

He arrived in Mauritius on 18 April. The climate was much less suitable for astronomy than that at the Cape, though he did manage a number of observations of the tilt of the earth's axis. Mainly, he occupied himself in preparing a detailed map of the island. Although his work on the islands is not particularly relevant to this book, Carlier (La Caille 1776) relates an adventure from this time that throws an interesting light on La Caille's character, not to mention his own. As mentioned, the Island had been abandoned by its previous holders, the VOC, in 1710 and its only inhabitants in the intervening years had been abandoned slaves. After the French took occupation, these people had taken refuge in the inland forests, supporting themselves by brigandage of various kinds. However, they were liable to be hunted down by the colonists and shot like wild animals. On coming across a group of these unfortunates, including apparently a woman, La Caille pleaded with his escort not to shoot her. Only after he paid a bribe would they comply with his request. After the event, it turned out that the woman was there against her will, having been kidnapped.

Carlier, when describing this incident, went on sanctimoniously:

> The practice of hunting down negro fugitives and brigands like wild animals should not shock European delicacies. From the moment when men useful to society renounce their position from a spirit of libertinage and cupidity, they degrade themselves to being below the animals and merit the most rigorous treatment (La Caille 1776, p. 225).

Grisgris is said to have got lost in a bay which today bears the unfortunate dog's name.

La Caille himself suffered from a violent bout of dysentery that started on 23 September 1753 but it did not stop him from working. He was cured by neither eating nor drinking for 50 hours.

In a letter he wrote to La Condamine soon after his return to Paris the Abbé expressed his frustration at this unnecessary visit:

> From the Cape I went to the Isles of France and Bourbon where I was extraordinarily bored. After having observed some satellites there I returned here by the first vessels. It seems that people are happy with my work, which will be my only reward, but I don't ask for any other.[2]

Altogether, he stayed on Mauritius for nine months, leaving on 16 January 1754 for Réunion. On 27 February he departed in turn from that island for France on the vessel L'Achille (1200 tons, 24 cannons, Captain Antoine-Levesque de Beaubriand), doubling the Cape of Good Hope on 25 March. His only stop was five days spent on the island of Ascension. Here the crew gathered tortoises to eat—'an excellent remedy against scorbutic illnesses [scurvy] and good nourishment for several weeks'.[3] The Abbé determined its latitude and longitude, helped by an accurate time he got from an emergence of Jupiter's satellite Io from behind the planet, observed simultaneously by colleagues in Paris.

Return to Paris and the Academy

At two-thirty pm on 4 June 1754 the Abbé finally set foot again in Lorient, the port from which he had departed, 'after having made one of the shortest and happiest crossings that one could hope for'. He left there on the 14th and got back home to Paris on the 28th. He had been absent for 44 months, of which no fewer than eight had been spent at sea.

On his return, he found that he had become a celebrity. He was given a hero's welcome when he re-appeared at the Royal Academy of Sciences on 3rd July. He had brought with him 'not the spoils of the orient but...those of the southern sky' and was compared to a star that had returned from below the horizon. It was declared that his discoveries had extended the sphere of human knowledge, and so on. 'But Mr de La Caille ignored these plaudits, which would have violated his modesty if he had listened to them'. He was completely embarrassed, which made the people who came to stare at him all the more curious. He kept a low profile, 'hiding himself in the bosom of his friends' and showed himself in public only occasionally at first, to avoid the praise that was heaped upon him.

Some of the Abbé's results, sent from the Cape, had already been presented to the Academy during his absence by Maraldi and Cassini

[2] La Caille to La Condamine, dated Paris, 20 August 1754., National Library of South Africa, Cape Town, ms 13297.1 (4).
[3] Manuscript version of his speech to the Academy of 5 November 1754; in the ms book of his *Journal Historique*.

II. However, his main paper on the results of his voyage, *Various astronomical and physical observations made at the Cape of Good Hope . . .* (La Caille 1751, pp. 398–456) was read in several parts from 10 July to 3 August 1754.[4] It contains *inter alia* the details of his geodetic survey, the description of his observatory, his magnetic and his meteorological work.

In his letter to La Condamine of 20 August 1754 (see previous page), he mentioned that he was at that date working on the construction of his planisphere of the southern sky.

On Wednesday 13 November 1754, after the feast of St. Martin when the Academy gathered after its annual break, he gave a public lecture about his voyage, presided over by the botanist Bernard de Jussieu. It was published as *An Abridged Relation of the Voyage Made by Order of the King to the Cape of Good Hope* (La Caille 1751, p. 519). At that time, the Academy's publications were running four years late but it was decided that his speech was sufficiently important to be published immediately, in the 1751 volume (pp. 519–536, published in 1755) instead of waiting for the usual four years (as was the paper *Various astronomical and physical observations . . .* already mentioned). A different version of this paper, probably a draft, can be found in the manuscript notebook that contains his *Journal Historique*; the changes are insubstantial.

La Caille's map of the Cape

With La Caille's paper presented to the Academy was a map of the Cape (see Fig. 5.1) which was to be the basis for many others of the same region published over the following decades (Stewart, 2009). As in the case of La Caille's planisphere, it was engraved by John Ingram. Another version of this map, with an out-dated and primitive inset view of Cape Town and Table Mountain, was incorporated into the *Journal Historique* (La Caille 1763). The same basic map was used by Everest (1821) nearly seventy years later in his discussion of La Caille's results. In comparison with a modern map (Fig. 3.1), it will be seen that a great many of the features are little more than guesswork. Of course, the positions of his geodetic stations are shown accurately.

The coastal details shown on the map may have been based on a detailed chart by d'Après de Mannevillette dated 1752,[5] except for the part north of Saldanha Bay. La Caille does not mention any travels which would have given him the opportunity to map the coastline himself. However, in the *Journal Historique* he mentions that the ship on which d'Après returned to France, 'Les Treize Cantons', spent from

---

[4] See also Procès-Verbaux de l'Académie Royale des Sciences, Tome 73, 1754.
[5] See, for example, Bibliothèque National de France, Département Cartes et Plans, ark:/12148/btv1b77595845.

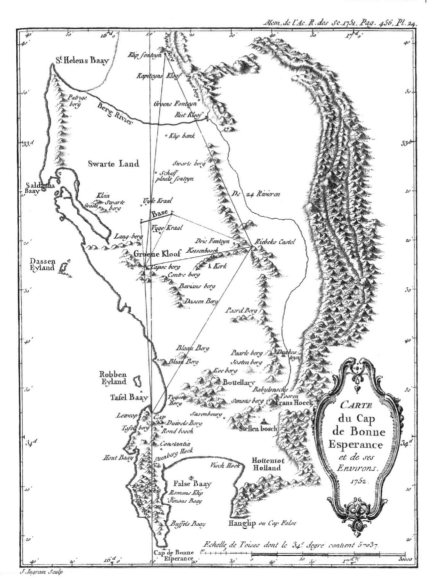

Mem. de l'Ac. R. des Sc. 1751. Pag. 456. Pl. 24.

Fig. 5.1 La Caille's map of the Cape, showing his survey triangles in the Swartland. Many of the farms he visited are marked. The site of the Zwartelandkerk (present-day Malmesbury) is given as 'kerk'. His longitudes are based on the Paris meridian (La Caille 1751, Plate 24).

3 March to 17 April 1752 at the Cape. This may have been when the coastal survey was carried out.[6]

The map of Hout Bay that La Caille mentions having prepared for the Governor (see Chapter 4, Extracts from La Caille's *Journal Historique*) has not been found.

An established scientist

In his last eight years La Caille remained a professor at the Collège Mazarin, where he had his own apartment. His salary was small but later he was granted a further 500 French pounds per annum by the Academy. As a deacon, he could have obtained a benefice (a church appointment which may or may not have involved some duties), but this was of no interest to him. In fact, he even resigned one that he had (Carlier, in La Caille 1776, p. 89). He was however offered 'an advantageous proposition' by a cardinal, which he accepted in spite of himself, but the prelate concerned died before it was put into effect. He was an official of the Collège Mazarin chapel and 'if this little appointment did not help him much at least it did not take up much of his time' (Delambre, 1827, p. 542). In fact, La Caille rarely mentions religious matters in his diary except for occasional attendance at Mass when French vessels were in Table Bay.

During his later years he was as busy as ever. He gave some thought to moving to Provence, in the south of France, to take advantage of the better weather there and for peace and quiet. His friends however persuaded him that he would be more useful to society if he remained in Paris.

His daily routine, according to Carlier (see La Caille 1776), was as follows:

He would rise at five in the morning, work until midday without stopping, read while dining, go out for an hour, continue working until eight in the evening, sup while reading his letters and then go up to his observatory, where he passed part of the night. He called *peaceful days* those which he spent in this way, as opposed to those which he spent in active or passive visits, even for private business.

He sustained this way of living by a sobriety that has no equal. He ate his meals out of habit and good sense, never because of need. However, he never regretted the time he spent at table with his friends in honest enjoyment.

[6] According to Briot, 'At the Cape of Good Hope, at the end of his mission, he found La Caille again. The sailor and the astronomer exchanged observations and before his departure they promised to write'. See Briot, Claude, 1990. *D'Après de Mannevillette Réhabilité*, Lecture presented to Congrès des Sociétés Historiques de Normandie. www.premiumorange.com/de-verrazano-au-france/d'Apres_de_Mannevillette.htm

Once absorbed in calculating, he was more difficult to see than Mercury or Venus when these planets meet on the solar disc [sic]. Devoted to his aim, he looked with an evil eye on those who distracted him. Three things put him in a bad mood; flattery, useless ideas and the presence of people he suspected lacked probity and a sense of honour. Apart from these encounters one found in him all the qualities of an amiable and amusing man in society (pp. 86–7).

Learned in just about every field, excellent in some, unique in his own, he hid the extent of his knowledge. Erudition flowed from his mouth unconsciously . . . To get out of him what you wanted, you had to avoid tackling him head-on; then you got nothing. Taking him on the flank you caused an inexhaustible flood of science to issue from his mouth (p. 93).

There are several stories concerning his utter disdain for financial matters. When returning to France he was offered a large sum of money to smuggle in some goods, by hiding them with his equipment, for which he had been granted customs immunity. He refused indignantly both 'as an ecclesiastic and an honest man' (although presumably either one of these should have been sufficient!).

It is also said that on being told he would have an income of 20,000 French pounds when he died he replied 'Good for death, because alive I would have been most embarrassed'. It is not clear where such an amount of money would have come from; possibly some of it arose from his very successful textbooks.

In the report on his expedition to the Royal Treasury it was revealed that of the grant of 10,000 French pounds he had received he had only spent 9144 and 5 sous. The officials did not want to accept the balance—'you must keep it', they said!—and this was in spite of the extra work on the mapping of Réunion and Mauritius for which most others would have asked for an extra grant (Delambre 1827).

His accuracy questioned

The Abbe's life of scholarly calm was soon disturbed by an accusation of error on his part in a Memoir on the shape of the earth written by the Swiss mathematician Leonhard Euler. In order to fit his theory, Euler claimed that Cassini de Thury and La Caille (see Chapter 1, survey of the Paris Meridian) must have made a mistake of 125 toises (246 m) in their measurement of the distance between Paris and Amiens. This assertion by one of the most famous scientists in existence touched him to the quick:

I cannot accuse Mr Euler of aiming to vex us. He is not the only person, nor the first one, who has written that our measure is inaccurate. He believed he could trust the judgement of certain Parisian academicians and, no doubt, without having read the history of our operations or those of Messrs Bouguer and La Condamine, has conjectured that it was an acknowledged thing and one recognised by the Academy of Sciences in Paris that the size of a degree in France was not determined with the requisite precision.

I would have hoped that [such people] made little impression just as had happened with other opinions propagated in their books. Besides, these people have only spoken in general, they have not deigned to indicate in what way our measures are defective; I know only too well what has brought them to express themselves in this way. I had therefore decided to say nothing, content to rely on those who have taken the trouble to examine our operations. But because I have been deceived in my hope that these judgements would only do harm to those who expressed them; and because I see they have imposed on a scientist of the first order, whose talents and writings are admired by all the mathematicians of Europe; and because our work could wither away because of what has been said in a book that will be consulted forever, I feel obliged to appeal to those who do not take sides until after a mature and unprejudiced examination, without any interest other than the truth. I am going to give some clarifications which will show the origin of these claims that Mr Euler has found in several writings (not endorsed by the Royal Academy of Sciences).

He then went on to list in detail all the checks and balances that had gone into the measurement of the baselines and to demolish all the arguments, such as they were, one by one.

Without denigrating other measures, I am convinced, and by the experience that I have acquired in this sort of work, and by the pains I have taken and the precautions we have taken at the time, that there is no terrestrial distance more accurately determined than the one from Paris to Amiens; that there could not be 10 toises (19.5 m) of error. I feel myself quite justified in saying that those who have written in such a vague manner that the length of the degree measured in France is uncertain, have done so without examination and without sense and by consequence have gone against all the rules of method and justice (La Caille 1755, pp. 53–59).

In the 'Remarks' that follow the biography of La Caille by Carlier (La Caille 1776, p. 102), an unnamed former colleague says that 'he demonstrated there that he would have to have been stupid or ignorant, mal-adroit or imbecillic to have committed in this measurement of the Paris degree the error that somebody had dared to suspect, and certainly nobody has doubted since this document [appeared] the exactitude of this operation . . .'

On 16 June 1756 Le Monnier presented a memoir to the Academy of sciences which resulted on the 19th June in the appointment of two commissions to re-check the distance from Paris to Amiens. The first commission consisted of Godin, Clairaut, Le Monnier and La Caille and the second of Bouguer, Camus, Cassini de Thury and Pingré. The results were favourable to La Caille (Maheu, 1966).

La Caille's circle: some pupils and friends

If his surviving correspondence is anything to go by, the Abbé seems to have drawn his friends mainly from among the members of the Royal Academy of Sciences. Perhaps his lengthy working hours did not allow him much time for socialising. Jean-Dominique Maraldi and Alexis-Claude Clairaut seem to have been those closest to him.

Antoine Laurent Lavoisier

La Caille's most distinguished student, the chemist Antoine Laurent Lavoisier, entered the Collège Mazarin in 1754 at the age of 11. He was very much impressed with the methods and teaching of La Caille, whose mathematical lectures he attended when aged 17, in 1760. In recollecting La Caille he wrote: 'I was accustomed to the rigorous reasoning of mathematicians. They never take up a proposition until the one preceding it has been determined. Everything is connected, everything is linked, from the definition of the point and the line up to the most sublime truths of transcendent geometry' (quoted by Bell 2005).

Later on, Lavoisier applied such precise and quantitative techniques to the study of chemistry and became famous for his discovery of new principles such as the conservation of mass in reactions. He helped to destroy the old phlogiston chemical theory of combustion and was one of those who discovered the nature of oxygen, as well as giving it its name. At the same time as he worked on his chemistry, he used some of his considerable private wealth to buy a partnership in the *Ferme Génerale* or General Farm, the hated private agency which collected taxes. He became very wealthy from this investment but, like other Fermiers Géneraux, he incurred the wrath of the more extreme elements in the French Revolution and was executed in May 1794.

Jean-Sylvain Bailly

Bailly, who was a pupil and friend of La Caille towards the end of the latter's life, was one of only two people to have been a member of all three French Academies—Sciences (1763), Française (1784) and Inscriptions (1785). Originally inclined towards painting and literature, he met La Caille at the salon of Anne-Louise Le Jeuneux (see section

Anne-Louise le Jeuneux, further on). He was attracted into learning astronomy and worked at several projects including the editing of a catalogue of stars by La Caille. He did original astronomical research for about a decade; for example, on the satellites of Jupiter. Besides this, he wrote extensively on the history of science and on the lives of famous people.

Later in life he was appointed to various commissions that brought him into politics, in which rôle he became a leader among the more moderate revolutionaries, i.e. the middle-class constitutionalists who hoped that the abuses of the old regime could be ameliorated by means of non-violent reforms. He was made a deputy from Paris to the States-General. During his brief political career he became president of the Third Estate and presided over the proceedings in the 'Tennis Court' which led to the formation of the National Assembly. After the fall of the Bastille he became the first mayor of Paris (1789–91), under the Commune. He was in favour of a settlement with the monarchy and tried to slow the Revolution. Unfortunately for him, during an attempt to keep the peace as mayor, he ordered a popular demonstration to be fired upon and this caused him to be hated by the radical elements. Although he saw the writing on the wall and fled the capital, he was caught and ended up being executed in November 1793, during the Jacobin Terror.

Père Michel Benoît

According to Carlier (see La Caille 1776, p. 104), this Jesuit father (also called Benoist), who had taken six months of practical instruction from La Caille, went to Beijing in 1745 as an astronomer but made the mistake of presenting the Emperor Ch'ien Lung of the Qing dynasty with a print showing fountains in a garden. The emperor was very fascinated by these and, having heard that the father had the knowledge and skill required to make them, he made a prisoner of him to force him to construct fountains and cascades in the gardens of the western-style summer palaces at Yuan Ming Yuan outside Beijing. That was the end of astronomy for him!

Carlier's story of Benoît does not appear to have been exaggerated. He, like several other Jesuit missionaries to China, was forced to spend a large part of his life in the emperor's service. Besides waterworks, he was made to construct and maintain European-style clocks.

He persuaded another Jesuit astronomer, Antoine Gaubil, to send data in his place to La Caille.

Sad to say, the Yuan Ming Yuan complex was destroyed in an act of revenge by French and British forces during the second 'Opium War' in 1860. Only some of the water features remain today.

Anne-Louise le Jeuneux

Anne-Louise Le Jeuneux (?–1794) was a young artist (Jeffares, 2006) who La Caille seems to have had a soft spot for. They must have met before his trip to the Cape in 1751, since he repeatedly asked after her in his letters to Maraldi. After his return to Paris, she painted his southern sky map (see Chapter 2) and later, in 1762, his portrait (frontispiece). Her father, who was an amateur scientist, had a 'Cabinet of Curiosities' or private museum around 1786 in the Hôtel de Chavigny, mentioned in a guide book to Paris (Thiéry 1786–7). The Cabinet contained a disparate collection of odds and ends, including instruments of physics and mechanics, an electric machine, dried fish, a 'double child', and many other oddments.

As mentioned, Jean-Sylvain Bailly first met La Caille at her salon. Such salons were social gatherings of an intellectual nature, usually held at regular intervals by a 'literary hostess'. They were important forums for the propagation of new ideas.

Anne-Louise married André Baudin de la Chesnaye (1732–92), Commander of the Legion of the Paris Horse Guards, in 1790. He was involved in defending the Tuileries palace during the Revolution and was one of many nobles massacred in September 1792 by the Paris mob at La Force prison.

Anne-Louise committed suicide by throwing herself into the Seine on 15 April 1794, when the banishment of nobles was decreed by the Committee of Public Safety (see La Lande 1803, p. 731).

Joseph-Jérôme Lefrançais de Lalande

An early interest in astronomy while he was at school in Lyon caused Joseph-Jérôme Le Français (Fig. 5.2) to think of becoming a Jesuit. His parents were none too pleased at the prospect and sent him to study law in Paris. There he came into contact with Joseph-Nicolas Delisle of the Collège Royal (now Collège de France), who had no other pupil besides him. His lessons proceeded at a fast pace, suited to such a studious and intelligent person. About this time he started to call himself Jérôme le Français de La Lande in order to sound more aristocratic. He attended physico-mathematical lessons from Le Monnier, also at the Collège Royal. The latter recognised what an able student he had on his hands and tried to steal him away from Delisle. His ploy was to take up La Caille's plea to fellow astronomers for simultaneous observations from Europe while he was at the Cape. Le Monnier arranged for Lalande to go to Berlin with his prize quadrant, the best then available in France, by the English instrument maker, Sisson.

He duly made observations simultaneously with those of La Caille in Cape Town to determine the distance of the Moon and planets. In spite of his youth he was accepted into the Prussian Academy. Thus,

Fig. 5.2 Joseph-Jérôme Lefrançais de Lalande in 1807. He is said to have become an atheist to get revenge on God for making him so ugly. Engraving from an old picture by Léopold Massard. Académie des Sciences – Institut de France.

by day he was exposed to the ideas of the mathematicians Euler and Maupertuis.[7] While still in Berlin he also met some of the most enlightened philosophers of the century. On return to Paris, on Le Monnier's recommendation. he was made an adjoint member of the Academy of Sciences at the exceptionally early age of 21 years.

In the course of working up his observations of the Moon, Lalande naturally came into frequent contact with La Caille, who he soon grew to admire. This aroused the jealousy of Le Monnier who, as mentioned, was no friend of the Abbé's, and led to a break between them. As von Zach (1799) put it:

> Le Monnier was naturally of a very irritable temper; as ardently as he loved his friends, as easily could he be offended; and his hatred was then implacable.... But Lalande's gratitude and respect for him always continued undiminished and were on every occasion with unremitting constancy publicly declared: patiently he endured from him undeserved ill-treatment; so much did he love and esteem his instructor and master to the day of his death.

La Lande's successful observations caused his career to blossom and he became Professor of Astronomy at the Collège Royale, where he remained for 46 years.

During the French Revolution he risked his life by hiding the economist Pierre Samuel du Pont de Nemours and some priests for

[7] Then working in Berlin.

Fig. 5.3 Alexis-Claude Clairaut by Charles-Nicolas Cochin, engraved by Cathelin. By permission, www.clairaut.com©.

some weeks in La Caille's former observatory in the Collège Mazarin. Dupont's son was later the founder of the chemical company E.I. Dupont de Nemours.

After the Revolution, which he survived in part because of his militant atheism, he thought it prudent to sound less aristocratic and merged the 'La' in his name with the 'Lande', becoming Jérôme Lefrançais de Lalande. He wrote a famous general textbook of astronomy that ran into three editions (Lalande, 1792).

Lalande was thus a disciple rather than a direct pupil of La Caille.

Alexis-Claude Clairaut

Clairaut (Fig. 5.3) was an almost exact comtemporary of La Caille, born in the same year (1713) and destined to survive him by only a short time. He came from a mathematical family and was himself a prodigy, being admitted to the Royal Academy of Sciences when only 18.

In the mid 1730s he became interested in astronomical questions, such as the shape of the earth, and was a member of the expedition to Lapland which reported its form to be a flattened ellipsoid.

In 1737 he claimed before a public meeting of the Royal Academy of Sciences that Newton's law of gravitation could not account adequately for the motion of the Moon's orbit. His calculations were in agreement with others by Maupertuis and Euler. However, in the face of widespread scepticism, he re-examined his method and found out that he had made too gross an approximation at a certain point. He gained much credit when he published a retraction of his earlier conclusion and showed that Newton's law in fact held.

It was Clairaut's misfortune that he often worked on the same problems as Maupertuis. Whereas he believed in detailed calculations that could be compared with observations, Maupertuis was more interested in abstract principles.

Although they were probably friendly before that time, in the late 1750s La Caille and he seem to have had a good deal of contact. It was, of course, the Abbé who provided the accurate data against which his numerical predictions of planetary movements could be tested.

A Hungarian visitor, the young mathematician Count Joseph Teleki de Szek, mentions having had dinner at Clairaut's home with La Caille and others present, on two occasions during his visit to Paris in 1760–61 (Teleki 1941).

Clairaut, aided by Lalande, devoted much effort to predicting the date of the return of Halley's comet in 1759. In this he was aided greatly by Madame Nicole-Reine Lepaute, the wife of a clockmaker, who unfortunately aroused the jealousy of his mistress, a *femme fatale* named Marie-Anne Gouilly, and received little credit for her work.[8] The success of the prediction led to widespread public acclaim but aroused in its turn the jealousy of d'Alembert and his ally Le Monnier.

It is clear that Clairaut valued his friendship with the Abbé and missed him after his death. In a letter to Daniel Bernoulli of 28 July 1763 he says 'There is nobody who can be compared to him [La Caille] for his science and his zeal, nor I believe for probity, at least among humans'.

He went on: Le Monnier, 'who is a good observer, knows nothing of theory and is extremely cantankerous. He is liked by nobody in the Academy and seems to make a point of annoying everybody. For myself, I have every reason to complain because he has sought to deprecate everything I have done on the Moon, the comet etc. He has been remarkably passionate about this.'[9]

On another occasion he informed a Jesuit colleague, Roger Joseph Boscovich , 'Our Paris publishers are asking for a second edition of the theory of the Moon ... I believe that if I had had the time to re-do all my calculations I would have arrived at something even more exact, but I would have had to have as good a friend as the Abbé de La Caille to give me new strength in this work'.[10]

---

[8] See Olivier Courcelle, *La mathématicienne la moins connue du monde (II)*, Images des Mathématiques, CNRS, 2011. http://images.math.cnrs.fr/La-mathematicienne-la-moins-connue,979.html.

[9] Clairaut to Daniel Bernoulli, dated Paris 28 July 1763; see Boncompagni 1894.

[10] Clairaut to Boscovich, dated Paris 23 February 1763; see Taton 1996).

Clairaut's *encyclopédist* enemies Diderot and Bossut, in their quite nasty obituaries (see www.clairaut.com) accused him of having been too much of a socialite 'with a lively taste for feminine company', good suppers and staying up too late. These proclivities supposedly shortened his life.

Bouguer and La Condamine

La Caille was friendly with both Charles-Marie de la Condamine and Pierre Bouguer, who had taken part in the geodetic expedition to Peru. La Condamine was an intrepid adventurer, which is why he was appointed leader. Bouguer did not, however, admire his scientific abilities and published an account of the expedition that claimed most of the credit for himself. A serious dispute then broke out between the two. Each published papers critical of the other and the disagreement became a scandal, offensive to the scientific community (Maheu, 1966). When La Caille returned from the Cape he was upset to find that their argument was still in full swing, a decade after the expedition had ended. In his letter to La Condamine of August 1754 already quoted (Journey to Paris and Réunion) he showed his displeasure in his frank and blunt way:

> I have received at different times the three pieces that you sent me. I would have wished that your matter had been put to sleep and I can only say to you that there will be no great glory for the one who wins. However upsetting it is to be attacked, it is certain that one gains a lot by appearing to ignore it because a response hardly ever lacks a reply and, in a case where there is no easy way to judge, the documents can multiply to infinity unless the public finds something else to amuse themselves with at the expense of the parties.

Bouguer was the more serious scientist of the two, though La Condamine was the more flamboyant. Apart from his presence on the Peru trip, Bouguer made several contributions to optics. Particularly, he is noted for early work on photometry (the measurement of brightness) and the absorption of light by the atmosphere of the earth. He also invented a specialised telescope for measuring small angles, called the heliometer. Whe he died in 1758, La Caille undertook to edit and expand his *Treatise on optics and the gradation of light*. According to Delambre (1827), he re-did all the calculations. He also revised Bouguer's *Treatise on navigation*, including new trigonometric tables.

An inopportune visitor?

Count Teleki, the Hungarian traveller, mentioned previously, recounted something unexpected in his Journal about a visit he made to the Abbé on 15 November 1760:

... I went to the Abbé de la Caille's place. I found him at home. Having been told by the porter that he was in, I went up. I knocked on the door, he opened up for me and seeing me in front of him the unfortunate fellow could not avoid letting me into his home, where I surprised a vulgar-looking woman.

Nevertheless I would not have been scandalised if the face of the Abbé had not showed so much confusion.

However, I was more uncomfortable than the Abbé. He called the woman, but she soon disappeared through a small door. Perhaps she was not a bad woman, but the circumstances confirmed my suspicions: above all the Abbé's confusion.

After that he invited me to come to see him when the weather was fine so that we could make observations together, if I would like. I thanked him for his civility and assured him that I would not fail to come to enjoy his teaching (Teleki, 1941).

Whether Teleki merely had a suspicious mind and had simply encountered a serving maid one cannot say. It is conceivable that the Abbé's uncharacteristic confusion was a result of his puritanical outlook and embarassment at even being suspected of impropiety.

Perhaps it *was* true that the Abbé had a *petite amie*, but no other evidence for such a relationship has emerged so far. French society in the eighteenth society was tolerant of such things. Besides, it should be remembered that La Caille was never a consecrated priest (if this should be regarded as important).

Later studies

Longitudes at sea

The question of finding longitudes at sea continued to exercise La Caille's mind. He had worked on it during the eight months of his return voyage from Réunion to France. He determined that, though the accuracy attainable when measuring distances on the sky with a reflecting quadrant was limited to about 4 arcmin, it was a relatively easy method to use.

This method of 'Lunars', which required measurement of the Moon's distance from a certain bright star, was turned into what he considered to be a relatively simple procedure that an ordinary navigator could complete within a half-hour using a ruler and a compass. Previously, it had taken five hours of work with logarithm tables and a knowledge of spherical trigonometry.

Essential to this approach was a set of tables of Lunar distances from certain bright stars, worked out in advance for every few hours. He prepared such a set for the month of July 1761 and published it in the almanac *Connaissance des Temps* for that year. His calculations were based on the theoretical work of Clairaut.

Today [1759], thanks to the profound researches of the geometers and especially to the indefatigable work of Mr Clairaut, we are sure that we have the true law of the Moon's movements and we no longer have to worry about having excellent tables for it; all this apparatus of periods or of *Saros*[11] has become a useless scaffold and we can assert boldly that the Lunar calculations no longer form an obstacle to the determination of longitudes at sea (La Caille 1759, p. 67).

The new procedure was judged so useful that it was reprinted several times by the Royal Academy of Sciences in various works. Owing to the success that the Astronomer Royal Nevil Maskelyne had in using these tables, similar ones were afterwards published regularly in the British *Nautical Almanac*, from 1767 onwards.

The method of 'Lunars' remained in use well into the nineteenth century and must have contributed enormously to the safety of ocean travel. It was only with the development of affordable marine chronometers that it fell into disuse.

Delambre (1827, p. 503) later complained that, while La Caille's graphical approach was as exact as he had stated, it was regrettable that he had taken so much trouble over it. Unusually critical of his hero for once, he said that in dreaming up these ingenious but obscure and complicated methods, La Caille must have wanted to put mariners off using them. A navigator, if he had even once tried the mathematical method, would prefer it!

More on the Cape data

Moon

The data collected at the Cape were the source for a number of papers produced during La Caille's later years.

He revised his ideas on the distance to the Moon several times. The data he had taken had to be combined with the near-simultaneous observations made by others in Europe. One big problem was to calculate the exact bases of the survey triangles between the two points on the earth that connected with the third point on the Moon. Much depended on the assumptions made about the shape of the earth (as explained, see Fig. 2.15). La Caille eventually adopted a flattening at the poles of one part in 200 (modern value: about 1 part in 300) and used a theoretical formula to get the radius at each latitude. Of course, the relative longitudes of the Cape, Stockholm, Berlin, Greenwich, Paris and Bologna were not accurately known and there was inevitably some time difference between each observation. A lengthy final paper on the

---

[11] i.e. the empirical corrections due to Halley.

subject appeared in 1763 (La Caille 1761, pp. 1–57). Since the distance between the earth and the Moon changes in a complicated way, he took its parallax to be the average of its minimum and maximum values, which he found to be 57′ 13″.1. A modern mean value is 57′ 02″.6, corresponding to a distance of 384,400 km (Allen, 1963).

Mars, Venus and the Sun

In 1760 he published his final results from observations made at the Cape in collaboration with European observatories on the distances of Mars, Venus and the Sun from earth. It is now known that his value for the distance of the Sun was several per cent too low.

The mean parallax[12] of the Sun, from which its distance can be calculated, that he arrived at from planetary observations, was 10″.2, and from certain other observations made at the Cape and in Paris, 9″.94. He took his final value to be realistically 10″, accepting that greater accuracy could not be expected. The Sun is now known to be about 14% further away than La Caille thought, based on modern observations. Its accepted parallax is 8″.794, corresponding to a mean distance of 1.496×10^{11} m.

Fundamental astronomy (1757) and Solar tables (1758)

In 1757 he completed his *Astronomiae Fundamenta Novissimus...The Latest on Fundamental Astronomy...* (La Caille 1757) which he did not publish commercially but merely sent copies of to his correspondents. It is reported to have cost him 1100 pounds (livres). According to Carlier (1776 p. 92), this kind of project would have ruined him but for the disinterestedness of his friend, the printer, who never sought to make a profit by him.

The aim of the book, published unusually for him in Latin, was to present his life's work on obtaining accurate fundamental data on astronomy. It starts off with tables that can be used to work out all the corrections (such as those discovered by Bradley) that must be applied to a positional observation to correct it to a standard epoch, for example 1750.0.

The book contains a catalogue of the 400 brightest stars in both hemispheres, the first to fully incorporate the new corrections. These stars define the background against which the positions of the Sun, planets and comets are measured. In addition, he included multiple observations of the brightest stars which showed that they had no

---

[12] See Appendix 1 on Astronomical terms.

detectable proper motion, after correction. Much of the information he included came from his work at the Cape.

He allowed himself a little touch of pride in his preface: 'If all these things seem to you to be accurately enough determined, you will have to admit that on them the foundations of astronomy are squarely established, as though on blocks of stone'.

Later on, he made an important statement on his methods:

Following the astonishing progress that has been made in astronomy we have learned not to believe anybody just on his word. To make use of an observed position with confidence we want to know all the details of the observation and all the elements of the data reduction. We may have the observations of Tycho, Hevelius and Flamsteed, we have their catalogues, but how did they do their calculations and what was the state of their instruments? ... before the beautiful discoveries of Bradley [see Chapter 1, Programme of research] one had no sure method for calculating the apparent movements of stars and it was impossible to assign their true positions.

When I was younger and in better health I had a project to determine the positions of all the stars visible in a two-feet long telescope with a reticle [similarly to his observations at the Cape].

...But in Paris the winters are so cloudy and rain is so common during the summer that I could not follow [my plan]..., which had been justified during my stay at the Cape, where in six months, without neglecting other observations, I was able to determine the positions of ten thousand southern stars. I found I had to abandon this ... part of my plan to those who enjoy a clearer sky.

He took a dig at an old enemy: 'Those who present as new [discoveries] the errors and discordances of their own observations, will be taken correctly for perturbers rather than promoters of astronomy'. These [remarks] seem to refer to Le Monnier who hassled him continually and who, with d'Alembert, kept up a quarrel which did not last for long because La Caille kept silent for the sake of peace and was averse to disputes (Delambre 1827, p. 506).

Le Monnier had been supported by d'Alembert, concerning a claim by him that the eccentricity of the earth's orbit is variable, against La Caille, who maintained that is not and, anyway, that the idea is not supported by theory. The Abbé's conclusions were, naturally enough, received negatively by Le Monnier and d'Alembert ('who maintained an attitude of superior scepticism', according to Wilson, 1980a,b). Actually it is now known that there really is a variation, but of a far smaller amount than Le Monnier had claimed.

In the following year (1758) he produced a book covering his final tables of the Sun, *Tabulae Solares*... (La Caille 1758), i.e. its apparent position versus time as viewed from the orbiting earth, taking into account the perturbing effects of Jupiter, Venus and the Moon. The formulae for the perturbations introduced by the planets were taken from the work of Clairaut.

In a criticism published after La Caille's death, Cassini de Thury was very indignant that he had presumed to use only his own observations in working out his Solar Tables and had ignored those of the Cassinis. Nevertheless, they were made the standard reference tables in the annual astronomical almanac, the *Connaissance des Temps*, edited by Lalande, for the next 17 years.

Interaction with Tobias Mayer

La Caille's tables formed the basis for those of Tobias Mayer which were to become the next standard. Mayer (1723–62), another of the century's great observational astronomers, was originally a mapmaker but in the later part of his life became superintendent of the observatory of the University of Göttingen, where he was known for his high accuracy. He was a little younger than La Caille and was interested in many of the same problems. These two great observers and their English counterpart James Bradley were all destined to die in the same year (1762).

In 1758 Mayer and La Caille corresponded in order to compare some of their precision observations, finding some small differences that both felt had to be explained (see Forbes and Gapaillard 1996). La Caille thought that the problem was due to errors in the refraction corrections that Mayer had used and Mayer thought that it lay in the calibration of La Caille's instruments. Although this issue was not resolved during their lifetimes, it was afterwards found that the fault had in fact lain with La Caille's instruments; see also Chapter 2, Other observation.

La Caille was not the only one who suffered at one time or another from criticism by d'Alembert. Mayer had published tables of the Moon's position which he had claimed to be the most exact so far published. D'Alembert had torn into him: 'I do not wish to destroy the pretensions of this author; but two things are necessary to affirm them, the details of his calculations, which he has not given, and a full and consistent comparison which he seems not to have made between them and the observations'.

Mayer complained in one of his letters to La Caille that d'Alembert's assertions were not only poorly founded but were injurious to his reputation. La Caille, who had suffered similarly from d'Alembert's attack on his solar theory, replied that their elements for the Moon's orbit agreed very well, 'which has given me as much surprise as it has given me pleasure'. However, he demanded rather sharply:

No doubt you will release to the public the method you followed for calculating the variations [in the law of refraction] because there is nothing more odious in the Republic of Letters than people who lay down the law to others without giving any other reason than their authority or their reputation for competence. That is the characteristic of our Encyclopedists.

This last reference was to the editors of the famous *Encyclopaedia*,[13] which was then in course of publication under the editorship of Denis Diderot and which involved d'Alembert as scientific editor, though he later dropped out. This work was a cornerstone of the trend in public awareness called the 'Enlightenment' that was responsible in part for the disintegration of the pre-revolutionary régime in France.

The last years of Mayer, covering the period of his correspondence with La Caille, were a time of great misery for him. Apart from being in failing health, his home town of Göttingen was occupied by French troops as part of the Seven Years War and his Observatory was turned into a powder magazine.

The return and naming of Comet Halley

In 1705 Edmond Halley had predicted that a comet seen in 1684 and on previous occasions was probably in orbit around the Sun and would reappear 74 years later, i.e. in 1758. However, Clairaut and Lalande, following an extremely laborious calculation (see Wilson, 1993), predicted that it would be delayed by perturbations due to Jupiter and Saturn. In April 1759, they said, it would be at its closest point to the Sun. The actual search for the reappearance of the comet was unfortunately left to the secretive Delisle of the Collège Royal, who had a private observatory. La Caille must have regretted this decision as he complained later to Wargentin in Stockholm that 'Delisle loves to keep to himself what others do not have' and that he 'pesters all and sundry to make them communicate their observations, though he is not at all communicative himself'. Lalande, Delisle's former pupil, felt the same about him (both are quoted by Widmalm, 1992). Meanwhile, 'the astronomers did not sleep', according to Voltaire.

In the event, it was first spotted in December 1758 by George Palitzsch and others in Saxony but the news travelled slowly. In Paris, Delisle, whose student Charles Messier saw it for the first time on 21 January, withheld this information from the rest of the French community, either because of his general bloody-mindedness or because his own crude prediction of the comet's reappearance had caused it to be looked for in the wrong part of the sky. Only on April Fool's

---

[13] *Encyclopédie ou Dictionnaire Raisonné des Sciences, Diderot (1751).*

day 1759 did he choose to reveal the news, which was understandably received with scepticism! The information from Germany arrived in Paris just after that. The comet was thereafter followed assiduously by the astronomical community for the next few months so that its orbit could be calculated. The actual date of perihelion was found to have been 13 March, a little earlier than had been expected, but within the anticipated error of about a month.

On 12 May 1759 La Caille (1759, p. 522) read a note about the comet to the Academy 'because everybody seems to be interested in the comet which is appearing at the moment and which can justly be called Halley's Comet . . .'. The name caught on and has been used ever since.

The successful prediction of the comet's return was a triumph for Newton's theory of universal gravitation, which had now been applied to a non-planetary object in Solar orbit for the first time. Any doubts that had remained in France were now dispelled. Clairaut's work nevertheless excited the jealousy of Le Monnier and his long-term rival d'Alembert who endeavoured to denigrate it, with little success (see Wilson, 1993). A fundamental difference between these two was that D'Alembert tended to believe in a purely theoretical approach to celestial mechanics, whereas Clairaut accepted the need for observational input to his models.

Some last observations

Rapid comet of 1760

Two observations carried out towards the end of La Caille's life were made in the company of the reformist politician and economist Anne-Robert-Jacques Turgot, then just starting his career after giving up on becoming a priest. The first of these was of Comet 1760A1, a bright comet noticed at Paris for the first time by Turgot as he crossed the Pont-Neuf. He informed La Caille about it and the latter followed it for several nights to compute its orbit. It was moving when first seen at the exceptional speed of 72' in one hour, though it later slowed down. The implication was that it must have been close to the earth and many people became worried about it. La Caille computed its elements and ridiculed those who were frightened (Delambre, 1827. p. 494).

Transit of Venus, 1761

The Transit of Venus of 6 June 1761 was visible from France and caused tremendous excitement among the astronomers. Many pages of the Mémoires of the Académie des Sciences were afterwards devoted to observations of this event. In spite of his scepticism about the value of Transits of Venus, La Caille took the trouble to go to Conflans-sous-Carrière, a few km outside Paris, to observe it (La Caille 1761, p. 1). His own observatory was not suitable for this observation (perhaps because the dome of the Mazarin chapel was in the way). He was accompanied by Turgot and Bailly. They brought a quadrant of two feet, a seconds pendulum, an equatorial mount and some telescopes of different sizes, all by boat on the Seine. Bailly set up and regulated the clock rate from solar observations over several days because La Caille could not stay away for the necessary time. The day was rather overcast but the Sun could be seen faintly through the clouds and the various stages of the passage of Venus across the solar disc could be timed successfully.

For the first time he used an achromatic telescope—one that focused all colours to about the same place, unlike the simpler ones that were available previously. The telescope in question had a focal length of 1.56 m and an aperture of 43 mm, with an eyepiece that gave it a magnification of about 40 times; much more than he usually used. The eyepiece was also equipped with a micrometer that could be used to measure the diameter of Venus.

Turgot with a 12-foot telescope (3.65 m focal length) differed from La Caille by 17 seconds earlier for the ingress time and 20 seconds later for the egress, whereas Bailly with a 6-foot telescope (1.83 m) estimated the egress about 4 seconds later (one of the problems of observing a Venus transit is that it happens so rarely that there is no chance to practise).

As La Caille had suspected, it was hopelessly difficult to time the ingress and egress of the planet. Clairaut, in his letter to Bernoulli after La Caille's death (see This chapter, La Caille's circle: some pupils and Friends), remarked 'It appears that in effect the transit of Venus has not come up to expectations. And that the astronomers do not agree with each other. My poor friend La Caille predicted it'.[14]

The presence of Turgot on these occasions is somewhat surprising. Turgot was close to some of the main figures of the enlightenment and was a contributor of articles to the *Encyclopédie* edited by Diderot (1751). Some years later, he was responsible for removing some of the economic absurdities that plagued pre-revolutionary France.

Transit telescope

In 1760 the Abbé acquired a transit telescope by Dollond (see Fig. 5.4) which he installed in his rooftop observatory. He had come to believe that this was the most efficient way to obtain accurate observations

---

[14] Clairaut to Daniel Bernoulli, dated Paris, 28 July 1763; see Boncompagni, 1894.)

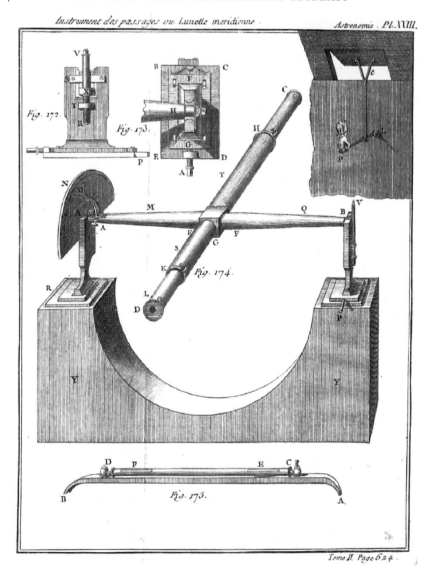

Fig. 5.4 Transit telescope by Dollond, installed 1760 in La Caille's observatory at the Collège Mazarin, above the Cardinal's tomb. This had a focal length of 50 inches (127 cm) and an axis of 2½ feet (76 cm). From Lalande 1792, Art. 2388.

of Right Ascensions. He took considerable trouble to erect a solid mounting for it in his observatory on the vault above Mazarin's tomb. He started using it on 15 September of that year but had to adjust it two months later. His idea had been to produce a highly precise catalogue of 800 stars along the Zodiac. Unfortunately he only managed to complete 515 of them before he died. The Catalogue was published in the end by his former pupil Bailly. Delambre (1827) in comparing positional results of his own with those from past observers, found La Caille's to be the best.

Last public lecture

On 14 November 1761 La Caille presented what was to be his swan song, a public discourse at the Royal Academy of Sciences on the progress that astronomy had made during the previous thirty years, later published in the introduction to his third and last volume of 10-year ephemerides (La Caille 1763). This and several other posthumous works were edited by Bailly, Maraldi and Carlier. It summarises beautifully the thinking of the French astronomers of the mid eighteenth century. He had never been far from the mainstream throughout his career.

> I believe that in this work, intended to help astronomers with all their operations, readers will see with pleasure an abridged account of the perfection that astronomy has acquired in our own times, by the singular support that the princes who govern Europe have accorded it, and by the competition between scientists that have made it the object of their studies. I imagine that this sketch will serve to make known what it is that occupies astronomers and to support this research spirit which has done so much honour to our century ...
>
> Though astronomers have in effect worked hard in the compilation of observations, it has to be admitted that, from about 1672 to 1725, practical astronomy made no significant progress. There was no successful effort to make observations more precise ... [in spite of suggestions by Hooke and Römer].
>
> Whilst practical astronomy remained in this sort of static and languishing state, theoretical astronomy rose to a level that one could not have dared to hope for, even from a century's worth of scientific effort put together; this was however the work of a single man, the celebrated Newton. But all these sublime speculations, founded on a principle that appeared unphysical, made almost no impression on most astronomers. They regarded the work of Newton purely as a geometric game; it has to be confessed that too few of them were able to understand him well enough to judge. So it happened, at least outside England, that for more than thirty years, just as with several useful inventions: astronomers neglected it until our own time ...
>
> Though for such a long time almost rejected by astronomers, Newton's celestial physics has since suddenly been universally accepted: one cannot attribute this revolution to the capriciousness of fashion as those do who only know its name and imagine that in a while some other system will take its place, causing that of Newton to fall into

oblivion…It is too well tied up and conforms too well to every kind of celestial phenomenon to be more than a simple hypothesis. Time may cause the word *attraction* to fall away, considered as a primitive quality attached to matter, but it will never destroy the laws of gravitation as we know them.

The revolution I have spoken of is in the order of the human spirit. The work of Newton appeared suddenly in 1687 without fanfare. It was too full of novel ideas and too obscure. The astronomers of the time…, mostly accustomed to the ideas of Descartes…, were not in the mood to immediately abandon the ideas of fluids, of a plenum[15] and celestial vortices…; even if they wanted to examine the proposed new physics, the cramped style of Newton, his analysis hidden in too concise a synthesis, made his work almost unintelligible. Its basis seemed unreliable. This was *attraction*, a hidden quality whose name was ridiculed by the philosophers from Descartes to Gassendi….National prejudice and the contrast between Newton and Descartes and Leibnitz led to the decision without further examination that the English geometer wished to introduce a false philosophy that was not worth serious refutation.

Then it happened that young mathematicians, struck by propositions as sublime as they were singular from Newton's book, tried to reconstruct the analysis [i.e. by algebra and calculus] that had led to them…; the success of these efforts made the material a bit more familiar…the singular agreement of all parts of the Newtonian system once understood really struck the mathematicians. Especially the young astronomers, who studied the parts necessary to them, arrived at a sufficient understanding that they could apply the Newtonian rules to the observations of the most remarkable phenomena that had always been thought the least susceptible to exact calculation, such as the movements of comets…

It was again in England that the first efforts were made to put more precision into astronomical measurements. The celebrated clockmaker G. Graham constructed new instruments with astonishing accuracy…[He] constructed a [zenith] sector of 24 English feet radius and another of 12, with whose aid the first astronomical discovery of the century was made[16]…This discovery was published in 1728 but was not made use of in France until about nine years afterwards.

In 1733 the preparation of a geometrically accurate map of France was started. In turn, it caused the Academy of Sciences to discuss the shape of the earth. It was resolved to decide the issue by up-to date observations, which the King duly ordered. The first large-scale operations revealed the need to construct more solid and convenient instruments. It was seen in effect how small errors, whether on the part of the observers

[15] The plenum was a mysterious material that filled interplanetary space in Descartes' theory.

[16] He is referring here to Bradley's discovery of aberration.

or the quadrants, became extended when one put together a long series of angular measures [This was a reference to his own work of 1744 (see Chapter 1, Member of the Academy of Sciences).].

Referring to instrumental developments, La Caille next mentions the development of reflecting telescopes using parabolic mirrors by Hadley around 1719, the transit telescope, temperature-compensated clocks (not used in France before 1762 according to Delambre 1827) and the Hadley quadrant of 1731 (see Chapter 2).

The next big discovery of the century was the 9 seconds of arc (radius) near-circular movement of the poles, or nutation of the earth's axis, by Bradley in 1737, but not published until 1748. This is caused by the action of the Moon on the bulging earth. Its period of 18 years 220 days corresponds to the rotation of the Moon's not quite circular orbit as a whole. It was theoretically explained by d'Alembert and Euler, which represented another triumph of Newtonian theory.

A matter of great concern to La Caille himself was long-term change in the earth's orbit. The angle between the earth's axis and the plane of its orbit[17] was changing, i.e. the tilt of about $23\frac{1}{2}°$ degrees that gives us the seasons was not quite constant. Also the orbit itself, which is elliptical, was rotating very slowly. Ever since ancient times, the height of the Sun at its summer highest seemed to be diminishing slightly, but the observations had on the whole been ignored on the grounds that they were too rough. It was due to La Caille that the phenomenon began to be observed more carefully. He compared measurements made from 1510 and the positions of ancient sundials with modern observations. Later it was found that the decreasing angle was part of a very long cyclic effect, the cause being the gravitational attraction of the other planets.[18]

Acknowledging all these new theories means that the places of stars in our best catalogues are uncertain because in reducing the observations only a uniform precession was allowed for. It is therefore necessary to construct a new catalogue where the positions of the stars, especially the brightest ones, are determined with all possible precision, having regard to their small apparent movements: that is the work I have been doing for the last 15 years and more . . . and why I went in 1750 to the Cape.

The other reason of course for going to the Cape had been to get good distances to the Sun and Moon. He mentions that previous observers had differed by large amounts, up to a factor of two.

---

[17] Formally known as the *inclination of the ecliptic*.

[18] The value of the tilt is now known to vary somewhat irregularly between 22° 38′ and 24° 21′ with a period of about 41,000 years. This is related to the climatic variability known as the Milankovitch Cycle, published around 1941.

He took the opportunity to criticise once again the attempts to get distances by the transits of Venus across the face of the Sun (see Chapter 1, The southern hemisphere plan, and This chapter, Some last observations). The measurements of 1761, in which he participated, showed this up only too well, even when the best instruments were used in the most favourable circumstances. He obviously regarded the costly expeditions sent overseas for this work as a waste of resources.

> In regard to the [distance] of the Moon, the difference between the tables of Halley and of Cassini are ... around one part in 56 of the distance, causing an uncertainty which hardly does honour to our century.

He then referred to his measurements due to be published in the *Mémoires* of the Academy (They were reported in La Caille, 1761, p. 1).

The study of comet orbits was one of the great successes of French astronomy at mid-century. Beside himself, his friend Maraldi was a pioneer in this area. Much progress was made in the computational methods used and understanding the perturbing effects of the planets that caused Halley's comet, for example, to have a variable period .

Instrumentally, in the last couple of years considered, the invention of the heliometer he regarded as one of the most important things. This was a telescope, popular until the end of the nineteenth century, for measuring small angles. In the hands of later astronomers such as Bessel and Gill it was to meet with great success in measuring the distances of the nearest stars. It is now, however, completely obsolete.

Next, he mentions the recently developed achromatic telescope (1758):

> Mr Dollond[19] has found also a new combination of materials for forming two lenses which together compose the objective of a telescope in which the colours of the rainbow to which ordinary telescopes are subject are almost completely annihilated, which makes this objective very powerful with a moderate focal length ...

In the days before practical calculating machines, let alone digital computers, the arithmetic work connected with astronomy was formidable:

> After the account I have just given, it should not appear surprising that astronomical calculations are at present prodigiously complicated in comparison with those of 30 years ago because of the corrections deduced from the large number of observationally confirmed theories ... one cannot avoid going to tenths of seconds in almost all astronomical calculations but one is compensated for the increased effort by the precision that can be obtained in the most delicate work ...

---

[19] Dollond was not the inventor, but rather was the developer and patentee of these telescopes.

After the observation of a star and of the Moon in the meridian, which take only 2 or 3 minutes of time, it doesn't take just a half-hour to derive the true longitude and latitude of the Moon. At present two hours are hardly enough for those most practised in astronomical reductions. Thus one should not judge the work of an astronomer by the number of observations he has made but rather by the number he has reduced...

It seems to me also that it is necessary not only to present observations together with the finished reductions, but even the principal elements of these reductions so that, if an error is suspected in the calculations, or even a misprint, one can verify it immediately. Lacking such care, today's geometers who want to work on Lunar theory can reasonably complain that in spite of all the volumes of observations printed by the observatories they find almost none to which they can compare the results of their work.

Last days

Three months before his death, the King offered La Caille an apartment in the Château de Vincennes on the outskirts of Paris, to allow him to devote his entire time to work. However, he never got around to moving there.

The last observation that La Caille was to obtain, of the Sun on the meridian, was made at Paris on 28th February 1762. Lalande wrote below his notebook entry: 'This great man died the 21st March 1762, of a neglected cold which he caught in his observatory'.

The Abbé Carlier, his colleague at the Collége Mazarin, must have been present at his end. Carlier was not a scientist, but rather a literary figure and agronomist. He wrote in his life of La Caille (see La Caille 1776):

At the end of February 1762 he again experienced the symptoms that he showed at the Cape in February 1752: exhaustion, a feeling of fullness, a 'rheumatism in the kidneys', a nosebleed and indigestion. He carried on with his ordinary activities until the 9th of March. A first bleeding of his foot brought out an inflammation of the chest, accompanied by suffocation and a cramp in the side. He could not hide from himself the danger of the situation and reconciled himself to a Christian end. Weakened by repulsive bleedings of his arms and legs, he recognised too late the nature of his illness. 'Alas!', he said,' if only they had treated me as they did at the Cape I would have had hope of recovery'. He saw death doubling its pace without being frightened. He disposed himself as a Christian and gave to those hearts hardened by the maxims of a blind incredulity the example of a sincere resignation to the orders of the Creator. He was administered the sacrament of penitence. He made his will on 17 March; he asked for the Viaticum[20] but because there were hopes of recovery he believed things would turn out differently; the danger was nothing more than exhaustion.

The night of the 19th/20th March he showed a periodic fever, a little stronger than before. The doctors, after a scrupulous combination of the rules of their art, believed that a new letting of blood from his foot would cut the root of the evil. It was done at six a.m. on the 20th March. He fell into a coma for 24 hours and died on the 21st, in the month of his birth: a sad anniversary which was celebrated by the tears of his friends.

The evacuation that had ended his sickness at the Cape happened a half-hour after his death, but his eyes were closed to the light; the effects of art had been more prompt than those of nature (Carlier, in La Caille 1776, pp. 82–84).'

The funeral service for La Caille was held in St. Sulpice and he was buried in the chapel of the Collège Mazarin. The following information is quoted from a book on the history of the Mazarin library and the Palace of the Institute (formerly the Collège Mazarin) by Alfred Franklin (1901) that gives an account of the ceremonies that then took place:

The Saint-Sulpice records state 'on 22 March 1762 convoy was made to the chapel of the College of Four Nations of Mr Nicolas-Louis de La Caille, professor of mathematics at the College Mazarin. Died at the college, aged around 48 years. Witnesses Mr Ambroise Riballier[21], 'procureur' of the college, Louis-François de la Tour[22], bookseller and printer, who have signed [p. 251].

The vast cellars beneath the chapel contained the bodies of Cardinal Mazarin as well as those of several famous professors such as La Caille.

The following is an extract of the letter sent to colleagues inviting them to the funeral:

You are invited to attend the convoy and interment of Messire Nicolas-Louis de la Caille, professor of mathematics at the Collège Mazarin who died there. Which will take place today, Monday 22nd March 1762 at 5 o'clock in the afternoon precisely, in his parish church of Saint Sulpice, and to the removal which will happen thereafter to the chapel of the Collège Mazarin where he will be inhumed. Requiescat in pace.

---

[20] This Latin word literally means provision for a journey; in the religious context it means the bread and wine of Holy Communion, intended to strengthen a dying person for the journey to the next world.

[21] The Abbé Ambroise Riballier was the 'Procureur' or bursar of the College and from 1766 its Grand-Master.

[22] H.-L. Guérin and L.F. Delatour were, as mentioned, the printers of most of La Caille's books.

A few days afterwards, a service was held at the College itself as the following note states:

You are invited by the Messieurs of the Collège Mazarin to do them the honour of attending the service they will celebrate on Wednesday 31 March 1762 in their chapel, at 10 o'clock precisely, for the repose of the soul of Messire Nicolas-Louis de la Caille, professor of mathematics at the College.

The cellar used for burials extends under the vestibule of the chapel. Researches that have been made there reveal the presence of a multitude of bones; but some inscriptions crudely written in pencil or charcoal on the vault preserve the only memory of these burials. I [Franklin] have collected the names of two Grand-Masters . . . , of three librarians . . . and three professors . . . [including La Caille].

No traces of coffins, nails or fabrics were found. The bodies seem to have been interred naked, perhaps covered in quicklime. These are in general disposed in three superimposed rows and have the feet turned towards the north [pp. 174–175].

Franklin did not state when this gruesome investigation was carried out or whether the bones were left in place.

Appreciations

La Caille's pupil Jean Sylvain Bailly wrote a loving appreciation of him:

His character was that of a lover of truth: he said straight out: bad luck to those who can be wounded by it. Perhaps in the great world he would have been reproached for this courageous attitude but he did not live in this world where so many considerations excuse this vice. 'My friend', he said to me, 'if good people express their indignation and make the evil ones better recognised as such, the vice thus unmasked can do no more harm and virtue will be better respected'. This was the man who honoured me with his friendship and for whom I grieve every day, and who merits the respect of men more than their praise.

He was cold and reserved with those he did not know well, but mild, straightforward, at ease and pleasant with friends. It was then that, stripping off the grave exterior that he presented in public, he showed a peaceful joy and honesty. Then his face lit up with the serenity of his soul which he seemed to communicate to all those around him. I never had more pleasant days than those I spent with him. His friends will never forget him; and his enemies if he has any, will have nothing to say against him. Happy is he who dies thus; because the reward of the sage is to say in dying: I have done nothing but good on the earth; and nothing after my death can be held against me (Bailly, 1770).

Grandjean de Fouchy (1762), who had helped La Caille from the very outset of his career, wrote in his éloge:

> He was above medium height, serious and cold with those who did not know him, but with his friends relaxing into a gentle, quiet gaiety, displaying the serenity of his soul: a friend of truth to the point of imprudence, he dared to speak it to a person's face, even though it might displease, though without any intention of shocking. One can easily judge that with such a character he was incapable of any subterfuge. He was extremely fair and moderate in all his conduct and perfectly disinterested; he never solicited any favours nor aimed to make a fortune; it happened so to say, that fortune herself came looking for him; but his extreme modesty and the modesty of his desires took the place of opulence and he was perhaps happier in suppressing desires than in setting about satisfying them. His mind was of the greatest precision, one could say when he spoke that the most abstract ideas arranged themselves in his speeches into the most methodical order. The same order and clarity were to be found in his writing, to which he joined a purity of style, without ornament. If no brilliant and exquisite thoughts are to be seen it is not that he did not scatter them around. He had an extensive knowledge of literature and the accuracy of his memory was such that he almost never forgot what he had read or heard, but he did not make use of this to ornament his writings; content with the precise expression of his thoughts, he rarely dreamed of embellishing them. Never was a man more faithful or exact in all his duties; two violent attacks of gout that he had in 1760 were unable to stop him from giving his lessons at the Collège Mazarin; nobody was more assiduous than him at our assemblies or more exact in carrying out the duties imposed by the status of academician ... In a word, one can say that he lived as full of virtues as of knowledge and that he lacked none of the virtues of a perfectly honest man, a dignified cleric, a great astronomer and an excellent academician.

Lalande, who gloried in having been his disciple, after having been admitted to the Academy of Sciences, said of him that 'by himself alone he had made more observations and calculations than all other astronomers who were his contemporaries, put together'.

Will of La Caille

Although we do not have the Abbé's complete will, the following is an extract[23] quoted in its 'Insinuation', or legal registration.[24] It is

---

[23] There may be some errors in the copying or in the translation.

[24] Conserved at Direction des Services d'Archives de Paris, Département de Paris, ref. DC6 243 f 279v–280.

especially interesting because it contains the only references we have to his living relations: two of his sisters, his cousin and his aunt. It also makes the only mention of his manservant Germain.

Will La Caille 17 March 1762

Validated[?] 18 May 1762

Gratis by order

From the will of Mr Nicolas Louis La Caille, deacon of the diocese of Rheims, Professor of Mathematics at College Mazarin, Quay of Quatre Nations near [?] St Sulpice, received by Janvry [?], notary at the Paris Chambers, on the seventeenth of March seventeen sixty-two, that which follows has been extracted.
I give and bequeath to the Royal Academy of Sciences the original registers of my astronomical observatory.

I give to Mr Maraldi, member of the same academy, my roughwork notebooks containing the calculations of astronomical research.

I give and bequeath to the [person] named Germain, who served me, the sum of twenty-four livres paid once.

I give and bequeath to each of my two religious sisters, one at St Aubin and the other at Nogent le Rotrou, sixty livres annuity, which makes one hundred and twenty livres for both of them, the annuity to run from the day of my death and to be payable each year, six months at a time, without any deduction.

I give and bequeath to the widow Norion my Godmother to enjoy during her lifetime, to count from the day of my death, the quarter of her estate that I received from Jeanne Brejean [?] my aunt, consisting of land at Rumigny, and to Dame Le Bar, wife of Sr. Gobreau, labourer, near Rozoy, diocese of Laon, the possession and usufruct of the said quarter of the combined fund and property after the decease of the said Dame Norion.

As to the surplus of all the goods that I leave on the day of my death, whatever it all consists of, I give and bequeath it to Dame Nicolle Coubron, my cousin-German[25], wife of Denis Janvier, who I make and institute my universal legatee, to enjoy, use and dispose of as [her] property, counting from the day of my death.

Insinuated at Paris the fifteenth of June seventeen sixty-two. Thirty-two livres ten sols have been paid for the right [i.e. as a fee].

Disposal of his effects

On 24 May 1762 the Academy of Sciences instructed Grandjean de Fouchy and Lalande to retrieve the Academy's belongings from his

---

[25] First cousin.

apartment. They reported back that they had collected a number of instruments and manuscripts.

Many of his scientific documents were left to the Royal Academy of Sciences and others went to Maraldi II, described as his best friend by Delambre (1827, p. 250). Maraldi also saw to the posthumous publication of La Caille's southern star observations (see Chapter 2, The Caelum, Australe Stelliferum). When Maraldi left Paris to retire to his native Perinaldo, he gave these manuscripts to Lalande, who eventually passed them on to the Paris Observatory, where they remain.

His personal books, his mathematical and astronomical instruments and other effects were disposed of in a sale between 12 and 20 July 1762, held at the Collège Mazarin. They were listed in the printed catalogue of the event.[26] Copies of this Catalogue still exist in the Bibliothèque Sainte-Geneviève in Paris. There were 854 lots consisting of books and 27 of instruments. A very large fraction of the books consisted of astronomical, mathematical and other scientific texts, including most of the major publications of the previous two centuries. Only about a third dated from his own century. He had many books on philosophy, classics, travels and the law. There were very few of a religious nature, perhaps a dozen or so. Kolbe's book did not appear in the list!

Among the instruments were quite a few telescopes and parts, a 'seconds watch', globes, drawing instruments and a counting device. Interestingly, he possessed a heliometer. The last item on the sale list was a complete laboratory with bench, forge and assorted tools.

Memorials to La Caille

Among other things, La Caille is remembered today for his catalogue of southern stars. Since he was the first person to number or name most of these, they are usually referred to by their Lacaille numbers, even though they all appear in later catalogues. He is also commemorated by an Asteroid: 9135, discovered in 1960 at Palomar, and by a lunar crater (23.8S, 1.1 E, 67 km diameter). The constellations he named are perhaps the most permanent reminder of his pioneering southern hemisphere observations.

In terms of physical memorials, La Caille is remembered by monuments at his birthplace, Rumigny, and Curepipe, Mauritius. A beautiful bronze plaque designed by the famous architect Herbert Baker (see Fig. 5.5) was installed close to the site of his observatory in Cape Town

---

[26] *Catalogue des livres de feu Monsieur l'Abbé de la Caille, de l'Académie Royale des Sciences; de celles de Pétersbourg, de Berlin & de Stockholm; des Sociétés Royales de Londres & de Gottingue; de l'Institut de Bologne; Professeur de Mathématiques au Collège Mazarin*, 1862. Paris, Damonneville, veuve de Michel—Musier fils.

Fig. 5.5 Plaque to the memory of La Caille set up by the South African Philosophical Society in 1903 on the site of his observatory. It was designed by the famous architect Herbert Baker. (W. Cape Archives & Record Service M127).

in 1903. Unfortunately it was stolen by metal thieves in 2010 and never recovered. Roads named after him exist in Cape Town and Curepipe.

On 21 September 1913 a plaque was fixed to the house of his birth in Rumigny in commemoration of his 200th anniversary (Boquet 1913). A number of his collateral descendants were present on this occasion. Following the First World War, a monument was erected by international subscription in 1921. The latter was destroyed during the Second World War. However, in 1962, the 200th anniversary of the Abbé's death, a replacement monument was erected in a ceremony presided over by André Danjon, Director of the Paris Observatory (see also Danjon & Fischer de Cugnac 1962 and Giret 1962).

The only portrait that we have of La Caille was painted by his friend Anne-Louise Le Jeuneux in 1762 (see frontispiece). We do not know whether it was done from life or was posthumous.

A summing up

La Caille was a progressive who helped to propagate Newtonian ideas in France and to sweep aside the cobwebs of outdated theories. As a teacher and writer of textbooks he had a strong influence on scientific education. But his greatest achievements were in the fields of positional astronomy and geodesy to which he introduced new levels of accuracy and accountability.

Today's astronomers tend to look with pity on their predecessors of one or two centuries ago, who spent their time on what seems to have been boring and endless labour-intensive visual positional work. Yet their increasingly precise observations of the movements of celestial bodies led to discoveries of fundamental importance.

Though not mentioned by previous biographers, La Caille deserves recognition as the first person to have made a systematic survey of the sky using a telescope. Many of the constellations of the southern sky were named by him. Their strange shapes to modern eyes were based on the eighteenth-century scientific instruments after which they were called.

He clearly recognised that the nebulae that emerged from his survey were something that would be worthy of investigation but his instruments were not powerful enough to follow them up.

On a practical level he showed the viability of 'Lunars' for the determination of longitudes at sea. He constructed tables to give the angular distance of the Moon from various bright stars and showed how to make the necessary observations. This procedure, after some further development by others, was of great benefit to seafarers for several decades

He is remembered today as the most meticulous of observers. His data sustained a group of brilliant theoreticians who worked mainly in Paris in the mid eighteenth century. While not associated with any outstanding individual discovery, he very clearly saw how to get the most out of the instruments that he used. Not only did he keep a close watch during their manufacture but, in the finest tradition of instrumental astronomy, he devoted enormous care to their calibration and to understanding the limits to the accuracy that they were capable of.

Only with the development of a method for the statistical treatment of observational errors early in the nineteenth century were his methods of calculation improved upon. In 1805, the mathematician and astronomer Adrien Marie Legendre published the 'Method of Least Squares' and, in 1809, Carl Friedrich Gauss followed the method up by making its basis more secure.

In his choice of what to observe, La Caille always had clear goals. In the design of his campaigns he worked to achieve what he needed with extraordinary clarity and direction. The effort he expended to attain a given result was just right; the precision of the observations was such as to achieve what he wanted with maximum economy. His measurement of the radius of the earth in the southern hemisphere, though incorrect for reasons that were not then understood, was an outstanding example. He took only a few weeks to complete his programme with the help of two or three moderately educated assistants and a team of slaves, whereas at a later time Maclear took much longer to achieve very little more, though having access to greater resources of every kind. The clarity of La Caille's thinking was exceptional.

6

Paradox resolved

Various eighteenth-century astronomers and physicists were sceptical about La Caille's conclusion that the earth is pear-shaped. For example, in 1775, the Italian mathematical physicist Paolo Frisi conjectured that because the sea to the south of the continent was less dense than the land, the difference might have affected the latitude determinations. A similar suggestion was made by the wealthy and taciturn English scientist Henry Cavendish in 1775 (see Todhunter 1873, §671).

The earth is in fact quite close to ellipsoidal in shape, contrary to what La Caille's measurement implied and its shape in both hemispheres is similar. As will be seen, the problem with his result arose from the latitude determinations at the end points of his arc. The measurements had depended on the plumb line of his sector giving a true reading of the vertical and this had not always, in fact, been the case. The bob had been pulled slightly sideways in opposite directions by the masses of Table Mountain at the southern end and the Piketberg at the northern end.

It is surprising that the Abbé did not think of gravitational attraction as a possible explanation for his anomalous result, which even he found hard to accept. Newton himself had estimated the attraction due to an idealised mountain, which he regarded as too small to be measurable. It is also the case that La Caille's friends and colleagues Pierre Bouguer and Charles-Marie de La Condamine had, while in Peru, actually tried to measure the deflection of a pendulum due to the mountain Chimboraçao or Chimborazo in 1738 (Bouguer 1749), though they felt that their results were unreliable (see Todhunter 1873, §363).

In 1772, a team under the Astronomer Royal in England, Neville Maskelyne, undertook an expedition to a somewhat symmetrical mountain called Schiehallion, in Scotland. By measuring an isolated mountain with a relatively simple shape they hoped it would be easy to calculate its mass theoretically as well as its centre of gravitational attraction. Using Newton's law of gravitation, its effect on a plumb bob could then be estimated. They measured the apparent latitude differences of two places on each side of the mountain by an astronomical method similar to La Caille's and followed this by determining the true

Fig. 6.1 Diagram of the Cavendish (1798) experiment that first demonstrated directly the attraction due to gravity between masses in the 'laboratory'. Two small balls were supported on a very delicate torsion balance and their positions could be measured through the microscopes. When the large balls were swung around they caused the small balls on the balance to move slightly (from Cavendish, 1798).

latitude difference from a ground-based trigonometrical survey. They found a discrepancy of 11.6 arc seconds between the two. Their result was used to estimate the mean density of the earth, which was their motivation for undertaking the expedition in the first place.

In 1797–8 Cavendish conducted an extremely delicate and famous experiment that demonstrated the gravitational attraction between masses directly. This was a difficult project to carry out because the effect is such a small one. The idea had originally occurred to a geologist, John Michell, but he died before he could carry the project to fruition. His experimental equipment eventually found its way to Cavendish. Figure 6.1 shows the special sealed building set up to house the apparatus and keep it free of drafts and other disturbances. From Cavendish's result it is possible to determine the 'Constant of Gravitation' usually referred to by physicists as 'G', or 'big G',[1] though he did not do this himself, being more attuned to the contemporary interest in the density of the earth. The value of 'G' is still one of the least precisely known constants of physics, being good to only about half of one per cent.

---

[1] According to Newton, the force F between two spherical bodies with masses m_1 and m_2 is given by the expression $F = G\frac{m_1 m_2}{r^2}$, where r is the distance between their centres.

In 1813 Lieut-Col William Mudge (see Rodriguez, 1813), director of the Ordnance Survey in the United Kingdom, who was interested in the shape of the earth and had made a measurement of the meridian over three degrees in England, worked out that La Caille's measurement of the latitude difference between his end points had to be in error by about 10 arcsec, if the earth is taken to be similar in both hemispheres. This corresponds to a distance on the surface of 309 m. 'An error of ten seconds, by an astronomer so skilful and scrupulous as Lacaille, is too extraordinary to be admitted as probable'. He made the suggestion that Major William Lambton (of the Survey of India) should be encouraged to repeat La Caille's measurements (since the Cape was conveniently on the way to India) and that more southern measurements should be carried out in other places. He was certainly aware that local attractors such as mountain masses could have been responsible for anomalous results such as this one.

Visit of George Everest to the Cape

The first serious attempt to check on the Abbé's work was made a few years later by George Everest (Fig. 6.2), after whom the famous mountain is named (though he never saw it). He was the Chief Assistant of the Geodetic Survey of India and was then serving under Lieut-Col William Lambton, its Superintendent. He had been in India since 1806 at the age of sixteen and had avoided catching any tropical diseases, the bane of Europeans in India, until October 1819. While conducting survey work in a jungle area he had succumbed to typhus or malaria. As many as 150 members of his team became sick; work was temporarily abandoned and several perished on the way back to their base. Everest had thought himself well enough to work again by June 1820, but soon relapsed. In the hope of recovering his health more permanently he applied for leave and departed from India in October 1820 for the Cape, where he expected that the mild climate would cure him. In fact, so-called 'Indians', i.e. people born in the British Isles but who lived in India, were a regular feature of the Cape scene, where they were apparently regarded by the locals as lazy and supercilious.

Everest arrived in Cape Town on 25 November 1820 (Smith, 1999). Unfortunately, nearly all of his correspondence was destroyed at some point so that it is impossible to find out how he occupied himself for most of the time he spent there. However he did write a fairly detailed paper about his investigation into La Caille's work which was published in the Memoirs of the Royal Astronomical Society (Everest, 1821).

Fig. 6.2 George Everest. While Chief Assistant of the Geodetic Survey of India he spent a year (1820–21) recuperating from an illness at the Cape and tracing the locations of La Caille's survey points (Photo: Courtesy J.R. Smith).

The land measurement revisited

Everest's paper starts off by mentioning that this project had in fact been instigated by Lambton, who asked him to 'examine the tract of country in which the geodetical operations of M. l'Abbé de la Caille were conducted'. He had no access to any of La Caille's publications when he arrived but by June 1821 he had managed to get hold of the printed *Journal Historique*. Although the details of the measurements had actually been published in the papers in the *Memoirs of the Royal Academy of Sciences*, he had not seen them and was unfortunately unaware of the methods the Abbé had employed and the scrupulous care he had taken.

He reproduced the Abbé's map (Fig. 5.1) with a faint dotted line that presumably shows the path that he had taken on his tour of inspection. He found the rock on the Kapokberg that La Caille had described and mentioned that on the second peak from the north of the Kasteelberg 'there are the remains of an old pile of stones, having (about five feet to its N.W.) a considerable quantity of half-burned wood in a state of partial decay'. La Caille (1751) in his *Diverse Observations* gives some offsets, which were presumably the distances of his signal fires from the survey beacons, but Everest did not know about these.

Next he looked for La Caille's baseline. Using the angles from the western end of the base to Kapokberg, Kasteelberg and Klipfontein, he succeeded in locating a 'ridge of quartz rock, somewhat resembling marble in whiteness and lustre, [which] protrudes itself through the soil, and where the angles answered the given conditions'. There were no remaining signs of the exact spot. Following a line 27 degrees north of east, 'I was enabled, after several trials, to reach a small mound of raised earth [the eastern end] in the vicinity of Coggera [the present Kochra], where the angles...nearly corresponded with those taken from the plan; and though there are neither artificial nor natural marks to designate the site of the station, yet...little doubt remains in my mind of its being the point to be sought...'. The baseline had covered undulating and irregular land covered with brush and Everest doubted that a good measurement could have been made by the means in use in La Caille's time. According to him, the measuring rods should have been supported by 'Coffer's tripods',[2] an aid which did not then exist.

Everest finally visited the farm at Klipfontein where the northern end of the arc had been. He was accompanied by William Frederick Hertzog, the Assistant Surveyor General of the Cape.

> ...it may not be amiss to mention, that the daughter of the quon-dam proprietor, now an aged lady called Letchie Schalkeveck, is still in existence, and not only gives a narration perfectly agreeing, but has pointed out the very platform on which the granary [barn?] once stood; and states further, that the signal fires were so large and bril-liant, that those of Riebek's Castle were visible from Klip Fonteyn, a distance of more than forty-five miles, with the naked eye at night.

Letchie also remembered La Caille's little dog Grisgris by name, which added apparent authenticity to her account.

The platform mentioned was in Everest's time partly a threshing floor and partly the remains of a house foundation (see Fig. 6.3). It is the only man-made built feature in the area that is still there today.

La Caille had stated that he placed his signal fire 36 toises to the west of his observatory. Mrs Schalkeveck told him that his instrument (presumably the quadrant) was placed some paces in front of this. Everest then quite wrongly concluded in his ignorance of the scientific details that 'not only the signals in these operations were ill defined, but that the instrument for measuring horizontal angles was not placed over the centres of the stations'.

---

[2] Evidently a levelling device used in connection with baseline measurements.

Fig. 6.3 View from Klipfontein towards the west, over the threshing floor ('Corn floor', No. 9, on Fig. 6.8) which Everest thought was the site of La Caille's barn or granary and where Maclear later installed his instruments. Maclear's camp lower down is visible. From a lost drawing of 1842 by C.P. Smyth (McIntyre, 1951).

The latitudes of the ends of the arc

Next he considered the astronomical measurements that determined the latitudes of the northern and southern ends of the arc.

He pointed out that the Klipfontein site is surrounded from northeast to southwest by mountainous masses. 'It would be a work of extreme difficulty, if not of absolute impossibility, to calculate the attraction which they would be likely to exert upon the plumb-line ... if any such lateral attraction did exist, it would all lie on one side, and principally in a N.W. direction'.

The Cape Town end of the arc he located through the recollection of a 'female slave belonging to Mrs Hertzog' at No. 7, Strand Street.[3] She remembered that No. 2 had been the residence of Mr Bestbier but was now that of Mrs De Witt. 'But there is a mark in existence which furnishes another corroborating fact, namely, that a brass plate perforated with a small hole, and fixed horizontally in a vertical wall, with a black line traced immediately below it, for the obvious purpose of determining the sun's passage over the meridian, still stands at Mr. De Witt's house, and is said to have been placed there by the Abbé De La Caille' (see Fig. 6.4). By coincidence, the house where he himself was staying was next door.

---

[3] Slavery was abolished at the Cape in 1834.

Fig. 6.4 Nineteenth-century photograph of the wall of the kitchen wing of 2 Strand Street showing a type of sundial erected by La Caille and believed to have been of use in aligning his instruments (W. Cape Archives & Record Service M126).

He expressed doubt as to whether an observatory erected within a month by government workmen could have been substantial enough to be stable! Further, Table Mountain behind the town 'could not have existed so near to the site of the observatory without affecting the plumb-line of the instrument used by M. De La Caille in 1751, 1752.'

Everest's conclusions

Based on the earth's shape derived from the Bouguer-La Condamine (1738) result in Peru and that of Cassini III (1740) in France, which had in fact been, as mentioned, the work of La Caille, he estimated that the La Caille's measurement had to be in error because of a total deflection arising from the mountains at each end of 8.99 seconds of arc. This could be compared to La Condamine's measured but rather dubious deflection of 7.5 arcseconds caused by Chimboraçao in Peru. He concludes 'I think it must be admitted, that the measurement in this quarter of the globe is by far too dubious to establish the theory which would assign to the southern meridians a different ellipticity from that found to obtain in the northern hemisphere'.

It is interesting to note that, at the time of Everest's visit, plans were already afoot to erect the Royal Observatory, Cape of Good Hope. The first of His Majesty's Astronomers, Rev Fearon Fallows, arrived at the Cape on 12 August 1821 and was referred to by Everest as 'My excellent friend, Mr Fallows'. They certainly met and discussed the idea of re-measuring the La Caille Arc.

Everest felt that, while a repeat of La Caille's observations could be made, it would merely serve to satisfy curiosity and have no useful purpose. Instead, it would be much better to make a new series of triangles extending far northwards towards Namaqualand and covering about 4 degrees of latitude. This would set the question 'for ever at rest' by avoiding the problems associated with the nearby mountains.

No doubt thinking of the difficulties he had experienced in India, he continued:

> In no country indeed could a datum of this nature and of equal importance be obtained with less personal toil and suffering to the individuals engaged in it; for the climate is perhaps without a parallel on earth, the face of the country presents no appalling difficulties, and there is a degree of hospitality and readiness to oblige on the part of the colonists in general, which would render a sojourn amongst them highly pleasing and satisfactory.

Everest probably only departed from the Cape at the end of October. He resumed his interrupted Indian career, though he continued to be plagued by periods of ill-health. He retired in 1843, after which he returned to England. There he married a lady 33 years his junior in 1846 and had six children. A late milestone in his life was the conferring of a knighthood in 1861. He died in 1866 and was buried in Hove, Sussex.

Fallows, in spite of Everest's remarks, was enthusiastic about the idea of re-measuring the arc and applied for additional instruments such as a theodolite, a zenith sector, measuring chains and the necessary Coffer's tripods (Warner 1995). Unfortunately he was not a good lobbyist and his request was turned down. Thus the matter rested until the arrival of the third HM Astronomer, Thomas Maclear (Fig. 6.5).

Fig. 6.5 Thomas Maclear as a young man (Professor Brian Warner).

Thomas Maclear

Maclear was HM Astronomer at the Cape during the years 1833 to 1870. Around 1838 he visited the sites associated with La Caille in the hope of identifying the precise positions of his survey stations.

Later, the formidable Astronomer Royal, G.B. Airy, took a close interest in the project, obtaining the services of Captain Alexander Henderson of the Royal Engineers and a number of sappers and miners to help Maclear in conducting survey operations. Maclear also managed to borrow 14 soldiers from the garrison in Cape Town.

To measure latitudes, a venerable zenith sector was borrowed from the Royal Greenwich Observatory. This was the original instrument that had been used in 1729 by Bradley in his discovery of the aberration of light (see Chapter 1, Programme of research). It was a heavy, rather clumsy, instrument that required a great deal of effort to move around and set up. It was capable of exceptional precision but required delicate handling.

The survey equipment available to Maclear was much more precise than La Caille's and used the latest techniques of the time. The rods for measuring the baselines were specially commissioned and were supported on adjustable stands rather than being placed on the ground as in La Caille's time. The triangulations were made with state-of-the-art theodolites.

A new baseline close to La Caille's was measured by Maclear between 30 October 1840 and 3 April 1841. Over the next few years, from October 1841 to March 1848, he performed a geodetic survey incorporating, as suggested by Everest, La Caille's points but extending further north and south to cover a total arc of 4° 37′.

His overall geodetic result was to show that the southern hemisphere was not significantly less curved than the northern one. However, in the following discussion, we will concentrate on his re-measurement of La Caille's arc.

Maclear and the site of La Caille's observatory

To confirm Everest's identification of the site of La Caille's Cape Town observatory and get a more exact position for it, he had the Deeds Office in Cape Town searched for Bestbier's name (Maclear 1840). He was able to construct a complete history of the property at No. 2, Strand Street (formerly Zeestraat). It had been granted by Governor van der Stel in 1701 to one Johannes Blankenberg and had been transferred to Jan Laurens[4] Bestbier in 1737. He in turn[5] was succeeded by Arend de Waal in 1766 and Petrus Johannes de Witt in 1794. Finally the property had been transferred to Johannes Henricus de Witt in 1797. The widow of the last-mentioned was still living there.

La Caille had remarked that:

> The corner of the street called Heerenstreet, in Cape Town, is at 73 degrees East of South from the east corner of the Observatory, at a distance of 111½ feet [36.22 m]. It is easily distinguished [when viewed from his beacon at Kasteelberg], being whitewashed, and projected against the wall of the large workshop of the Company, which is painted black and very high.

The dark VOC workshops (seen in Fig. 2.6) had burnt down in 1798 and been replaced by this time, but Maclear assumed that the existing building occupied the same ground plan. He was then able to pinpoint the position of the Observatory in Mrs de Witt's yard and enter it on a map he had made (see Fig. 6.6) of the city block. The sundial arrangement noted by Everest (see Fig. 6.4) on the kitchen wall running northeast was still there. What were probably unobstructed gardens in La Caille's time had gradually become encrusted with small houses and the site of the observatory had been covered by a warehouse. Waterkant Street now ran along the sea end of the properties and a guardhouse had

---

[4] Spelling as given by Maclear.
[5] Bestbier died in 1754; his widow married Jacobus Blankenberg.

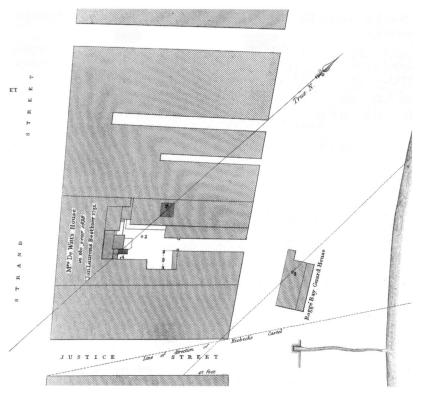

Fig. 6.6 Diagram of the city block around the site of La Caille's observatory in 1838. The dark hatched square shows its calculated position. The shoreline is to the right. Justice Street is now part of Adderley Street (extracted from Maclear, 1866).

been built on the sea side of that. Those familiar with present-day Cape Town should note that since his time Justice Street has been widened to form an extension to the Heerengracht and St George's Street has been driven right through the city block shown on Maclear's map. In the twentieth century, Rogge Bay was filled in to allow the City to expand seawards.

Maclear set up the Bradley sector in Mrs de Witt's yard to measure the latitude of La Caille's observatory but soon found this to be less than an ideal situation, being very cramped and sandy. Later, he moved it to the Rogge Bay guardhouse (see Fig. 6.6) nearby, which was more satisfactory. Using survey techniques, he also derived the coordinates of La Caille's observatory from those of the Royal Observatory a few kilometres away.

In 1845, Mrs de Witt died and the new owner of the property made alterations to the warehouse, built in 1798, that covered the site of La Caille's observatory. Maclear (1866, pp. 411–12) obtained permission to excavate the floor of this building but found nothing that seemed to

Fig. 6.7 View from Maclear's 'Signal Rock' on Kapokberg, towards the south. The author is sitting on La Caille's beacon rock, now heavily overgrown, though about 2 m high. Table Mountain is seen faintly in the distance (Photo: H. Glass, July 2011).

relate to La Caille. He did, however, find a 'dressed block of gneiss' on the other side of the yard which he thought might have been the support for the latter's quadrant. This he removed and used to support an instrument in what is now the photoheliograph dome at the Royal Observatory.[6]

The mountain beacons

The station on Kapokberg (see Fig. 6.7) seems to have been visited several times by Maclear's team in the years 1842 to 1847 (see Maclear 1866, p. 446). Maclear at first identified the wrong rock (called by him the 'Signal Rock') as having been used by La Caille. His measurements were made from a mark placed at this position. A heliostat was used to make his station visible to observers at the comparatively distant northern and southern termini of the La Caille arc. Later Maclear realised his mistake: the real La Caille rock was about 128 English feet (39 m) from the Signal Rock at an azimuth of about 158°. He measured the distance between the two points with care so as to be able to reduce his observations to La Caille's rock for comparison purposes[7].

> The signals on the triangulating points of Riebeck's Castel and Capoc Berg are easily recognised, and are well described by Captain Everest. I covered over the charcoal remnant of the signal fire on Riebeck's Castel with stones,[8] previously abstracting a portion as an interesting relic. The top of this rugged mountain offers nothing inviting to visitors; the ascent is laborious and difficult: hence the reason why the signal remained

[6] No obvious trace of the block remains.

[7] The Signal Rock and La Caille's beacon (as identified by Maclear, see Figs. 3.4 and 6.7) may still be recognised, though with difficulty since they are both now overgrown by dense bush about 2m high. Maclear's mark on the Signal Rock is covered by a stone platform on which now stands a Trigonometrical Survey beacon.

[8] A bottle of charcoal from La Caille's fire is kept in the Astronomical Museum at the South African Astronomical Observatory.

undisturbed, and we were able to enjoy the sight of one undeniable mark of La Caille's work (Maclear 1866, pp. 19–20).

The summit of the Kasteelberg used by La Caille consists of several rocks separated by fissures. Maclear chose to leave La Caille's pile of stones undisturbed and to make his measurements from a nearby rock that offered more space for his theodolite tent. His measurements were made from February to April 1842 (Maclear 1866 pp. 452–3).

La Caille's pile was unfortunately dismantled by the South African Trigonometric Survey when they established a beacon on the site in the early twentieth century (Warner and Rourke, 1990).

Maclear's observations at La Caille's northern terminal

The precise situation of the northern terminal at Klipfontein was much more difficult to determine. Maclear questioned Mr Hertzog, the surveyor who had accompanied Everest, about his visit to Klipfontein and was able to borrow some drawings made by him at that time. When he saw the platform or threshing floor described by Everest as the location of La Caille's granary (barn?) he compared its dimensions with La Caille's statement and noted its distance from the oldest house. He strongly doubted the identification since normally a granary was built near the farmer's dwelling house.

> I beg it to be understood, that I by no means undervalue Captain Everest's exertions ..., but without charging the inhabitants with a desire to mislead, I may state that a longer residence in this colony has taught me that, in their readiness to afford an affirmative answer on all occasions, they are apt to affect a knowledge of circumstances which they do not possess (Maclear 1866, p. 4).

It was found that very little still existed that was likely to have been there in La Caille's time. Similarly today, there is very little that can be identified with the items on Maclear's map from around 1838. Only the threshing floor that he used as a platform for his measurements and which is the site of a monument to his efforts, a spring and some remains of a ditch that carried water to the houses can be distinguished.

He spoke to a certain Jerrit Coetzee (Gerrit Coetzee) (see Chapter 3, footnote 10) who informed him that the foundation overlapping the threshing floor had been that of his father's house and that the granary had been to the east of it, close to the foot of the hill. It emerged that Everest's witness, Mrs Schalkeveck, was the daughter of a tenant, Oker van Schalkeveck, who had lived in another house, also demolished.

The people that Maclear found at Klipfontein were extremely poor and the property had changed hands many times since La Caille's time (see Maclear 1866, p. 16, footnote). It is quite likely that when a building became too old or was no longer needed, its bricks and other building materials were taken away and re-cycled, since they were relatively valuable. By questioning as many locals as he could find and by setting a group of sappers to work on excavating various ruins, he was able to locate what he believed to have been the foundations of the house of Oker van Schalkeveck. To the west he excavated a small mound and found there the stone and clay foundations of a building 22 × 12 (English) feet which he identified with the granary used by La Caille for his sector. It is marked on Fig. 6.8 as 13. The site of the signal fire, according to La Caille, was 36 toises (70.2 m) further to the west, which fell in Maclear's time in a ploughed field (15). At the end of his operations at Klipfontein, he had the excavations covered up again to preserve the foundations for any possible future investigation (this was unusually far-sighted for the time!). Maclear then took 13 to be the defining northern point of La Caille's survey and reduced his later measurements to that point. Fig. 6.9 gives a general view of the area.

He set up Bradley's sector and the Dollond Repeating Circle that he was using on the Corn floor (9) that was part of Coetzee's farmhouse ruin, the place that Everest thought was La Caille's granary station. This was a large firm circular area formed of hard pot-clay and offering a solid foundation for the instruments. It is marked on Fig. 6.8 and still exists (2011).

The conclusion (Maclear 1866, p. 111) from Maclear's measurement of the latitude with Bradley's sector was that the astronomical length of the La Caille arc was 1° 13′ 17″.12, which can be compared to La Caille's (revised) value of 1°13′17″.5. Maclear here took the Abbé's observatory to be the southern point and, as mentioned, the spot marked 13 on the map (Fig. 6.8) to be the northern point.[9]

> Although this work does not clear up the anomaly of La Caille's arc, it redounds to the credit of that justly distinguished astronomer, that with his means, and in his day, his result from 16 stars is almost identical with that from 1133 observations on 40 stars made with a powerful and celebrated instrument.

Of course, the mountains affected Maclear's plumb lines in exactly the same way that they did in La Caille's case.

Maclear's baseline

To carry out the ground-based survey Maclear had to set up an impeccably correct baseline.

---

[9] Reminder: one second of arc corresponds to 30.1 m on the ground.

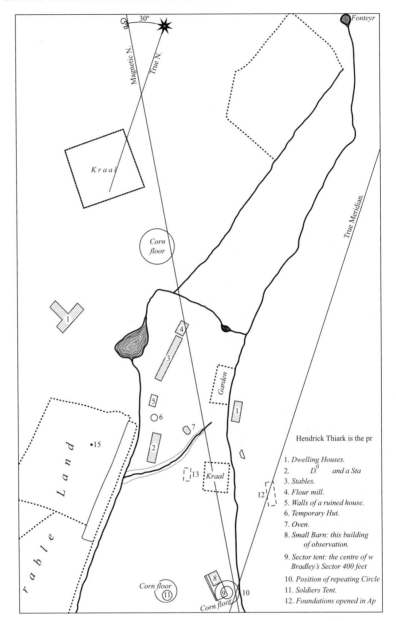

The following labels appear within the figure:

30°

Fonteyr

Magnetic N.

True N.

True Meridian.

Kraal

Corn floor

Kraal

1

4

3

Garden

1

5

○6

7

2

•15

arable Land

13 Kraal

12

Hendrick Thiark is the pr

1. *Dwelling Houses.*
2. *D⁰ and a Sta*
3. *Stables.*
4. *Flour mill.*
5. *Walls of a ruined house.*
6. *Temporary Hut.*
7. *Oven.*
8. *Small Barn: this building of observation.*
9. *Sector tent: the centre of w Bradley's Sector 400 feet*
10. *Position of repeating Circle*
11. *Soldiers Tent.*
12. *Foundations opened in Ap*

8

10

Corn floor

⑪

Corn floor

Fig. 6.8 Part of Maclear's (1866) diagram of Klipfontein around 1840. Everest took the spot marked 'Corn floor', No. 9, (centre bottom) to be the site of La Caille's sector. Maclear at first thought it was at the spot marked 13 (to the left of 'Kraal'), which he excavated. Later, however, he decided that it was at 2, then occupied by a house (See Fig. 6.9). Only the 'Fonteyn' (spring) at the top of the map, some of the ditch leading from it and the 'Corn floor' at the bottom are still extant.

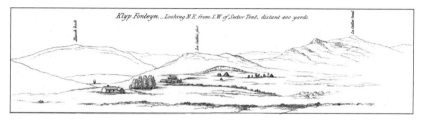

Klyp Fonteyn. – Looking N.E. from S.W. of Sector Tent, distant 400 yards.

Fig. 6.9 Drawing of Klipfontein made by a member of Maclear's expedition. The artist's position was to the left of the area shown on the map (Fig. 6.8). The bigger tent was on the 'Corn floor' and contained Bradley's sector. 'House 2' is to the right of the trees (Maclear, 1866).

He located the terminals of La Caille's Swartland base, 'by a series of tentative operations' (Maclear 1866 p. 233), i.e. by trial and error, using La Caille's published bearings towards Kapokberg and the Kasteelberg. They turned out to be inconspicuous small mounds without any surviving markers. The white quartzite of the western terminal provided confirmation that he had found the right place as it was probably the 'white marble' referred to by La Caille. However, he stated that the terrain of La Caille's baseline passed over water in one place and sandy and spongy ground in another, so that he had to choose a slightly different line.

The line that he eventually chose started 462 yards (422 m) south-west of La Caille's western terminal and passed through it. 'As viewed from the west end, the line is more inclined to the north than La Caille's by about two degrees'. Its east end was about 520 yards (475 m) from La Caille's 'on the same undulation' (Maclear 1866, p. 234).

To help with the measurement he obtained the services of Lieut Cust, a non-commissioned officer, and twelve men. At the conclusion of the work, small masonry pyramids were erected at each end to form permanent markers. The pyramids are still in existence today. Table 6.1 summarises the positions of the main beacons used by La Caille.

Comparison with La Caille's work

The results of Maclear's triangulation, carried out over the next few years, showed that the three angles of La Caille's southern triangle, connecting La Caille's Observatory, Kapok Berg and Kasteelberg, were respectively $+8''.0$, $-2''.2$ and $-5''.8$ arcseconds different from his own values. This was acceptable because they were well within the expected observational errors.

However, the three angles of the northern triangle, connecting Klipfontein, Kapokberg and Kasteelberg, differed much more from Maclear's measurements, namely by $+29''.4$, $-72''.6$ and $+43''.2$. Because his values had been based on the assumption that the foundations he had located were the true site of La Caille's granary, Maclear had to admit that he might have been in error and that the site might not have been identified correctly. According to him (Maclear 1866, p. 616), the differences in the angles meant that the true site of the granary was most likely within the house marked 2, erected in about 1820 as an outhouse. Like almost every other building on his map, this one no longer exists and only an archaeological investigation could settle the question.

Finally, quite independently of anything to do with La Caille, Maclear compared the latitudes of the Royal Observatory and those of the Sector Station (i.e. his incorrect position for the granary) at Klipfontein, as determined astronomically by him and by his triangulation involving stations to the south of Table Mountain and far to the north of the Piketberg. These measurements should have been unaffected by the mountain masses. He concluded that Table Mountain had deflected La Caille's plumblines by $1''.36$ and the Piketberg by $7''.19$ and that this explained his anomalous result (Maclear, 1866, p. 625).

In a section called *Discussion of La Caille's Measure*, Maclear (1866, p. 623) found that La Caille's measurement of the distance from Kapokberg to Kasteelberg was 44.6 English feet (13.6 m) too long. If this is true, his measurement of his base had to have been 2.1245 toises (or 4.14 m) too long, or one part in 3044. Similarly, his measurement of length of the arc of meridian was 144 feet (43.9 m) too great.

Maclear's report was published only about 20 years after his campaign. It is a massive work, in two volumes, without an index. Isaac Todhunter, a well-known Cambridge mathematician, published an article in Monthly Notices of the Royal Astronomical Society (Todhunter, 1872) which was highly critical of this publication, finding it to be

Table 6.1 Positions of various stations determined by Maclear (1866), p. 589.

Station	Latitude	Longitude[1]
La Caille's Obsy	$-33° 55' 16''.07$	$+0° 3' 13''.86$
Riebeek Casteel	$-33° 20' 53''.707$	$-0° 21' 25''.020$
Kapoc Berg	$-33° 25' 05''.874$	$+0° 4' 47''.81$
Royal Observatory	$-33° 56' 3''.2$	$0° 0' 0''.0$
East end of base[2]	$-33° 13' 55''.650$	$-0° 1' 52''.270$
West end of base[2]	$-33° 16' 9''.995$	$+0° 6' 6''.994$

Note 1: The longitudes were referred to the centre of the Transit Instrument of the Royal Observatory. The longitude of the Airy Transit was determined in 1926 from radio time signals to be $18°28'38''.940$ (Horrocks, 1927). The declination of the same instrument was $-33°$ 56 03.5. However, it could be that Maclear was referring to the earlier Troughton transit instrument about $0''.6$ to the west of this.

Note 2: Refers to Maclear's Swartland base.

diffuse and inconsistent. He claimed that it did not address the issue of its title, the Verification of La Caille's Arc, at all sufficiently.

One is left with the impression that Maclear was less clear in his thoughts and plans than La Caille. La Caille was a better planner. The effort expended and the accuracy of the observations were much better judged in relation to his aims than were Maclear's. Though Maclear does seem to have achieved what he set out to do, he went overboard on details, costing him and his team huge effort.

A modern determination of Maclear's baseline and the coordinates of the sites on Kapokberg and Kasteelberg using the Global Positioning Satellites would not be very difficult and would enable a check to be made of the accuracy of the work of both these astronomers.

Appendix 1
Astronomical terms

DECLINATION

The *Declination* of a star is analogous to geographical latitude and it is the angle between the celestial equator and the star, measured in the direction of the north or south pole. It is given in degrees, arcminutes and arcseconds

EPOCH

Because the apparent positions of stars change with time due to precession, aberration and nutation it is usual when making a catalogue to specify a particular date, called the *Epoch*, to which all entries have been reduced.

KEPLER'S LAWS

Kepler's laws are:

  I. The planets revolve in ellipses with the Sun at one focus.
  II. The line between a planet and the Sun sweeps out equal areas in equal times.
  III. The square of the period of revolution of a planet is proportional to the cube of its mean orbital radius.

MERIDIAN

The *Meridian* is an imaginary line in the sky joining the celestial poles and passing through the zenith of a particular place.

PARALLAX

The *Parallax* of a star is the angle, as viewed from it, subtended by the radius of the *earth's orbit*. It is measured, for example, by photographing a nearby star against the background of much more distant stars on two occasions six months apart. Knowing the size of the earth's orbit, the distance of the star can then be be worked out.

The *Parallax* of a solar system object is the angle, as viewed from it, subtended by the *earth's radius*. It is measured, for example, by photographing the object against the starry background from two well-separated points on the earth's surface simultaneously. Knowing the earth's radius, the distance can be worked out.

PRECESSION

The axis of the earth is not fixed in space but moves in a circle of angular radius about $23\frac{1}{2}°$ over a period of about 25,800 years. This movement is called *Precession* and is a much larger effect than the axial nutation discovered by Bradley and described in Chapter 1, Programme of research.

RIGHT ASCENSION

The *Right Ascension* of a star is analogous to its geographic longitude. It is simply the exact time, measured by a sidereal clock, when it is seen to cross the meridian, i.e. when it goes from the eastern side of the sky to the west due to the rotation of the earth. It is measured in hours, minutes and seconds.

SIDEREAL TIME

Just as ordinary time is given by the rotation of the earth beneath the Sun, *Sidereal time* is given by the rotation of the earth beneath the stars. A sidereal day is about four minutes shorter than a solar day because the earth goes around the Sun in 365 days.

ZENITH

The *Zenith* is the direction straight up from a particular place.

Appendix 2
Currency and length conversions

Money

The value of money in the eighteenth century is hard to estimate realistically. La Caille's salary of 500 livres per annum seems to have been only about that of an *average* French worker.

At the Cape, the Governor received 3400 guilders per year including allowances; a skilled worker perhaps 200 (Mentzel **1**), which translates to about 1200 French livres if Mentzel's exchange rate (quoted later in this section) is correct. Such people were probably better paid than they would have been in Europe. Dutch rates of pay were in addition high compared to the rest of Europe.

According to Mentzel (**2**, p. 90) 'a strong and healthy slave can be purchased at a price varying from 80 to 120 Rds'. The hire of a slave cost 4 Rds per month, plus his food and tobacco, but not his clothes.

FRENCH

1 Louis d'or = 24 livres
1 écu = 6 livres
1 French pound (livre) = 20 sous or sols
The economist Quesnay writing around 1760 took 500 livres per annum as the income of the average worker.

DUTCH

1 Cape Rijksdaalder (Rd) = 48 stuivers
1 Dutch guilder = 20 stuivers
1 Skilling (schelling) = 6 stuivers
1 Stuiver = 4 duit(en) in VOC territories

SPANISH

Piastres or pieces of eight

EXCHANGE RATE

In Chapter 4, LaCaille's *Remarks:*
    In 4. Vegetables and Fruits there is the statement that 2 local sous = 4 French ones. 'Local sous' must be another name for stuivers.
    In 6. Economy of Farming 1 shilling (skilling) = 12 French sols (or sous).

Mentzel **1**, p. 29 states that 1 Piastre = 1 Rijksdalder.

In the letter quoted in 14, Wine, La Caille states that 46 $\frac{4}{9}$ Piastres is equivalent to 242 livres and 10 sous in French money. Using the other rate information given above, it should have been 222 French livres. Probably there were variations with time of the exchange rates, which would explain the discrepancy.

Linear measure

The following table shows the relation between the old French units of linear measure and modern ones:

Table A2.1 Linear measure

French unit	Modern equivalent
Toise (fathom)	1.949 m
Pied (foot)	0.3248 m
Pouce (inch)	2.706 cm
Ligne (line)	2.256 mm

Appendix 3
Note on the *Journal Historique*

———◦◦◦◦———

The Observatoire de Paris manuscript C3 26 is a leather-bound notebook, some of whose right-hand pages are numbered. It has never been printed in full, either in French or in translation. The whole notebook is written in La Caille's usually tidy hand, though there are frequent corrections and insertions.

It contains the following items:

(a) *Journal Historique de mon Voyage au Cap de Bonne Esperance avec les Rémarques et Réflexions faites en diverses occasions* (Historic Journal of my Voyage to the Cape of Good Hope with the Remarks and Reflections made on various occasions).

At first the *Journal* was written only on the right-side pages and the left-side were blank. The latter were often used for insertions which seem to have been written after the actual *Journal*. Later, both sides were made use of.

Opposite page 4 is a list *Essay d'observations de longitude* (Attempted observations of longitude).

Opposite page 23 is a short memo *Raisons qui m'ont déterminé a entreprendre le catalogue general des Etoiles Comprises entre le Pole Australe et le Tropique du Capricorn* (Reasons that made me decide to undertake the general catalogue of stars between the South Pole and the Tropic of Capricorn.).

(b) *Copie du Discours remis au M. le Governeur du Cap. Sur la Mésure du 34 degré de Latitude Australe* (Copy of the Discourse sent to the Governor of the Cape. On the Measurement of the 34rd degree of Southern Latitude), (3pp).

(c) *Discours Sur Mon Voyage au Cap de Bonne Esperance Pour etre lu à une Assemblée publique de L'Académie* (Discourse On My Voyage to the Cape of Good Hope to be read at a public Assembly of the Academy), (12pp).

(d) *Observations Géodésiques* (Geodesic Observations), (5pp). These are the same as the relevant section in La Caille (1751, p. 425).

(e) Notes about the Cape (no heading, 7pp). In printed French *Journal*.

(f) *Notes et réflexions critiques Sur la description du Cap de Bonne-Esperance par P. Kolbe* (Notes and critical Reflections on the Description of the Cape of Good Hope by P. Kolbe), (6pp). These were also in the printed French Journal.

(g) *Observations Meteorologiques faites pendant mon Séjour au Cap: avec les reflexions et les conclusions que j'en ai deduit* (Meteorological Observations made during my sojourn at the Cape: with the reflections and the conclusions I have deduced from them).

JOURNAL

HISTORIQUE

DU VOYAGE

FAIT AU CAP

DE

BONNE-ESPÉRANCE.

Par Feu

M. l'Abbé DE LA CAILLE,

DE L'ACADÉMIE DES SCIENCES;

*Précédé d'un Difcours fur la Vie de l'Auteur,
fuivi de remarques & de réflexions fur les Cou-
tumes des Hottentots & des Habitans du Cap.*

AVEC FIGURES.

A PARIS,

Chez GUILLYN, Libraire, Quai des Auguftins,
près le Pont S. Michel, au Lys d'or.

M. DCC. LXIII.

Avec Approbation & Privilége du Roi.

Fig. A3.1 Title page of the first printing of La Caille's *Journal Historique* ... (Courtesy University of Cape Town).

A version of the *Journal Historique* and La Caille's accompanying remarks was edited by his friend and colleague, the Abbé Claude Carlier, Sous-Maître (under-master) of the Collège Mazarin, where he taught. It is evident that, though Carlier was an important historian and also a scientist (agronomist), he was not knowledgeable about astronomical matters and had a tendency to embellish 'facts' in general. His edition, which omitted a number of passages, as well as numerical data about longitudes, latitudes and magnetic observations, was published after La Caille's death, by Guillyn (Paris) in 1763 (See Fig. A3.1). It was reprinted 'chez Nyon aîné' in 1776 (La Caille 1776). It commences with the biography already mentioned. Also included were a set of unreliable remarks, supposedly derived from the Abbé's conversations, on the customs of the indigenous people of the Cape, then called Hottentots. Some irrelevant material from other sources was interspersed in the text, though this is distinguished by quotation marks. A German edition appeared in 1776 (Taton 1978).

The modern translation by Raven-Hart (1976) was based on the printed *Journal*. Although Evans (1992) worked from the manuscript he also did not include the numerical data. The placing of some of the later interpolated text must necessarily be somewhat arbitrary as it was not always precisely specified.

In the National Library of South Africa (Cape Town) there is a translation by Mrs E. Melck *Lacaille: Historical journal of the voyage made to the Cape of Good Hope (1750–53): Accompanied by Notes and reflections upon Kolbe's work by Lacaille*. This I have not examined.

Appendix 4
Timeline

———◦◦◦———

15 March 1713: birth
School at Mantes sur Seine
1729: Rhetoric and philosophy at the College of Lisieux
1732–36: Theology at the College of Navarre
1736–40: Paris Observatory
1738–1742: Paris Meridian survey
1739: appointed to chair of Mathematics, Collège Mazarin
8 May 1741: Adjunct Astronomer, Royal Academy of Sciences
1745: Associate Astronomer, Royal Academy of Sciences
21 Oct 1750: leaves Paris for Cape
25 Jan 1751–22 Feb 1751: in Rio de Janeiro
20 Apr 1751: arrives at Cape
6 Aug 1751–18 July 1752: sky survey
9 Sept 1752–2 Nov 1752: measures earth's radius
8 March 1753: leaves Cape
18 April 1743–16 Jan 1754: in Mauritius
22 Feb 1754–27 Feb 1754: on Réunion
15 Apr 1754–19 April 1754: on Ascension
28 June 1754: return to Paris
21 March 1762: death.

Appendix 5
Sources and acknowledgements

The main sources of information on the life of La Caille are: (a) a biographical introduction to the eighteenth century French printed version of his diary or *Journal Historique* by his friend and colleague, the Abbé Claude Carlier, (b) a lengthy section of Delambre's *History of Astronomy in the Eighteenth Century* (1827), concentrating on his astronomical contributions[1], (c) a eulogy by Jean-Paul Grandjean de Fouchy (1762), Permanent Secretary of the Royal Academy of Sciences and one of his earliest supporters, (d) another eulogy by his ex-pupil Jean Sylvain Bailly (1770), (e) a further eulogy in Latin by Gabriel Brotier in La Caille's (1763) posthumous catalogue of southern stars already mentioned and (f) a small number of personal letters that have survived.

A useful summary of La Caille's science was published in modern times by Armitage (1956) and a highly detailed account of the problems that occupied eighteenth-century astronomers and La Caille in particular has been given by Wilson (1980a,b). It is the latter writer who demonstrates most clearly how the developments in celestial mechanics of the time were keyed into physical reality by the precise observations of La Caille and his colleagues. Several issues relevant to this book are addressed in Taton & Wilson (1995).

La Caille's private philosophy is revealed by the introductions to his various textbooks and in a public lecture on the progress of astronomy that he gave at the Royal Academy of Sciences in 1761, just a few months before he died.

An inventory of his publications and manuscripts was published by Taton (1978). The manuscripts of most of La Caille's printed works are in the Archives of the Institut de France and the Paris Observatory. However, his letters have not yet been catalogued. Taton also lists references to La Caille in the minutes (Procès-Verbaux) of the Royal Academy of Sciences, which still exist. Not all of his publications are referred to in this book. Not mentioned by Taton are a letter to de la Condamine of 1754 in the National Library of South Africa, Cape Town, and a notebook containing data from his Cape expedition and other matters in the library of the University of the Witwatersrand, Johannesburg.

---

[1] Delambre was a fervent admirer of the Abbé and a harsh critic of many other eighteenth century astronomers.

Most of what we know about his visit to the Cape comes from the manuscript *Journal Historique*,[2] in the Abbé's own handwriting, that still exists in the library of the Paris Observatory. Further details are given in Appendix 3.

A later writer on the Cape was Otto Mentzel (1785, 1787) who had visited long before La Caille, namely during the years 1733 to 1741, but who wrote his own account many years afterwards. He agreed with the Abbé's low opinion of a book on the Cape written by Peter Kolbe (1719), a Prussian visitor in the years 1705–1713, but felt he had sometimes been too harshly critical and had even perpetrated further inaccuracies.

In my translations of the Abbé's work I have made occasional use of the publications by Evans (1992) and Raven-Hart (1976). The Abbé's sentences were often very long, interspersed with colons and semi-colons, and I have sometimes split them up to make them easier to grasp. My interpolated comments are enclosed in square brackets.

Though some measures have been translated into metric ones (see Appendix 2), others (inches, feet, toises) have been left as the original French amounts (i.e. pouces, pieds and toises) if not critical to the text.

The Abbé's scientific results were usually published in the annual Memoirs of the Royal Academy of Sciences. The references in the present text are to the dates on which the work was presented and not to those of publication, which could be several years later. The latter are given in square brackets [ ] in the bibliography. I have also given page references in the text because in some years La Caille published more than one paper and this seemed the least cumbersome way to refer to them.

Proper names are sometimes quoted with strange spellings. For example, Maclear's 'Letchie Schalkeveck' was probably better known to her friends as Letjie Schalkwyk. Usually I have left them in the original form. La Caille[3] himself wrote his name as 'Lacaille' at the ends of his letters though he used 'de La Caille' in his publications.

I have made use of material in the following libraries and archives: Bibliothèque Saint-Geneviève, Paris, Fehr Collection (Cape Town Castle), Gallica.bnf.fr (web site), Institut de France, Paris, National Library of South Africa, Cape Town, Observatoire de Paris, South African Astronomical Observatory, University of Cape Town, University of Kyoto, Walters Museum, Philadelphia, www.clairaut.com and and the Western Cape Archives and Records Service, I thank the relevant archivists and librarians for their help.

I also thank John Rennie (Architect) and Dr Antonia Malan for historical information about Cape Town. Marina Musi, Osservatorio Astronomico 'G.D. Maraldi', Perinaldo, is thanked for the portrait of J.-D. Maraldi. Professor Brian Warner (University of Cape Town) is thanked for images and Dr Olivier Courcelle (Versailles) for an image and certain information.

---

[2] Full title in translation: *Historical Journal of the Voyage made to the Cape of Good Hope by the Abbé de La Caille*. Bibliothèque de l'Observatoire de Paris, ms C3 26.
[3] 'Caille' is French for quail (the bird).

Early versions of the manuscript have been read by several people. Dr Dan Sleigh (Pinelands, Cape) made several corrections and has provided information about Jan Lourens Bestbier, La Caille's landlord at the Cape and guide to the Swartland. J.R. Smith, Editor of *Survey Review* and Professor James Lequeux, Observatoire de Paris, have also suggested improvements and corrected some errors.

Appendix 6
Bibliography

Notes: In the cases of the Histoire and Mémoires of the Académie Royale des Sciences, two dates are given. The first is usually the year that the work concerned was accepted for publication and the second is the year in which it was actually printed.

When two papers by La Caille are from the same year, the page numbers reveal which is being referred to.

Alder, K., 2002. *The Measure of All Things*, Free Press, New York.

Allen, C.W., 1963. *Astrophysical Quantities*, Second Edition, Athlone Press, London.

Anon., 1751 [1755]. Sur Plusieurs Observations Astronomiques, Géographiques et Physiques, Fait au Cap de Bonne-espérance. *Hist. Acad. Roy. des Sci.*, 158–169. This was a summary of La Caille's article appearing in the Mémoires on pp. 519–536.

Armitage, A., 1956. The Astronomical Work of Nicolas-Louis de Lacaille, *Annals of Science*, **12**, 163–191.

Baily, F., 1847. *A Catalogue of 9766 stars in the Southern hemisphere, for the beginning of the year 1750, from the observations of the Abbé de Lacaille, made at the Cape of Good Hope in the years 1751 and 1752, reduced... under the immediate superintendence of the late professor Henderson...*, R. and J.-E. Taylor, London.

Bailly, S., 1770. Éloge de M. L'Abbé de la Caille, in *Éloges de Charles V, de Corneille, de l'Abbé de La Caille et de Leibnitz*, Chez Delalain, Paris, 99–128.

Bell, M.S., 2005. *Lavoisier in the Year One*, Norton, New York.

Bernardin de Saint-Pierre (1773) *Journey to Mauritius*, tr. Wilson, J., 2002. Signal Books, Oxford.

Bernoulli J., 1771. *Lettres Astronomiques où l'on Donne une Idée de l'État Actuel de l'Astronomie Practique dans Plusieurs Villes de l'Europe*, Chez l'auteur, Berlin.

Bigourdan, G., 1895. Variétés. Lacaille et l'invention du micromètre circulaire, *Bulletin Astronomique*, Serie 1, **12**, 366–368.

Bigourdan, G., 1919. L'Observatoire du Collège Mazarin, aujourd'hui palais de l'Institut, *Comptes Rendus de l'Académie des Sciences*, **169**, 264–269.

Boncompagni, B. de), 1894. Lettere di Alessio Claudio Clairaut, *Atti dell'Accademia Pontifica dei Nuovi Lincei*, **45**, 233–291.

Boquet, F., 1913. La Bicentenaire de Lacaille, *L'Astronomie*, **27**, 457–473.

Bouguer, M., 1749. *La Figure de la Terre…*, Charles-Antoine Jombert, Paris.

Bradley, J., 1728. An Account of a new discovered Motion of the Fix'd Stars, *Phil. Trans. Roy. Soc.*, **35**, 637–661.

Bradley, J., 1748. An apparent Motion observed in some Fixed Stars, *Phil. Trans. Roy. Soc.*, **45**, 1–43.

Brice, G., 1725. *Nouvelle description de la Ville de Paris, et de tout ce qu'elle continent de plus remarquable*, 8th edition, Vol. 1, Gandouin & Fournier, Paris.

Brown, L.A., 1980. *The Story of Maps*, Dover Publications, New York.

Carlier, 1763 & 1776. See La Caille, 1763 & 1776.

Cassini de Thury, J.-D., 1740 [1744]. La Meridienne de l'Observatoire Royal de Paris Vérifiée dans toute l'étendue du Royaume par de Nouvelles Observations. *Suite Mém. Acad. Roy. des Sci.,* 1740.

Cassini de Thury, J.-D., La Caille, N.-L., Maraldi, G.-D., 1738 [1740]. Sur la Propagation du Son. *Mém. Acad. Roy. des Sci.*, 128–146.

Cavendish, H., 1798. Experiments to determine the Density of the Earth, *Phil. Trans. Roy. Soc. London*, (part II), 469–526.

Clémencet, Charles et al., 1750. *L'Art de Vérifier les dates des Faits Historiques…*, Desprez & Cavelier, Paris.

Danjon, A. & Fischer de Cugnac, L.-M., 1962. Deuxième Centenaire de la Mort de la Caille et Rétablissement de son Monument a Rumigny le 30 Juin 1962, *L'Astronomie*, **76**, 239–249.

Dapper, O., ten Rhyn, W. and de Grevenbroek, J.G., 1933. *The early Cape Hottentots*, eds. Schapera, I. and Farrington, B., Van Riebeeck Society, Series 1, Vol. 12, Cape Town.

Delambre, Jean Baptiste Joseph, 1827. *Hist. de l'Astronomie au dix-huitième Siècle*, edited by Claude-Louis Mathieu, Bachelier (successeur de Mme Ve Courcier), Paris.

Diderot, Denis, 1751 (and later). *Encyclopédie ou Dictionnaire Raisonné des Sciences, des Arts et des Métiers*, Briasson, David, Le Breton & Durand, Paris.

Evans, David S., 1992. *Lacaille: Astronomer, Traveler. With a new translation of his Journal*, Pachart Publishing House, Tucson, Arizona, USA.

Everest, G., 1821. On the Triangulation of the Cape of Good Hope. *Mem. Roy. Astr. Soc.,* **I, pt. II**, 255–270.

Fontenelle, B. le B. de, 1686. *Entretiens sur la Pluralités des Mondes*, Veuve Blageant, Paris.

Forbes, E.G. & Gapaillard, J. (1996). The astronomical correspondence between Abbé de Lacaille and Tobias Mayer, *Revue d'Histoire des Sciences*, **49**, 483–542.

Franklin, Alfred, 1901. *Histoire de la Bibliothèque Mazarine et du Palais de L'Institut*, 2nd ed., H. Welter, Libraire-Éditeur, Paris.

Gingerich, O., 1960. Abbe Lacaille's List of Clusters and Nebulae, *Sky and Telescope*, **19**, 207–208.

Giret, A., 1962. Le Bicentenaire de l'abbé de la Caille. *L'Astronomie*, **76**, 194–196.

Grandjean de Fouchy, G., 1762. Éloge de M. L'Abbé de la Caille. *Hist. Acad. Roy. des Sci.*, 197–212.

Greenberg, J.L., 1995. *The Problem of the Earth's Shape from Newton to Clairaut*, Cambridge University Press, Cambridge.

Guerlac, H., 1956. A Note on Lavoisier's Scientific Education, *Isis*, **47**, 211–216.

Hadley, J., 1731. The description of a new instrument for taking angles. *Phil. Trans. Roy. Soc.*, **37**, 147–157.

Herschel, W.F., (1800). On the Power of penetrating into Space by Telescopes..., *Phil. Trans. Roy. Soc.*, **90**, 49–85.

Horrocks, H., 1929. The longitude of the Royal Observatory Cape of Good Hope from Wireless Signals October-November 1926. *Mon. Not. Roy. Astr. Soc.*, **89**, 611–615.

Jeffares, N., 2006. *Dictionary of pastellists before 1800*. Online edition: www. pastellists.com.

Kolbe, P., 1719. *Caput Bonae Spei Hodiernum . . .* , P.C. Monath, Nuremberg.

La Caille, N.-L., 1741. *Leçons Élémentaires de Mathématiques, ou Élémens d'Algèbre et de Géométrie*, Collombat, Paris.

La Caille, N.-L., 1741 [1744]. Calcul des différences dans la Trigonométrie sphérique. *Mém. Acad. Roy. des Sci.*, 238–260 + 1 plate.

La Caille, N.-L., 1742 [1745]. Projet d'un nouveau Catalogue des Étoiles Fixes. *Hist. Acad. Roy. des Sci.*, 63–71.

La Caille, N.-L., 1746. *Leçons Élémentaires d'Astronomie Géométrique et Physique*, Guérin, Paris.

La Caille, N.-L., 1750. *Leçons Élémentaires d'Optique*, Guérin, Paris.

La Caille, N.-L., 1750. Avis aux astronomes, à l'occasion des observations qu'il va faire par ordre du Roi dans l'hémisphère austral. Paris, 4pp.

La Caille, N.-L., 1751 [1755]. Diverses Observations astronomiques et physiques faites au cap de Bonne-Espérance pendant les années 1751 et 1752, et une partie de 1753. *Mém. Acad. Roy. des Sci.*, 398–456 + 2 plates.

La Caille, N.-L., 1751 [1755]. Relation Abrégée du Voyage Fait par ordre du Roi, au Cap de Bonne-espérance. *Mém. Acad. Roy. des Sci.*, 519–536

La Caille, N.-L., 1752 [1756]. Table des Ascensions Droites et des Déclinaisons Apparentes Des Étoiles australes renfermées dans le tropique du Capricorne; observées au cap de Bonne-espérance dans l'intervalle du 6 Août 1751, au 18 Juillet 1752. *Mém. Acad. Roy. des Sci.*, 539–592 + 1 plate.

La Caille, N.-L., 1755 [1761]. Sur les Étoiles Nébuleuses du ciel austral. *Mém. Acad. Roy. des Sci.*, 194–199.

La Caille, N.-L., 1755 [1761]. Sur la Précision des Mesures Géodésiques Faites en 1740, pour déterminer la distance de Paris à Amiens; A l'occasion d'un Mémoire de M. Euler, Inséré dans la neuvième tome de l'Académie de Berlin, *Mém. Acad. Roy. des Sci.*, 53–59.

La Caille, N.-L., 1757. *Astronomiae fundamenta novissimis solis et stellarum observationibus stabilita Lutetiae in Collegio Mazarinaeo et in Africa ad caput Bonae Spei*, J.J. Stephani Columbat, Paris (privately printed).

La Caille, N.-L., 1758. *Tabulae solares quas è novissimis suis observationibus deduxit N.L. de la Caille*, H.L Guerin and L.F. Delatour, Paris.

La Caille, N.-L., 1759 [1765]. Mémoire sur l'observation des longitudes en mer par le moyen de la Lune, *Mém. Acad. Roy. des Sci.*, 63–98 + 1 plate.

La Caille, N.-L., 1759 [1765]. Sur la Calcul des Éléments de la Théorie de la Comète qui Paroît Maintenant, *Mém. Acad. Roy. des Sci.*, 522–524.

La Caille, N.-L., 1760 [1765]. Mémoire sur la parallaxe du Soleil, qui résulte de la comparaison des observations simultanées de Mars & de Vénus, faites en l'année 1751 en Europe & au Cap de Bonne-Espérance, *Mém. Acad. Roy. des Sci.*, 369–387.

La Caille, N.-L., 1761 [1763]. Mémoire sur la Parallaxe de la Lune, *Mém. Acad. Roy. des Sci.*, 1–57.

La Caille, N.-L., 1761 [1763]. Observation du Passage de Vénus sur le Disque du Soleil, *Mém. Acad. Roy. des Sci.*, 78–81.

La Caille, Nicolao-Ludovico, 1763. *Coelum Australe Stelliferum; seu Observationes ad Construendum Stellarum Australium Institutae, in Africa ad Caput Bonae-Spei*, H.L. Guerin & L.F. Delatour, Paris (with a life of La Caille in Latin by Gabriel Brotier).

La Caille, M. l'Abbé De, 1763. *Journal Historique du Voyage Fait au Cap de Bonne-Espérance...*, Edited anonymously by Abbé Claude Carlier. Guillyn, Paris (1st printing).

La Caille, N.-L., 1763. Discours Sur les Progrès que L'Astronomie a fait depuis une trentaine d'années, in *Ephémérides des mouvemens célestes pour dix années, VI; Depuis 1765 jusqu'en 1775...*, J.-T. Hérissant, Paris.

La Caille, M. l'Abbé De, 1776. *Journal Historique du Voyage Fait au Cap de Bonne-Espérance...*, Edited anonymously by Abbé Claude Carlier. Chez Nyon ainé, Paris (2nd printing).

La Lande, J. le Français de, 1792. *Astronomie*, 3rd. Ed., 3 Vols, Chez la Veuve Desaint, Paris.

La Lande, J. de, 1803. *Bibliographie Astronomique avec l'Histoire de L'Astronomie Depuis 1781 Jusqu'à 1802*, Imprimerie de la République, Paris.

Lequeux, J., 2008. François Arago, Un Savant genereux: Physique et Astronomy au XIXe Siècle, EDP Sciences, Paris.

Lydekker, Richard (ed) 1894. *The Royal Natural History*, Frederick Warne and Co., London and New York.

Maclear, T., 1840. On the Position of La Caille's Stations at the Cape of Good Hope, *Mem. Roy. Astr. Soc.*, XI, 91–137.

Maclear, Sir Thomas, 1866. *Verification and Extension of La Caille's Arc of Meridian at the Cape of Good Hope*, Vol. 1, Lords Commissioners of the Admiralty, London.

Maheu, G., 1966. La vie scientifique au milieu du XVIIIe siècle: Introduction à la publication des lettres de Bouguer à Euler, *Revue d'Histoire des Sciences et de leurs Applications*, **19**, 206–224.

Maupertuis, P.L.M. de, 1732. *Discours sur les Différentes Figures des Astres... avec une Exposition abrégée des Systemes de M. Descartes & de M. Newton*, Paris, Imprimerie Royale.

Maupertuis, P.L.M. de, 1768. *Oeuvres de Maupertuis, Nouvelle Édition*, Bruyset, Lyon.

Maupertuis, P.L.M. de, Camus, C.É.L., Clairaut, A.-C., Le Monnier, P.-C., Celsius, A., 1738. *Observations made by order of the French King at the Polar Circle*, London, T. Cox.

McIntyre, Donald, 1951. *An Astronomical Bi-Centenary. the Abbé de Lacaille's Visit to the Cape 1751–1753*, Astronomical Society of South Africa, Observatory, Cape, South Africa, pp. 12 + 9 plates.

Mentzel, O.F., 1785, 1787. *Beschreibung des Vorgebirges der Guten Hoffnung*, Vols I and II, Glogau, C.F. Günther; Translated as *A Complete and Authen-*

tic Geographical and Topographical Description of the...African Cape of Good Hope...; Vol I tr. in two parts by H.J. Mandelbrote, Van Riebeeck Society, Series 1, Vols. 4 & 6, 1921, 1925; Vol II tr. by G.V. Marais and J. Hoge, Van Riebeeck Society Series 1, Vol. 25, 1944, Cape Town. Vol. 1 part 1, Vol. 1 part 2 and Vol. 2 are referred to here as **1**, **2** and **3** respectively.

Michaud, J., Michaud, L.G. 1843–65. *Biographie Universelle Ancienne et Moderne*, Nouvelle Édition, Desplaces, Paris & Brockhaus, Leipzig.

Montucla, J.F., Lalande, J., 1802 (An. X). Histoire des Mathématiques, **III**, Agasse, Paris.

Murdin, P., 2009. *Full Meridian of Glory*, Springer, New York.

Peiffer, J., 2009. Le *Traité de Géométrie* de Varignon et l'apprentissage mathématique du jeune D'Alembert, *Recherches sur Diderot et sur l'Encyclopédie* **38**, *La formation de D'Alembert*, put on line 30 March 2009, URL: http://rde.revues.org/index301.html.

Raven-Hart, R. (tr., ed.), 1976. *Nicolas Louis de la Caille: Travels at the Cape 1751–53*. Balkema, Cape Town and Rotterdam.

Rigaud, S.P. (ed.), 1832. *Miscellaneous Works and Correspondence of the Rev. James Bradley D.D., F.R.S.*, University Press, Oxford.

Rodriguez, Don Joseph, 1813. Observations on the Measurement of three Degrees of the Meridian conducted in England by Lieut.-Colonel William Mudge. *Phil Mag.*, **XLI**, 90–100.

Shank, J.B., 2008. *The Newton Wars and the Beginning of the French Enlightenment*, University of Chicago Press, Chicago.

Smith, J.R., 1999. *Everest: The Man and the Mountain*, Whittles Publishing, Caithness, Scotland.

Stewart, R., 2009. A mystery resolved: Lacaille's map of the Cape of Good Hope, *Journal of the International Map Collector's Society*, Winter 2009, pp. 7–11.

Taton, R., 1978. *Inventaire des Publications et des manuscrits de Nicolas-Louis Lacaille (1713–1762)*, in *Science and History, Studies in Honor of Edward Rosen*, ed Czartoryski, P., Polish Academy of Sciences, Wrocklaw, pp. 317–333.

Taton, R., 1996. Les relations entre R.J. Boscovich et Alexis-Claude Clairaut (1759–1764), *Revue d'Histoire des Sciences*, **49**, 415–458.

Taton, R., Wilson, C., (eds.), 1995. *The General History of Astronomy* Vol. 2, Part B, Planetary Astronomy...The Eighteenth and Nineteenth Centuries, Cambridge University Press, Cambridge.

Teleki, J., 1941. *La Cour de Louis XV: Journal de Voyage du Comte Joseph Teleki*, ed. Tolnac, G., Presses Universitaire de France, Paris.

Terrall, M., 2002. *The Man Who Flattened the Earth: Maupertuis and the Sciences in the Enlightenment*, University of Chicgo Press, Chicago and London.

Thiéry, L.V., 1786. *L'Almanach du voyageur à Paris*, chez Hardouin & Gattery, Paris.

Todhunter, I., 1872. On the Arc of Meridian Measured in South Africa, *Mon. Not. Roy. Astr. Soc.*, **33**, 27–33.

Todhunter, I., 1873. *A History of the Mathematical Theories of Attraction and the Figure of the Earth...*, Macmillan, London (2 Vols).

Trystram, F., 1979. *Le Procès des Étoiles*, Seghers, Paris.

Verne, J. 1872. *Aventures de 3 Russes et de 3 Anglais dans l'Afrique Australe*, Hetzel, Paris.

von Zach, F., 1799. Memoirs of the Celebrated Astronomer Le Monnier, in *Monthly Mazagine and British Register, Part II for 1799*, **VIII**, Sept. 1799, pp. 626–628.

Warner, B., (ed.), 1989. *The Cape Diary and Letters of William Mann, Astronomer and Mountaineer 1839–1843*, Friends of the South African Library, Cape Town.

Warner, B., 1995. Royal Observatory Cape of Good Hope (1820–1831): *The Founding of a Colonial Observatory*. Kluwer Academic Publishers, Dordrecht.

Warner, B. and Rourke, J., 1990. Riebeeck Kasteel: in the footsteps of De la Caille and Thunberg, *Sagittarius*, **5**, 12–17 (Published by the South African Museum, Cape Town).

Westfall, R.S., 1980. *Never at Rest: A Biography of Isaac Newton*, Cambridge University Press, Cambridge.

Whitaker, R., 2005. *The Mapmaker's Wife, a True Tale of Love, Murder and Survival in the Amazon*, Bantam Books, London.

Widmalm, S., 1992. A Commerce of Letters: Astronomical Communication in the 18th Century. *Science Studies*, **5**, 43–58.

Wilson, C.A., 1993. Clairaut's Calculation of the Eighteenth-Century Re-appearance of Halley's Comet, *J. Hist. Astr.*, **xxiv**, pp. 1–15.

Wilson, C.A., 1980a,b. Perturbations and Solar Tables from Lacaille to Delambre : the Rapprochement of Observation and Theory, *Archive for History of Exact Sciences*, Part I, **22**, pp. 1–136; Part II, **22**, pp189–304.

Wolf, C., 1902. *Histoire de L'Observatoire de Paris de sa Fondation à 1793*. Gauthier-Villars, Paris.

Zuidervaart, H.J., 2006. 'The latest news about the heavens: The European contact- and correspondence-network of Dutch astronomers in mid-18th century', in *The Global and the Local: The History of Science and the Cultural Integration of Europe*. Proceedings of the ICESHS (Cracow, Poland, September 6–9, 2006) Ed. by M. Kokowski, pp. 825–837. URL: http://www.cyfronet.pl/~n1kokows/home.html.

Index